Dr.-Ing. Frank Kupke

Robust Distributed Software Transactions for Haskell

Dr.-Ing. Frank Kupke

Robust Distributed Software Transactions for Haskell

Freedom from Deadlock without the Headache

Südwestdeutscher Verlag für Hochschulschriften

Impressum/Imprint (nur für Deutschland/only for Germany)
Bibliografische Information der Deutschen Nationalbibliothek: Die Deutsche Nationalbibliothek verzeichnet diese Publikation in der Deutschen Nationalbibliografie; detaillierte bibliografische Daten sind im Internet über http://dnb.d-nb.de abrufbar.
Alle in diesem Buch genannten Marken und Produktnamen unterliegen warenzeichen-, marken- oder patentrechtlichem Schutz bzw. sind Warenzeichen oder eingetragene Warenzeichen der jeweiligen Inhaber. Die Wiedergabe von Marken, Produktnamen, Gebrauchsnamen, Handelsnamen, Warenbezeichnungen u.s.w. in diesem Werk berechtigt auch ohne besondere Kennzeichnung nicht zu der Annahme, dass solche Namen im Sinne der Warenzeichen- und Markenschutzgesetzgebung als frei zu betrachten wären und daher von jedermann benutzt werden dürften.

Coverbild: www.ingimage.com

Verlag: Südwestdeutscher Verlag für Hochschulschriften GmbH & Co. KG
Dudweiler Landstr. 99, 66123 Saarbrücken, Deutschland
Telefon +49 681 37 20 271-1, Telefax +49 681 37 20 271-0
Email: info@svh-verlag.de

Zugl.: Kiel, CAU, Diss., 2010

Herstellung in Deutschland:
Schaltungsdienst Lange o.H.G., Berlin
Books on Demand GmbH, Norderstedt
Reha GmbH, Saarbrücken
Amazon Distribution GmbH, Leipzig
ISBN: 978-3-8381-2736-1

Imprint (only for USA, GB)
Bibliographic information published by the Deutsche Nationalbibliothek: The Deutsche Nationalbibliothek lists this publication in the Deutsche Nationalbibliografie; detailed bibliographic data are available in the Internet at http://dnb.d-nb.de.
Any brand names and product names mentioned in this book are subject to trademark, brand or patent protection and are trademarks or registered trademarks of their respective holders. The use of brand names, product names, common names, trade names, product descriptions etc. even without a particular marking in this works is in no way to be construed to mean that such names may be regarded as unrestricted in respect of trademark and brand protection legislation and could thus be used by anyone.

Cover image: www.ingimage.com

Publisher: Südwestdeutscher Verlag für Hochschulschriften GmbH & Co. KG
Dudweiler Landstr. 99, 66123 Saarbrücken, Germany
Phone +49 681 37 20 271-1, Fax +49 681 37 20 271-0
Email: info@svh-verlag.de

Printed in the U.S.A.
Printed in the U.K. by (see last page)
ISBN: 978-3-8381-2736-1

Copyright © 2011 by the author and Südwestdeutscher Verlag für Hochschulschriften GmbH & Co. KG and licensors
All rights reserved. Saarbrücken 2011

The nett effect was that I was extremely ill-equipped to appreciate functional programming when I encountered it: I was, for instance, totally baffled by the shocking suggestion that the value of a function could be another function.

Edsger W. Dijkstra, 1995

Abstract

This book motivates and develops a robust distributed *Software Transactional Memory (STM)* library for Haskell. Many real-life applications are distributed by nature. They either control geographically wide spread hardware resources or utilize redundant hardware components to minimize system failure. STM is an abstraction for synchronizing shared resources in concurrent applications. It helps to prevent deadlocks and thus facilitates composing program code.

We extend the STM abstraction to distributed systems and present an implementation efficient enough to be used in soft real-time applications. Further, the implemented library is robust in itself, offering the application developer a high abstraction level to realize robustness, hence, significantly simplifying this, in general, complex task.

Keywords   deadlock-free, distributed, robust, software transactional memory

Contents

1. **Introduction**   1

2. **Foundations**   3
   2.1. Haskell 3
       2.1.1. Type System 6
       2.1.2. Monads 10
       2.1.3. Concurrent Haskell 15
       2.1.4. Haskell Exceptions 18
       2.1.5. Dynamically-Typed Exceptions 19
   2.2. Concurrency and Distribution 20
       2.2.1. Hardware Development 20
       2.2.2. Concurrent Systems 22
       2.2.3. Lock-based Synchronization 25
       2.2.4. Distributed Systems 28
   2.3. Software Transactional Memory 33
       2.3.1. Database Transactions 34
       2.3.2. Transactional Memory 35
       2.3.3. Transactions for Concurrent Haskell 35

3. **Using Distributed STM**   41
   3.1. Library Interface Design 41
   3.2. Distributed System Setup 44
   3.3. Introductory Example 47
   3.4. Robust Library Interface 49
       3.4.1. Design Pattern of a Robust DSTM Application 50
       3.4.2. The DSTM Exception 51
   3.5. Complete API 53

Contents

4. Implementing Software Transactional Memory for Distributed Haskell — 55
- 4.1. Transaction Paradigm 55
  - 4.1.1. Transaction Monad 56
  - 4.1.2. Transactional Variables 58
- 4.2. STM Protocol 63
  - 4.2.1. Synchronizing Transactions 64
  - 4.2.2. Transaction State 64
  - 4.2.3. Controlling Transactions 66
  - 4.2.4. Execution Protocols 72
  - 4.2.5. Creation Protocols 75
- 4.3. Distributed Communication 78
  - 4.3.1. Network Messaging 78
  - 4.3.2. Communicating Mutable Variables 84
  - 4.3.3. Retry Variables 86
  - 4.3.4. Distributed Garbage Collection 87
- 4.4. Intra-Transaction State 93

5. Implementing Efficient Transactional Communication — 95
- 5.1. Individual Line 96
- 5.2. Dedicated Line 97
- 5.3. Line Stack 101
- 5.4. Line Bundle 103
  - 5.4.1. Logging Transactions using Bundle Logs 108
  - 5.4.2. Collecting Bundle Logs 110
  - 5.4.3. Executing Bundle Logs 116
  - 5.4.4. Logging Retry Variables 118
- 5.5. Reading Uncommitted TVar Values 119
  - 5.5.1. Empty Commit Log 121
  - 5.5.2. Host TVar 122
  - 5.5.3. Link TVar 123
- 5.6. Benchmark Tests 124

6. Implementing Robustness — 131
- 6.1. Dependability 132
  - 6.1.1. Fault Tolerance in a Distributed Library 133
  - 6.1.2. System Levels 134
- 6.2. Transaction Failure 135
  - 6.2.1. Error Detection 136
  - 6.2.2. Fault Scenarios 137
  - 6.2.3. Active Transaction 138

	6.2.4. Inactive Transaction	139
	6.2.5. Reactive Transaction	140
6.3.	Robust DSTM Protocol	144
	6.3.1. Database Transactions and STM	144
	6.3.2. Reactive Transaction Status	146
	6.3.3. Controlling Reactive Transactions	149
	6.3.4. Library Exception	153
	6.3.5. Coordinator Election	154
	6.3.6. Life-check	156
	6.3.7. Controlling Active Transactions	162
	6.3.8. Consolidated Log	165
	6.3.9. Robust Protocol for Active Transactions	167
6.4.	Synchronization Caveats	170
	6.4.1. Protocol Inversion	170
	6.4.2. Transaction Trap	172

7. Conclusions and Related Work   175

- 7.1. Conclusion . . . 175
- 7.2. Transactional Systems . . . 176
  - 7.2.1. Data Invariants . . . 176
  - 7.2.2. STM optimizations . . . 177
  - 7.2.3. STM in Mainstream Languages . . . 177
- 7.3. Distributed Systems . . . 178
  - 7.3.1. Erlang . . . 179
  - 7.3.2. Curry . . . 179
  - 7.3.3. Oz . . . 180
  - 7.3.4. Glasgow Distributed Haskell . . . 181
  - 7.3.5. Haskell with Ports . . . 181
  - 7.3.6. Holumbus . . . 181
- 7.4. Future Work . . . 182

A. Application Programming   183

- A.1. Name Server . . . 183
- A.2. Complete DSTM Library API . . . 187

B. Sample Applications   189

- B.1. Dining Philosophers . . . 189
- B.2. Chat . . . 191
- B.3. Bomberman . . . 196

C. Proof of STM Monad Laws   201

Chapter 1

Introduction

In this book we present a Haskell library extension for distributed programming in an internet network environment based on a concurrent Software Transactional Memory abstraction model. We call this library robust *Distributed Software Transactional Memory* (DSTM).

The library facilitates the development of easy to compose, robust, distributed, strictly typed Haskell applications. We realize a fully transparent distributed synchronization, offering distributed transactional variables. The application designer is able to focus on the application logic itself rather than on avoiding deadlocks using lock-based synchronization measures. The high-level DSTM synchronization abstraction naturally extends to robustness. The programmer simply manages abstract transactional variables instead of a complex low-level network interface recovery. Thus, developing a recovery logic becomes a task of managing logical program resources.

We begin with an introduction to the lazy, pure, functional programming language Haskell in Chapter 2. In Chapter 3 we introduce the augmented STM application programmer interface (API).

The main part consists of the following three chapters detailing design and implementation of our library. In Chapter 4 we present a first distributed transactional implementation. With the major performance improvements described in Chapter 5 the library becomes useable for practical applications. Chapter 6 introduces the additional robustness functionality to our library, essential to real-life distributed applications, entailing a profound rewrite of the library.

We conclude in Chapter 7 with an overview of related approaches of both transactional and distributed systems. We position our library and suggest further improvements for future work.

1. Introduction

Appendix A guides the application programmer using the robust distributed transactional library and Appendix B details three real application examples as an exercise. We present a semi-formal proof of the monad laws for the STM monad in Appendix C.

Formal Notes

Throughout this book we show a major portion of the developed code supporting the design ideas behind. We present each code sample with line numbers, resetting the line counter at the beginning of every chapter. We refer to these line numbers within chapter boundaries only.

The code shown is running and mostly complete. However, we omit all module, import, and export information to keep the code concise. We also omit most comments and derived class information using the `deriving` keyword, like `deriving Show` converting data types into printable string values. We reveal such information when it explicitly supports our explanations. We show examples of functions following a common template rather than all their occurrences. We define partial functions omitting pattern match alternatives revealing library programming errors only.

In this book we emphasize newly introduced terms or references to introduced terms if their names may be ambiguous by printing them in an *italic* font. As an example we refer to a *lock* protocol which eventually locks a variable.

We print textual references to code fragments or names in a `monospaced` font, like `Bool` or function `foo`. In general, such a code reference stands for the literal word, like the data type name `Bool` or the function name `foo`. There are two noteworthy exceptions to this rule because we reference them so often throughout this book. When denoting `TVar` and `RetryVar` we reference either the literal type names `TVar` or `RetryVar`, respectively, or, as in most cases, we refer to a variable of either type when explaining its usage in an algorithm or design idea. We use the latter reference also in a plural form. The difference becomes apparent from the context.

We refer to global variables as variables having a global scope in respect to the process they are used in. Their names always begin with the letter g, like `gMyEnv` denoting the environment of the current process.

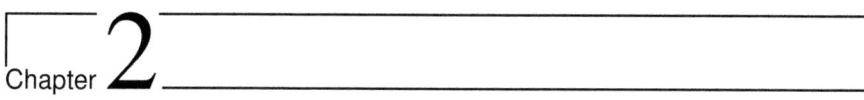

Foundations

The practical part of this work has been implemented in Haskell. In this chapter we first describe the most fundamental aspects of Haskell and highlight those language features that are essential to this work like the type system and monads. A full description of the Haskell 98 Standard can be found in The *Haskell 98 Report* [PJ+02]. In addition we introduce the *Concurrent Haskell* [PJGF96] extension to this standard.

Next, we lay out the basis of distributed programming. We show that both concurrent and distributed programming are motivated by improvements in computer hardware leading to software concepts for sharing common resources.

We end this foundation chapter with an introduction to *Software Transactional Memory* as described by Harris, Marlow, Peyton Jones and Herlihy in [HMPJH05] which represents the core inspiration to this work.

2.1. Haskell

Haskell is a lazy, pure, functional programming language.

Functional languages like *LISP*, *ML*, *Erlang* and *Haskell* are declarative as opposed to imperative programming languages like *Pascal*, *C*, *Java* and many others. Further declarative language types are logic (*Prolog*) or functional-logic languages (*Curry*).

Imperative programs describe a solution to a problem by listing a sequence of state changing commands to be executed strictly step by step. The programmer tells the computer what to do and when to do it. Those programs are abstractions of the *von Neumann* architecture[vN45] they are running on which

3

2. Foundations

in turn is based on the mathematical *Turing machine* model [Tur37, PVE93].

Declarative programs describe a problem as a collection of mathematical definitions. The programmer tells the computer what the problem definition is. Functional languages are based on the *lambda calculus* on variables, function expressions (lambda abstractions) and function applications. A variable in functional programming denotes a fixed mathematical value, not a memory location with variable content. A function is an operation which may be applied on one thing (the arguments) to yield another thing (the value[1] of the function) [Chu85]. Functions are first class citizens as they are regular data objects. Function objects can be used like any other data object in the program. In particular, they can be applied to other functions (*higher-order* functions) and yield functions as results. Partial application of a function yields another function as its result. The resulting function can then be applied to the remaining arguments.

More than technical differences it is the software creation methodology that differs between imperative and functional programming [Pep03].

A simple example algorithm to increment a list of elements shows the idea. We want to change all elements of an array. In an imperative language, we would loop over the array and change its elements in place. In Haskell we may define a mapping function which we then call with a function parameter and a given list to create a new modified list. The `map` function shown here is already defined in the Haskell *Prelude*[2]

```
1 map :: (a -> b) -> [a] -> [b]
2 map      f      (x:xs) = f x : map f xs
3 map      _      []     = []
```

Line 1 is the function type declaration (see Section 2.1.1 for type system) in curried[3] form. The function `map` takes two arguments, a function with an argument of type `a` returning a result of type `b` as its first argument and a list of elements of type `a` as its second. The result of `map` is a list of type `b`. The type variables `a` and `b` denote arbitrary types. The mixfix operator `[]` surrounding an element denotes a list type of those elements. Line 2 is the main function definition in declaration style [HHPJW07] calling `map` with a function `f`, and a list with head element `x` and tail list `xs`. The result is a new list with `f` applied

---
[1]Here, value means the result of the function, not a variable.
[2]The Prelude is a library of functions useful for general Haskell programs.
[3]Currying is the process of transforming a function that takes multiple arguments into a function that takes just a single argument and returns another function if any arguments are still needed [Y+09].

2.1. Haskell

to x followed by a recursive call with f and the tail list as arguments. Line 3 finally terminates the recursion by returning an empty list when the tail list itself is empty.

In order to increment a list of integer numbers, we would simply use map to apply a function to this list:

```
> map (1+) [1, 2, 3]
[2, 3, 4]
```

The function parameter (1+) in this example is a partial application of the + function with the parameter 1 grouped together by enclosing parenthesis. The resulting function (1+) of arity 1 requires another parameter. This is exactly the function type map requires for its function parameter. Instead of implementing memory cell modifications, our small sample program consists of consecutive mathematical function definitions and applications.

This leads to purity, an essential Haskell property. A *pure* functional program consists of (higher-order) functions taking (function) parameters and returning (function) results, nothing else. There are no *side effects*, thus, no state that could be changed and no mutable variables. The calculation of the program functions solely relies on their arguments and not on the time or order of execution. We call pure function expressions *referential transparent*. A pure programming language prohibiting side effects enables a safe modular programming style but it would prohibit any input and output. If the program should have any effect on the real world, only mutable content is of interest. Input into a program is read from mutable memory locations and output is written to mutable memory locations like a file or video buffer. In Haskell there is a special solution to this problem, called *IO-Monad* (see Section 2.1.2 for monads).

Functional languages are executed by evaluating the initial expression, the main function. Expressions are reduced by repeatedly replacing function applications by their function bodies substituting formal parameters with actual arguments until the most simple form, the normal form, has been reached. Pure functional languages enable a special kind of optimization, *lazy evaluation* which in turn allows for a different programming style as well. As the order of execution does not matter in pure languages the evaluation of an expression might as well be (lazily) deferred until its result is needed. If a result is not needed for a particular application, it is not evaluated at all. The lazy evaluation order will find the normal form if it exists [PVE93]. Thus, we can program with infinite data structures and still create terminating programs using lazy languages. However, a terminating program cannot be guaranteed since the

2. Foundations

halting problem is in general undecidable [Tur37]. We take the **head** function, also defined in the Prelude, as an example.

```
4 head :: [a] -> a
5 head  (x:_) = x
6 head  []    = error "Prelude.head: empty list"
```

On non-empty lists **head** returns the first element. Note that applying **head** on empty lists raises an exception. The **error** function outputs a message and terminates the execution of the program (line 6).

Because of lazy evaluation, we can map a function onto the infinite list of positive integers [1..], calculate the head element,

```
> head (map (1+) [1..])
2
```

and still get a result. As only the head element is requested, the function (1+) is applied only to the head element 1 of the original list yielding the result 2. It is irrelevant how long the original list is as only its head element is evaluated.

2.1.1. Type System

Types are a programming abstraction which aids the programmer to write programs according to their specification. A type system is the implementation of this abstraction for a particular programming language and can be seen as a built-in modeling language.

Haskell uses a polymorphic, strong, static type system. It is an extension of a Hindley-Milner[4] or ML[5]-like type system with decidable type inference [Pie05]. The Haskell compiler checks and maintains type consistency using type inference and unification. The compiler creates a set of type constraints from the program code and tries to solve it. If the constraints can be solved, the types are inferred and the program is well-typed. Haskell does not require the programmer to declare types used in the program. The compiler infers the types automatically. However, Haskell allows to annotate every function and variable with the desired type signature. The Haskell type checking mechanism then detects mismatches between inferred and annotated types, giving the programmer a compile time feedback on possible design errors.

---

[4]J. Roger Hindley and Robin Milner independently provided the type inference algorithms associated with their names.

[5]Standard-ML is a general purpose functional programming language used as a meta-language (ML) within a theorem prover.

2.1. Haskell

```
7  intTail :: [Int] -> [Integer]
8  intTail  (_:xs) = xs
9  intTail  []     = error "intTail: empty list"
```

An attempt to compile the `intTail` function would result in a compiler error message like this:

```
Couldn't match expected type 'Integer' against inferred type 'Int'
Expected type: [Integer]
Inferred type: [Int]
In the expression: xs
In the definition of 'intTail': intTail (_ : xs) = xs
```

The type inference constraints demand an identical type of the parameter list elements (`Int`) and the function result list elements (`Integer`) for our `intTail` function. The existing type mismatch forces the *strong static* type system to generate a compile time error. When we change the result type of `intTail` to `[Int]` we have a well-typed function that returns a list of all but the head element of a given non-empty list. Even then, the function `intTail` only accepts input lists of type `Int`.

A *polymorphic* type system introduces the use of type variables. The programmer can define expressions to be of any type and describe their type relations to other expressions. Polymorphic types allow abstraction from implementation details by focusing on the *structure* of a function or problem solution.

```
10 tail :: [a] -> [a]
11 tail (_:xs) = xs
12 tail []     = error "Prelude.tail: empty list"
```

The `intTail` function has the same functionality as the `tail` function except that the latter is polymorphic and thus can be applied to lists of any type. The type declaration in line 10 is implicitly universally quantified. It defines a potentially infinite number of functions for structurally equal types.

The structure to focus on for the `tail` function is a list. A list is an ordered collection of elements. It is recursively defined as shown in line 13. Note that this is not real Haskell syntax. Lists are predefined data types. A list is either the empty list or it is an element followed by another list of the same element type.

```
13 data [a] = [] | a : [a]
```

2. Foundations

The data type *list* shows another concept of the Haskell type system, polymorphic data types. Like polymorphic functions, polymorphic data types define an infinite number of types with the same (just defined) structure. Here, this common structure is to be a list of any type with [] being the type constructor for these list types.

Polymorphic functions define structurally equal functions in a single definition. By definition a polymorphic function is defined for all possible types.

Haskell also knows *overloaded* functions which have a polymorphic type declaration but possibly structurally different definitions for each type. An example is the equality operator (==) (line 14) which denotes a set of equality predicates for many different types like Bool, Int, Integer and others.

```
14  (==)  :: a -> a -> Bool
15  (==)     x    y   = ...
```

An overloaded function may be implemented differently for each structurally different type. This definition then replaces, or overloads, a possible generic definition, hence the name. In general, however, there is no generic definition but individual implementations for concrete type structures. In the equality example above there are definitions for Bool, Int, Integer and others.

```
16  elem  :: a -> [a] -> Bool
17  elem     x = any (==x)
```

When an overloaded function is applied, both the programmer and the compiler have to be certain that such a definition really exists. In the above example the Prelude function elem (line 16) calls another function any[6] with the equality predicate applied to its first argument. This is only useful when equality is defined on the actual type a. Note that the function declaration does not use the second argument of type [a] and, therefore, defines a partial function which is equivalent to a complete declaration.

Haskell uses *type classes* which are collections of types, called *instances*, defining a common set of overloaded functions, called *signature*. Any type can be declared to be an instance of a type class. It then has to define the signature functions. A polymorphic function definition can be restricted to only such type variables which are instances of certain type classes. This restriction is called a *type constraint*. There is an equality type class Eq whose instances all define the

---

[6]The Prelude function any maps the predicate onto the given list and folds (cumulates) the result to the final boolean result.

2.1. Haskell

equality operator (==). Line 18 shows the complete elem function declaration restricted to types a which are instances of the Eq type class. Types can also be restricted to instances of more than one class by multiple type constraints.

```
18  elem  :: Eq a => a -> [a] -> Bool
19  elem           x = any (==x)
```

The (==) operator itself, naturally, is also restricted to types instantiating the Eq type class. Line 20 shows the complete definition.

```
20  (==) :: Eq a => a -> a -> Bool
```

The Eq type class signature consists of the equality and the disequality operator functions.

```
21  class Eq a where
22    (==), (/=) :: a -> a -> Bool
23    x /= y = not (x==y)
24    x == y = not (x/=y)
```

Lines 23 and 24 are default declarations. Equality and disequality are defined in relation to each other. An actual type instance needs to implement only either one of the two signature functions. The other one is predefined by this default.

The instance Eq definition of type Bool (lines 25–28) defines the equality function on expressions of type Bool, thus, overloading the class definition (==) operator for all combinations of Bool type constructors.

```
25  instance Eq Bool where
26    True  == True  = True
27    False == False = True
28    _     == _     = False
```

With the above declarations an application of the elem function (line 18) with parameters of type Bool like:

```
> elem True [False, False, True]
True
```

is type correct.

9

2. Foundations

2.1.2. Monads

As a pure language Haskell does not allow side effects. Input and output (I/O) of a program are side effects, however. As a general purpose language Haskell needs to support I/O operations. Haskell solves this contradiction with a programming abstraction called *monad*. Monads can be used as pure wrappers of I/O operations.

Although an important motivation of the monad abstraction is based on solving the functional I/O issue, it is a general programming abstraction useful in other areas as well. In fact, the monad concept is essential to this work (see also Section 2.3 on *Software Transactional Memory*). Monads are a programming abstraction without breaking the pure lazy functional paradigm. From a programmer's perspective, a monad can be used as a type-safe embedded program.

Mathematical Background

Monads have a mathematical foundation in category theory. A category in the mathematical sense is a thing consisting of objects and transformations, called morphisms, mapping objects onto each other. A functor maps categories (objects and morphisms) onto other objects and other morphisms. If there is only one category, the functor maps it onto itself (still mapping objects onto other objects and morphisms onto other morphisms, in general). Given also a set of *natural transformations* ensuring well-behaviour like identity and associativity, we call this construct a monad. As a consequence of this construction, a sequence of monad transformations forms again a monad transformation.

When we imagine a category with state objects and morphisms and monad transformations as state transition actions, monads become an interesting programming abstraction in functional languages. In fact, this abstraction bridges the gap between a pure functional language and I/O side effects when the states become a representation of the real world.

The Haskell analogy of a category is a type class, a functor is represented as a polymorphic data type, a constructor class[7] and a mapping function [PH06]. The type constructor maps the basis type onto another (functor) type and the mapping function maps functions on values of the original type to functions on values of the transformed type. The general mapping function is called `fmap`

---

[7]The instances of a type class (like `Eq`) are types, the instances of constructor classes are type constructors or polymorphic data types.

2.1. Haskell

(line 29) in Haskell with `Functor` being the Haskell functor constructor type class.

```
29  fmap  ::  Functor f => (a -> b) -> f a -> f b
```

A Haskell monad, finally, is also a constructor class with a defined set of functions and laws mimicking the mathematical model.

Haskell Monads

Besides the mathematical background, monads, as a constructor class, are fully integrated into the Haskell language. However, creating a monad type constructor requires both defining an instance of the monad class and fulfilling the *monad laws*. The latter cannot be enforced by the compiler, as the complexity of enforcing the monad laws at compile time is equivalent to solving the halting problem [CC07], and has to be assured by the programmer.

The monad class definition declares four functions on the constructed monad type: (>>=), the composition operator, also called *bind*; (>>), like bind but discarding previous results; `return`; and `fail`. (>>) and `fail` have default declarations and thus do not necessarily need to be overwritten by the instance declaration.

```
30  class Monad m where
31    (>>=)  :: m a -> (a -> m b) -> m b
32    (>>)   :: m a ->    m b     -> m b
33    return :: a -> m a
34    fail   :: String -> m a
35    -- default declarations⁸
36    m >> k = m >>= \_ -> k
37    fail s = error s
```

In line 36 the second argument of the bind operator (`\_ -> k`) is an anonymous function called λ-expression (`\` symbolizing the greek letter λ). The function definition `f x = y` is equivalent to `f = \x -> y`. The underscore `_` denotes an always matching wildcard pattern where the matching value is not assigned to a variable because it is not needed further in the program.

The `bind` operator (>>=) describes the monad composition operation. It composes two monadic functions (called monadic actions or computations) to form a compound action. When the compound action is executed, the first

---
[8] This line is a comment. Comments in Haskell start with two dashes (--)

2. Foundations

action is evaluated first, feeding its result into the second action which generates then the result of the compound action.

The `return` function generates a monadic action out of an arbitrary base type value. We cannot bind base type values directly to monadic transformations, only actions can be combined with other actions. Informally, `return` creates a transformation passing on the given value as its result.

Every Haskell monad has to obey the monad laws. The first law (line 38) formalizes what we just informally said. It requires return to be a left identity function for `bind`. The second law (line 39) requires return to be a right identity function. The third law (line 40) finally requires `bind` to be associative. All monad laws are usually fulfilled when creating *normal* monads and should be proved for newly created monads.

```
38  return x >>= f    == f x
39  m >>= return      == m
40  (m >>= f) >>= g   == m >>= (\x -> f x >>= g)
```

The beauty of the monad abstraction is that it is possible to let each action perform also an (implicit) state transformation of a monadic state. A compound monadic action is then effectively a sequence of state transformations like a sequence of statements in imperative programming. However, using the Haskell constructor type `Monad`, we are certain to confine any state transformation, which is a side effect, type-safely to the monad. The monad wraps the side effects and purity is fully maintained. We make the state transformations explicit and use it in our program as we do in this work (see Section 2.3) but we are not required to.

Monads, finally, have to be started to unwrap the value out of the monadic computation. A start function extracts the value of the compound monadic computation.

IO Monad

The `IO`-Monad, predefined in Haskell, manages an implicit state, the *RealWorld*. Of course, nothing like the real world could be fed through a computer program. Modelling the sequential nature of side effects, we can think of the `RealWorld` data type as being like a baton in a relay race passed from action to action [Y[+]09]. In fact, the *ghc* [Mar10] implementation uses a token to be passed between `IO`-actions. The side effect is that the real world is being modified when passed on which is not modeled within Haskell and does not have to be.

When we had to define the IO-Monad it would look like the following. Note that this is not real Haskell.

```
41  type IO a = RealWorld -> (a, RealWorld)

42  instance Monad IO where
43    -- (>>=) :: IO a -> (a -> IO b) -> IO b
44    (a >>= k) world0 = case a world0 of
45                        (r, world1) -> k r world1
46    -- return :: a -> IO a
47    return a world -> (a, world)
48    ...
```

Every Haskell program consists of a main function. It is declared as

```
49  main :: IO ()
```

which makes it a real world state transformation function. The run-time system implicitly starts the IO-Monad when the main function is called. The () type is called *unit*, a single element data type consisting of only the () constructor. The Haskell main function generates an action representing the whole program yielding a () result. We ignore the result as we are only interested in the state transformation as a side effect of the program. Now, we can write programs like

```
50  main =
51    putStr "Hello World. " >>
52    putStrLn "How are you?" >>
53    getLine >>= \answer ->
54    putStrLn answer
```

with functions

```
55  putStr, putStrLn :: String -> IO ()
```

to output and

```
56  getLine :: IO String
```

to input String type values yielding a possible result of:

2. Foundations

```
> main
Hello World. How are you?
> fine
fine
```

The monadic portions of a Haskell program can be written in a more convenient way, called the do notation.

```
57  main = do
58    putStr "Hello World. "
59    putStrLn "How are you?"
60    answer <- getLine
61    putStrLn answer
```

What looks like an imperative program in lines 57–61 is merely *syntactic sugar* for monads. The above program is equivalent to the one in lines 50–54. In fact, the compiler translates the do notation into the monadic bind and return functions. The do notation expresses the imperative character of a monad.

State Monad

The IO-Monad is a specialized version of a *state monad* implementing explicit state transformations. A state monad is defined as a data type State s a representing the monadic action.

```
62  data State s a = ST (s -> (a, s))
```

It is a function taking a state and returning both the result and a new state which possibly differs from the input state.

```
63  instance Monad (State s) where
64    -- (>>=) :: State s a -> (a -> State s b)
65    --                   -> State s b
66    (ST st0) >>= f = ST (\s0 -> let (r1, s1) = st0 s0
67                                    (ST st1) = f r1
68                                in (st1 s1))
69    -- return :: a -> State s a
70    return x = ST (\s -> (x, s))
```

14

2.1. Haskell

Bind (>>=) defines a sequencing function composition of two monadic actions (lines 66 – 68). Action st0 is applied to state s0 resulting in an intermediate result r1 and state s1. The composition function f is applied to r1 yielding another monadic action st1 which, applied to the intermediate state s1, delivers the final result and the final state of this monadic composition. The return function creates a monadic action simply returning the result and the unmodified state.

The state monad requires an explicit start function to finally unwrap the monadic value back into the functional world. The start function is applied to the initial state. Thus, it can be defined as:

```
71  runState :: (State s a) -> s -> a
72  runState (ST tr) s = fst (tr s)
```

Then the following program is a very simple example of a state monad application:

```
73  update :: (s -> s) -> State s s
74  update f = ST (\st -> (st, f st))

75  test :: State Int [Int]
76  test = do
77      x <- update (+3)
78      y <- update (+(-2))
79      z <- update id
80      return [x, y, z]

81  main = print (runState test 1)
```

The test function executes a series of state updates and returns an update record as a list of state changes, update generates a monadic action which returns the old state as its result and the updated state. The result is:

```
> main
[1,4,2]
```

In Section 2.3 we give a more sophisticated example where we describe how software transactions are embedded in a state monad.

2.1.3. Concurrent Haskell

As we will see in Section 2.2 in more detail, concurrent systems need thread management and synchronization to enable a mutual exclusive access to shared

2. Foundations

resources. *Concurrent Haskell* [PJGF96, PJ01] is an extension to *Haskell 98* to enable writing concurrent Haskell applications. Concurrent Haskell is also the basis for building distributed Haskell frameworks as we will see in the following chapters.

Concurrent Haskell provides IO-Monad functions to manage threads. Most important are thread creation and termination functions:

```
82 data ThreadId
```

`ThreadId` is an abstract datatype identifying a thread.

```
83 forkIO :: IO () -> IO ThreadId
```

The IO-action `forkIO` takes an `IO ()` action, creates a new child thread returning immediately to its caller with the child `ThreadId`, and executes the action within the new asynchronous thread running concurrently to the calling parent thread. The child thread terminates when the child action is completed. The `killThread` action terminates a running thread identified by the `ThreadId` parameter.

```
84 killThread :: ThreadId -> IO ()
```

Additionally *Concurrent Haskell* offers IO-Monad functions to synchronize concurrent threads on shared variables:

```
85 data MVar a
```

The abstract data type `MVar a` is a *mutable* synchronization variable. The intuition of an `MVar` is a box being either empty or full. If the box is full it contains a value of type `a`. Regular Haskell variables are *immutable* as Haskell is a pure language (see Section 2.1). Mutable variables like `MVar`s can only be modified with IO-actions.

```
86 newMVar :: a -> IO (MVar a)
```

`newMVar` creates a new `MVar` filled with the given value of type `a`.

```
87 takeMVar :: MVar a -> IO a
```

`takeMVar` empties the given `MVar` and returns its value. If the `MVar` is already empty the calling thread is suspended until the `MVar` is filled by another thread. In this case, the calling thread resumes and `takeMVar` finally returns its value.

2.1. Haskell

```
88  putMVar :: MVar a -> a -> IO ()
```
putMVar fills the given MVar by writing the given value into it. If the MVar is already full, the calling thread is suspended. It resumes when the MVar is emptied by another thread and putMVar finally writes the value.

An example shows how these concurrency constructs can be used in practice. We want to implement a simplified version of the producer/consumer problem. A producer thread generates continuously numbers into a shared storage. Another thread continuously consumes these numbers out of that storage. We need to model the system such that access to the storage is mutual exclusive. Further, no number should be dropped because a fast producer fills the storage before it can be consumed by a slower consumer thus overwriting a previously produced value.

```
89  producer :: MVar Int -> Int -> IO ()
90  producer mVar i = do
91    putMVar mVar i
92    producer mVar (i+1)


93  consumer :: MVar Int -> IO ()
94  consumer mVar = do
95    i <- takeMVar mVar
96    print i
97    consumer mVar

98  loop = loop

99  main = do
100   mVar <- newMVar 0
101   tIdp <- forkIO (producer mVar 1)
102   tIdc <- forkIO (consumer mVar)
103   loop
```

The above simple program shows the idea. In line 100 the main program creates a new synchronizing MVar containing the initial value 0 and forks both a producer and a consumer thread in lines 101–102 initialized with that MVar. Additionally the producer is initialized with 1 as the first value to be produced. The loop function defined line 98 and called in line 103 is an infinite loop to keep the threads alive forever. The result in this example is that both threads run concurrently. If the producer thread accesses the MVar first it is suspended as the MVar is already full. The consumer thread empties the MVar which wakes

2. Foundations

up the producer thread to fill the `MVar` again. No matter what schedule the threads have, the end result will be a synchronized alternating consume-produce cycle outputting the numbers 0, 1, 2, 3, ... where each number is printed on a separate line.

Note that an `MVar` value could be modified by calling `takeMVar` immediately followed by `putMVar`. However, this is unsafe because the runtime system may switch the context between the two calls. Another thread may have accessed the `MVar`, in between. As a result, unexpected blocking may occur. The functions `modifyMVar_` (line 104) and `modifyMVar` (line 105) modify the `MVar` content safely. The latter function additionally returns a value.

```
104  modifyMVar_  :: MVar a -> (a -> IO a) -> IO ()

105  modifyMVar   :: MVar a -> (a -> IO (a, b)) -> IO b
```

2.1.4. Haskell Exceptions

Like many practical programming languages, Haskell supports exception handling. Exceptions can be seen as a programming abstraction to eliminate the possibly last remaining reason for the infamous `goto` statement [Dij68] by allowing multiple exit points of program scopes being caught in one defined place.

In Haskell 98, standard `IO` exceptions are raised synchronously to the program flow. These are extended in [PJ01] to integrate also synchronous exceptions in pure code as well as asynchronous exceptions. The difficulties to fully describe a semantic for the latter, in our view, support the relative closeness to the problematic `goto`. A thorough discussion and description of Haskell asynchronous exceptions can be found in [MPJMR01]. Hardware generated exceptions are always asynchronous by their nature.

The Haskell exception abstraction is that exceptions are thrown to exit a program scope arbitrarily and are caught by an error handler surrounding that scope. The ghc system defines a comprehensive exception interface. Essentially, the following three functions are sufficient for designing robust software.

```
106  catch    :: IO a -> (Exception -> IO a) -> IO a

107  throw    :: Exception -> a
108  throwTo  :: ThreadId -> Exception -> IO ()
```

2.1. Haskell

The `catch` function defined in line 106 executes its IO action argument. If, during execution, an exception is raised, the exception handler is called with the raised exception of type `Exception` as its parameter. Otherwise, `catch` returns the original execution result. A thread raises an exception of type `Exception` synchronously to its execution calling `throw` (line 107). It raises an asynchronous[9] exception in other threads, identified by their `ThreadId`, by calling `throwTo` (line 108).

The `Exception` type itself is predefined. There are numerous constructors for all kinds of machine and program generated error conditions. However, it is cumbersome to incorporate user defined error definitions. A `DynException` constructor allows to define own exception types but those must be handled differently thus not fitting the concise abstraction given above. Luckily, ghc now incorporates a very elegant mechanism allowing dynamically typed exceptions.

2.1.5. Dynamically-Typed Exceptions

Simon Marlow shows an implementation of an extensible dynamically-typed hierarchy of exceptions in [Mar06] allowing exceptions of user-defined types to be caught by a single overloaded `catch` operator for concise error handling.

```
109   catch    :: Exception e => IO a -> (e -> IO a) -> IO a

110   throw    :: Exception e => e -> a
111   throwTo  :: Exception e => ThreadId -> e -> IO ()
```

The application interface is almost identical to the previous one, only the predefined `Exception` type now becomes a type class which then can be instantiated by the user.

```
112   class (Typeable e, Show e) => Exception e where
113     toException   :: e -> SomeException
114     fromException :: SomeException -> Maybe e
```

The `Exception` type class predefines two conversion functions (lines 113, 114). The `toException` and `fromException` functions wrap and unwrap the exception type constructor, respectively. Thus, the type class mechanism enables a user-defined dynamic exception hierarchy. The type `e` is constrained by

---
[9]The ghc-implementation still synchronizes the delivery of an asynchronous exception with the throwing thread.

the `Show` class to ensure that the exception can be printed and by `Typeable` to ensure a type-safe type cast within `fromException`. Thus, the exception type can be compared with the supplied type.

```
115  data SomeException = forall e . Exception e =>
116                      SomeException e
117                      deriving Typeable

118  instance Show SomeException where
119    show (SomeException e) = show e

120  instance Exception SomeException
```

The exception type `SomeException` is the predefined root of the exception type hierarchy we can dynamically generate. It is defined as an existentially-quantified type, constrained by the `Exception` class. The quantification, made explicit by the `forall` keyword, hides the type parameter from the exception type. The required `Typeable` functions are generically derived.

It is possible to define further hierarchies or add branches to existing ones. We define our own Distributed Software Transactional Memory library exceptions in Chapter 6. For further insight into the exception extension beyond the scope of this book, we refer to the literature.

2.2. Concurrency and Distribution

Concurrent and distributed systems are closely related. Although their applications are quite different, the programming logic shares important similarities like managing commonly shared resources. A resource can be anything connected to the computer, like memory, devices, or interfaces. Conceptually, a resource is simply a memory location as all resources are eventually mapped to memory addresses. Computer hardware development[PF06] has inspired the development and improvement of concurrent and distributed systems as well as generated new theoretical concepts and abstractions.

2.2.1. Hardware Development

In the early days of electronic computing machines, in the middle of the twentieth century, programs were executed consecutively on one computer. This

2.2. Concurrency and Distribution

processing style is called batch mode. A batch of programs is executed one after the other. Naturally, the one program in execution can access all computer resources without interfering with other programs not running at that time. Each program only has to preserve the state of all used resources before and after the program run.

Later, the mainframe and then personal computers became powerful enough to easily execute multiple programs or *tasks* quasi parallel using a *scheduler*. A scheduler in a multitasking operating system alternatingly executes time slices of all active tasks until all tasks are terminated. Thus, the user has the impression of a parallel operation. In reality, each processing unit within a computer physically can still only execute one program task at a time. Changing the active executing program is called a *context switch*. The quasi parallel execution, however, raises the problem of two tasks conflictingly accessing the same resources at the same time. This conflict is in part resolved by virtually multiplying and *swapping* computing memory. Multitasking operating system circumvent parallel memory accesses by issuing an individual virtual address space to each program and swapping the virtual address spaces with the one real address space at each context switch.

A program, however, cannot duplicate physical resources and, therefore, needs to access them exclusively. Thus, the operating system temporarily confines those accesses to one task only. On a program task level, this is transparent to the application developer. The operating systems performs the necessary work under the hood using a locking mechanism. We look into lock-based synchronization in more detail in Section 2.2.3.

With increasing numbers of computers used, the need to exchange information among them pushed the development of computer networks. These networks enable efficient scaling of computing power using geographically distributed systems but create the additional problem of physically distributed memory resources. Every synchronizing mechanism for distributed memory has to exchange information by sending and receiving network messages.

Nowadays, computer networks consist not only of dedicated computers but of all kind of mobile and embedded devices, like washing machines and refrigerators. Distributed systems in general and mobile distributed systems in particular not only need to deal with shared resources but with fluctuating devices raising a need for increased security and robustness of the system. In our work we present a transactional memory based mechanism to create a robust distributed system in Chapter 6.

2. Foundations

Continued hardware improvements made processors become increasingly faster. In recent years further speed improvements reached a physical barrier, thus, leading to multi-core processor designs. Conceptually, this is also a shared resources problem. Each processor core could either execute a different program or one program could be executed in parallel on different cores. The operating system then has to assure the exclusive access to common resources. Current research works on improving the scheduling mechanisms for multiple programs running on multiple cores within one processor. Although the underlying problem of synchronizing shared resources is similar to distributed systems, we will not further discuss multi-core architectures in this book.

2.2.2. Concurrent Systems

The described hardware development triggered the development of concurrent programming concepts which are as well suited to implement natural solutions for many problems that could otherwise be modeled using sequential algorithms. Concurrent systems allow to use *threads* within one task rather than process tasks in a multitasking environment. Threads are the smallest processing units a run-time system can schedule. They can be looked at as lightweight processes within a process. A concurrent run-time system enables thread creation, scheduling, termination, and synchronization between different threads.

A classic example for using concurrent algorithms is the *Dining Philosophers* problem [Dij71]. *Dijkstra* used this example to illustrate problems like

Figure 2.1.: Dining Philosophers Problem

2.2. Concurrency and Distribution

deadlocks and unfairness occurring with lock-based synchronization of shared resources.

The story is that five philosophers are sitting around a table with a big plate of spaghetti in the middle (see Figure 2.1 [Lea08]). Between two philosophers there is one fork. Each philosopher continuously either thinks or wants to eat. Each philosopher decides independently of the others what to do which makes the overall system non-deterministic. In order to eat he or she needs to acquire two forks, one from next to each neighbor. After acquiring two forks, the philosopher eats for a while, then returns both forks, and thinks for a while. The story describes a repeated concurrent setting of five tasks and five resources where each task briefly requires exclusive access to two restricted resources.

A program fragment for a dining philosopher thread would look like:

```
121 phil i = do
122   thinkAWhile
123   eatAWhile i
124   phil i

125 eatAWhile i = do
126   enter i Left  -- acquire fork left of i
127   enter i Right -- acquire fork right of i
128   criticalEatingSection
129   leave i Left  -- return fork left of i
130   leave i Right -- return fork right of i
```

Lines 121–124 let the philosopher i alternately think and eat. Lines 125–130 define the eating function. The actual eating (line 128) is a *critical section*. Before the philosopher can start eating, he or she needs to acquire both the left and right hand side fork. We assume doing this with the function **enter** (lines 126–127). With the **leave** function (line 130) the philosopher returns the forks when the eating is finished. These functions restrict the access of philosopher tasks to the critical section so that only one philosopher can acquire a specific fork at any time. We call this a *mutual exclusive* access of the shared resources.

Figure 2.2 shows a possible schedule of the *Dining Philosopher* program running five philosopher threads (Ph.1–Ph.5). In the example there are enough resources (forks) for two threads (philosophers) to run (eat) in parallel provided the eating philosophers are no direct neighbors. The diagram shows that all philosopher threads may think at the same time. However, at any given time at most two philosophers may eat. Other threads (philosophers) who may wish

23

2. Foundations

thinkAWhile	blocked		crit
thinkAWhile	blocked	criticalEatingSection	thin
thinkAWhile	criticalEatingSection	thinkAWhile	bloc. c₀
thinkAWhile	blocked	criticalEatingSection	th
thinkAWhile	criticalEatingSection	thinkAWhile	blocked

→ time

Figure 2.2.: Possible schedule with critical sections

to enter the critical section (eat) are blocked until the shared resources (forks) become available.

The thread can either block itself actively by repeatedly checking the resource availability, called *busy waiting*[10], or the blocked process can suspend itself due to the unavailable resource. Usually, the suspension is transparent to the thread. When it tries to access a shared resource a signal is sent to the operating or run-time system that the thread currently can not continue properly because of an unavailable resource. The scheduler exempts this thread then from its schedule until the resource becomes available again.

We can see that the longer the critical sections are the longer are potential blocking periods. Therefore, each task should be designed to keep critical sections relatively short to not destroy the impression of a parallel execution of the concurrent program. The `enter` and `leave` functions controlling the critical section are assumed to take no execution time and are thus not shown in this schedule.

Concurrent threads execute non-deterministically. Depending on the implementation of the mutual exclusive access to the critical section (see *locks* in Section 2.2.3), deadlocks and other critical things can happen, hence its name. With the Dining Philosopher example we can show three typical scenarios occurring with concurrent systems.

---

[10] A blocked, busy waiting process unintentionally consumes computation power although it actually should do nothing.

24

2.2. Concurrency and Distribution

Cooperation All philosophers act cooperatively. Regularly each one has access to the necessary two forks. Two non-neighbor philosophers eat at the same time. When they are finished both their right (or left) neighbors start eating. The whole system works as intended.

Livelock One or two philosophers act uncooperatively. They acquire both forks again just after they returned them so that none of the other philosophers has a chance to eat and dies from *starvation*.

If the philosophers have different appetites and agree on an eating priority an uncooperative low appetite philosopher can lead to *priority inversion* by keeping a high appetite colleague waiting.

Deadlock All philosophers act uncooperatively. Each one either acquires, at first, the right fork or the left fork, respectively. None of them is able to take a second fork to start eating. The whole system is blocked.

The only successful and fair scenario is the cooperative one. Therefore, we have to synchronize access to the critical section in such a way that neither unfairness nor deadlocks can occur. This has to be true for every possible scheduling taking place. This last requirement can be very difficult to test or prove. If the result of the concurrent application depends on the order of execution we call this a *race-condition*. Therefore, sound and easy to use synchronization mechanisms are of utmost importance to concurrent programming.

2.2.3. Lock-based Synchronization

The intuition to synchronizing a critical section is a door lock. The critical section is locked and there is only one key. Whoever has the key may enter the critical section. When exiting the critical section the key-holder forwards the key to somebody waiting to enter or leaves it for the next one to come.

Lock Primitives

The programmatic solution for this intuition is a memory location (the lock) capable of holding two distinct values — unlocked and locked. A thread that wants to *enter* the critical section checks if the memory lock holds the value locked. In case of a locked section, the thread actively waits until it becomes unlocked by trying to *enter* again. This is called *busy waiting*. Otherwise, it

25

2. Foundations

writes the value locked into the memory lock itself and enters the critical section. When *leaving* it, the thread writes the value unlocked into the memory lock again.

```
131  enter cs = do
132     if (isLocked cs)
133        then enter cs  -- (busy) waiting
134        else lock cs   -- enter critical section

135  leave cs = unlock cs
```

This naive implementation[11], however, will not work for every schedule. Suppose a thread has verified that the critical section is unlocked and decides to enter it (line 134). Then the scheduler invokes a context switch and another thread verifies also the unlocked critical section and enters it. Then the first thread resumes operation and also enters the critical section now violating the mutual exclusive access property.

There are proven, purely software-based solutions to guarantee a mutual exclusive access ([Lam74, Pet81]). Although being sound, their main disadvantage is not being very practical because they do not scale well and rely on busy waiting. As we have seen, one of the reasons to use concurrent programming is to benefit from more powerful hardware. Busy waiting is therefore counterproductive.

A more efficient solution is hardware supported. Multitasking systems offer a machine command that tests a lock and sets it atomically. This test-and-set operation cannot be interrupted by the run-time nor the operating system. Either system omits busy waiting by suspending the thread during the execution of the test-and-set command when the tested resource is already locked. It resumes the thread as soon as the resource is unlocked by the other thread leaving this critical section.

Lock Abstractions

Multitasking operating systems offer locks in a variety of application interfaces [PF06]. Depending on the implementation, there are *Mutexes* which simply lift the test-and-set primitive to the application level and *semaphores*[12] which offer

---

[11] For better readability we show `enter` and `leave` for an arbitrary critical section. The Dining Philosopher example would require a slightly more elaborate version.

[12] Mutexes are sometimes referred to as binary semaphores because their lock state can be seen as a binary counter.

2.2. Concurrency and Distribution

an additional counter to model sharing a set of equal resources instead of only one.

Another lock abstraction is called *monitor* [Hoa74]. It models a critical section as an object with access methods and condition variables. The programmer can call `wait` and `signal` on condition variables. `Wait` causes the calling thread to suspend. `Signal` resumes another thread being suspended on the same condition variable. The monitor object manages the mutual exclusive access property as long as the programmer uses the condition variables properly.

Deadlock

Locks offer a simple and comprehensive interface to implement efficient concurrent applications. However, locks offer only a poor abstraction for the mutual exclusion of shared resources and their application is error prone. As seen in the dining philosopher example (Section 2.2.2), deadlocks can occur when access to a (logical) critical section is protected by multiple (physical) locks.

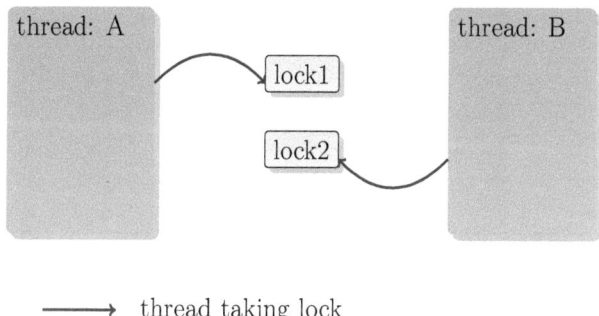

⟶ thread taking lock

Figure 2.3.: Multiple locks: Threads outside critical section

Figures 2.3–2.5 show the development of a deadlock with two threads A and B that are about to enter a critical section which is protected by both *lock1* and *lock2*. In Figure 2.4 thread A already holds *lock1* while thread B holds *lock2*. Now, both locks are taken and neither thread has a chance to acquire the other lock. Therefore, both threads wait for the additional lock to become available. As this will never happen, processing cannot continue with these threads. We

2. Foundations

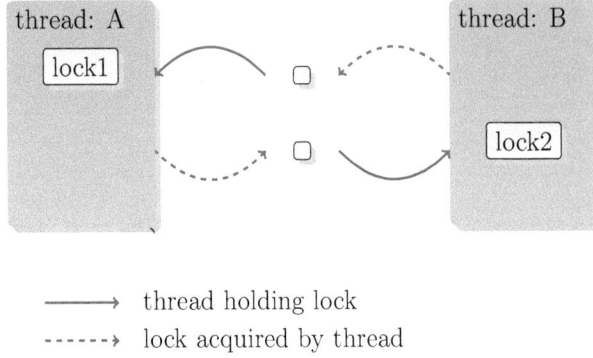

Figure 2.4.: Multiple locks: Threads acquiring initial locks

call this situation a *deadlock* (Figure 2.5) which can be seen as a cycle in a lock hold/acquire graph.

There are algorithms to detect deadlocks and software strategies to either prohibit or resolve those. One strategy is to enlarge the critical sections such that they encompass multiple resources. Instead of individual locks for each resource only one lock for the whole region is required. The downside of such coarse grained locking is then reduced concurrency and increased serialization of the program.

In this book we will not further discuss strategies in lock-based algorithms. Instead, in Section 2.3 we show that *Software Transactional Memory* is a more adequate solution for managing critical sections with multiple shared resources.

2.2.4. Distributed Systems

Tanenbaum defines a distributed system as a collection of independent computers that appear to its users as a single coherent system [TVS01]. The application programmer sees the system behaving transparently as one machine.

As we will see in the remainder of this section and in detail in the main part of this book, a library programmer regards the collection of computers indeed as independent *processes* assuming the responsibility of coordinating their behavior. The collection of computers is connected through a network. The *Internet* is the worldwide standard computer network. It is based on the

2.2. Concurrency and Distribution

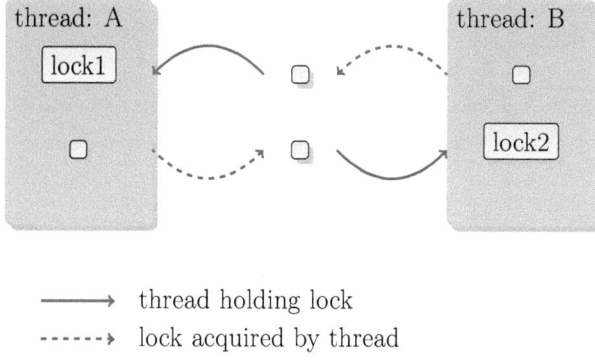

→ thread holding lock
⇢ lock acquired by thread

Figure 2.5.: Multiple locks: Deadlock (lock hold/acquire cycle)

internet protocol suite which we look at more closely later in this section. Multi-processing operating systems are capable of scheduling multiple processes on a single physical computer device. A network can be seen as a graph structure where the edges are called nodes and the vertices are network connections. Therefore, distributed processes are often called *process nodes* or just *nodes*. We use the term *process* when emphasizing the software aspect and *node* when emphasizing the network topology aspect of the distributed system.

There are problems naturally defined with distributed resources. Rather than using a sequential or a concurrent approach, we have to model those as *distributed systems*. If, for example, we wanted to control all ATM machines a bank operates, we would model a system consisting of independent ATM computers exchanging information with other system resources transparent to the application programmer.

Other problems can be modeled perfectly well using concurrent or sequential algorithms but we may want to explicitly profit from added reliability and scalability provided by distributed systems. Distributed systems like Glasgow Distributed Haskell [PTL01] enable scalability and reliability using additional resources. As an example we could model a database process providing information to client processes. When data traffic increases we could add proxy nodes between the database and the clients to relieve the database itself from computation load and thereby improve response times. We could also add redundant database processes which do nothing else than keeping themselves

2. Foundations

synchronized with the main database process. In case of a failure of the main process, a redundant process would replace it so that the distributed system as a whole continues to operate.

Distributed and concurrent systems are structurally similar. Both systems divide a complete program computation into parts executed in individual computing units coordinating their behavior by exchanging information. Table 2.1 summarizes the major characteristics of both systems.

CHARACTERISTIC	CONCURRENT SYSTEM	DISTRIBUTED SYSTEM
system boundary	process	network
computation unit	thread	process
communication	shared memory	network messages
synchronization	run-time/library	library
scalability	single process limit	unrestricted
redundancy	single process limit	unrestricted

Table 2.1.: Characteristics of Concurrent and Distributed Systems

A small concurrent system is illustrated in Figure 2.6. Distributed systems operate on a larger scale. In general, their computation units, the process nodes, form a concurrent or multithreaded system itself as shown in Figure 2.7. Therefore, distributed systems are, just as concurrent systems, prone to problems like deadlock, unfairness and race-conditions and in addition require additional coordinating effort which may not be underestimated. We look into these issues in detail in the following chapters.

Network Communication

In this book we focus on internet-based distributed systems. Our solution, presented here, will work with any internet-based network architecture like Local Area Networks (LAN) or Wide Area Networks (WAN) and different network hardware like wire-based networks or Wireless Local Area Networks (WLAN). Discussions of network topology details are, however, beyond the scope of this book.

Network communication within internet-based systems uses the internet protocol suite, also known as TCP/IP. It is a layered protocol where each hierarchy layer assumes a different role in the communication process as shown in Table 2.2. Application programmers use application layer protocols to create web

2.2. Concurrency and Distribution

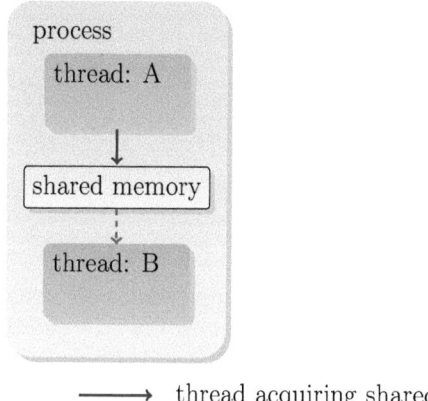

⟶ thread acquiring shared memory
┄┄► shared memory acquired by thread

Figure 2.6.: Concurrent System

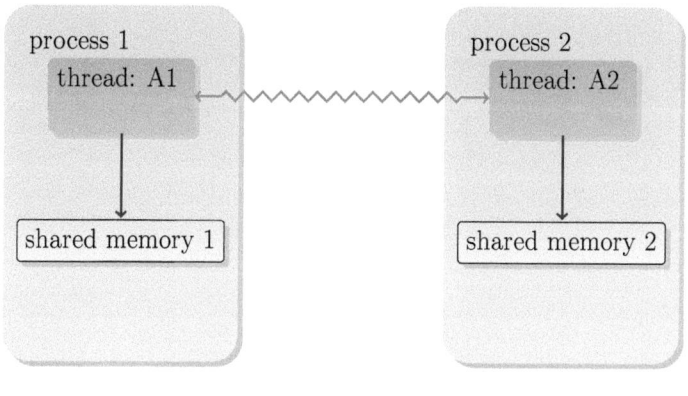

⟶ thread acquiring shared memory
⌇► network message

Figure 2.7.: Distributed System

2. Foundations

LAYER	PROTOCOL	ADDRESS
Application	HTTP, FTP, POP3, ...	*application specific*
Transport	UDP, TCP, ...	Port
Internet	IP, ...	IP-Address
Network Link	Ethernet, WLAN, ...	MAC-Address

Table 2.2.: Internet Protocol Layers and network message addressing

browsers (HTTP), file transfer programs (FTP), e-mail clients (POP3)[13] and many others. In Chapter 4 we define an application layer protocol ourselves.

These top layer protocols use in turn transport layer protocols to communicate between network node ports. Ports are logical addresses within a network node to identify a certain service provided by that node. As an example, port 80 is used for web services. There are connection-less (UDP) and connection oriented (TCP)[14] models. A UDP transport just sends application data packets (datagrams) to one or many receivers. There is no overhead for verifying the process. Therefore, this is a fast but unreliable transport method. TCP establishes a connection between two ports. All communication then takes place through this connection and includes exception handling and error recovery. This is a reliable transport method between two processes (*peer-to-peer*) including some managing overhead.

Either transport method uses the *internet protocol* (IP) or other internet layer protocols to send and receive its data to and from the recipients internet address. Each internet network node is associated with a logical address. As an example 134.245.12.21 is the IP address of the web server of the Christian-Albrechts-Universität. However, we mostly use human readable addresses like www.uni-kiel.de. There are internet name services that convert between both address types.

The lowest layer protocols used by the internet layer finally determine which hardware is used to actually communicate the internet layer data packets. Therefore, unique physical or *media access control* (MAC) addresses are used to address the packets.

The run-time system provides a socket interface to enable a connection-

---
[13]HTTP = HyperText Transfer Protocol, FTP = File Transfer Protocol, POP3 = Post Office Protocol version 3
[14]UDP=User Datagram Protocol, TCP=Transport Control Protocol

oriented network-communication. The socket interface maps a transport layer communication port onto a software socket that the application-program uses to communicate between a server node and a client node. We show the basic Haskell socket interface. The server creates a new socket based on a given port with the `listenOn` function (line 136). The `accept` function (line 137) prepares the server socket to receive network messages that a client sends. The client uses `connectTo` (line 138) to prepare sending messages to a given node address, defined by its IP address and TCP port. The client and server applications then use the resulting handle to read and write network messages. A detailed description of the Haskell socket interface and its types used can be found in [Tib09].

```
136  listenOn  :: PortID  -> IO Socket
137  accept    :: Socket  -> IO (Handle, Address, PortNumber)

138  connectTo :: Address -> PortID -> IO Handle
```

2.3. Software Transactional Memory

Herlihy and Moss proposed a lock-free solution to synchronize concurrent tasks in [HM93]. They called their hardware supported approach *Transactional Memory (TM)*. The term *Software Transactional Memory (STM)* was coined by Shavit and Touitou in [ST95], where they proposed a purely software-based approach built on the hardware-based ideas. Harris, Marlow, Peyton Jones and Herlihy proposed a further STM abstraction for Concurrent Haskell [HMPJH05]. Commonly, these approaches are based on the transaction[15] concept known from databases. They allow programmers to specify transaction sequences which are executed atomically. Much work has been published on TM. A comprehensive overview of the TM literature can be found in [HLR10]. The focus of this book is on Haskell STM, however.

In comparison to lock-based approaches (see Section 2.2.3), the TM concept provides automatic roll-back on exceptions or timeouts and freedom from the tension between lock granularity and concurrency, hence, freedom from deadlock and priority inversion. Note that programmers may still introduce dead-

---

[15] The English meaning of *transaction* is the action of conducting a business. Its latin origin (*trans* - across, beyond, through; *agere* - do, lead)[Qui08] more distinctively denotes an action that leads from one state across intermediate states to another state.

2. Foundations

locks to their applications, however, the powerful modular STM abstraction makes it much harder to do so.

2.3.1. Database Transactions

Database systems are among the early widely used applications for computer systems. Today, the world wide economic system relies heavily on well behaving database management systems. For this reason alone a lot of research is invested in databases, much of it in the last quarter of the past century. Therefore, it is no coincidence that the transaction concept has been chosen as a synchronization abstraction outside the database domain as well. It is obviously powerful enough to securely handle billions of bank transactions every day.

The database transaction concept derives from contract law [Gra81]. Two or more parties agree on a contract. An external party like a notary public verifies the agreement of all contract parties and either sanctions this agreement thus rendering it permanently valid or declares the agreement being invalid. Transposed to database or computer terms in general, a transaction is a series of permanent state transforming consistent actions of which either none or all are performed. Thus, a transaction has two possible outcomes. It can be *committed* or it can be *aborted*. Additionally, actions within transactions, especially when performed concurrently, need to be hidden from actions within other transactions. As a result, database transactions adhere to the *ACID* principles [HR83].

Atomicity Either all or no action is committed

Consistency Committed transactions always generate legal results

Isolation Actions have no effect outside their transaction until committed

Durability Committed transaction results are final

These principles lead to the implementation of current database management systems. The solutions are optimized for efficiency on large scale data input and reliability on current computer hardware.

2.3. Software Transactional Memory

2.3.2. Transactional Memory

The idea behind *transactional memory* is a mutable variable, called *transactional variable*. There are base operations like creating, reading from, and writing to transactional variables. These base operations can be combined to a collection of operations such that either the whole collection or none of it is executed.

We call a successfully executed collection a *committed* transaction and a not executed collection an *aborted* transaction. A committed transaction mutates its transactional variables. Thus, it has a visible effect on the outside world. A transaction commits, if there is no synchronizing conflict with other transactions. Otherwise, the transaction aborts. There is a synchronization conflict, if any of the transactional variables read in a transaction has been committed afterwards by another transaction. This constitutes an *inconsistent* view of the transactional memory. As a consequence, the former transaction aborts.

The Haskell STM solution is an *optimistic* transactional approach. It assumes that, in general, there are no synchronization conflicts. Therefore, Haskell transactions operate concurrently in isolation, at first. When the isolated operation is finished, the transaction synchronizes with all other concurrently executed transactions that are sharing any of its transactional variables. The synchronization itself requires a locking strategy. First, the transaction checks for synchronization conflicts and then either commits or aborts. We call this check a *validation*. When committed, the effect of all base operations within the transaction becomes visible to other transactions. When aborted, there is no outside effect. The transaction forgets all operations made in isolation[16] and the isolated operations are re-executed. Thus, the transaction restarts itself[17].

2.3.3. Transactions for Concurrent Haskell

Harris, Marlow, Peyton Jones and Herlihy efficiently implemented the STM abstraction as an external *C*-primitive library in current releases of the Glasgow Haskell compiler (ghc) [Mar10]. In this book we refer to this implementation as *Concurrent Haskell Software Transactional Memory*. The implementation relies on the fair implementation of Concurrent Haskell within ghc. There are

---

[16]Depending on the implementation, the transactional memory system inevitably generates visible effects and, hence, cannot simply forget its operations. Instead the effect of such prematurely executed operations is reverted. This is often called a *rollback*.

[17]There are implementations that do not restart an aborted transaction automatically.

2. Foundations

also lightweight Haskell library implementations [HK05, Sch09a] which allow porting STM to other implementations of Concurrent Haskell [Cla99], as in Hugs [OY06], and easily enable additions and changes of the STM application programming interface (API) which makes it more maintainable. *Concurrent Haskell Software Transactional Memory*, in addition to essential STM benefits like deadlock prevention, provides:

- Strong guarantee of proper STM-library application leveraging the Haskell type system

- Compositional transactions allowing small transactions to be safely composed to one large transaction

- Both sequential and alternative composition operations

- Composition aware modular blocking

Harris, Marlow, Peyton Jones and Herlihy modeled transactions as an abstract data type monad STM. The execution of a transaction is guaranteed to be atomic with respect to other concurrently executed threads. STM provides *optimistic synchronization* of *transactional variables* (*TVar*) which means transactions can be interleaved with other transactions. A transaction is committed only if no other transaction has modified transactional variables its execution depended on. Otherwise, the transaction is restarted. The STM library provides transactional variables as shared resources modeled as the abstract data type TVar which can only be used within the STM monad. The interface is defined as follows:

```
139  -- Transactional Monad
140  data STM a   -- abstract
141  instance Monad STM

142  -- Transactional variables
143  data TVar a   -- abstract

144  -- Running STM computations
145  atomic :: STM a -> IO a
146  retry  :: STM a
147  orElse :: STM a -> STM a -> STM a
```

2.3. Software Transactional Memory

```
148 -- Transactional variable access
149 newTVar   :: a -> STM (TVar a)
150 readTVar  :: TVar a -> STM a
151 writeTVar :: TVar a -> a -> STM ()

152 -- Exceptions
153 throw :: Exception -> STM a
154 catch :: STM a -> (Exception -> STM a) -> STM a
```

Transactions are started within the IO monad by means of **atomic**. When a transaction is finished, it is validated that the transaction was executed on a consistent system state meaning that no other finished transaction may have modified relevant parts of the system state in the meantime. In this case, the transaction is committed to the real (IO) world. Otherwise, it is aborted and restarted.

Accordingly, inconsistent application program states, as shared resources that are blocked by concurrent tasks, can be detected by programmers and solved manually by calling **retry** to explicitly abort and restart a transaction. The provided implementation of **retry**, however, avoids an immediate transaction restart and, thus, busy waiting. It rather suspends the thread performing **retry** until a re-execution again potentially can be successful because any of its read **TVars** has been mutated by another transaction. As such, **retry** enables an efficient transaction abort and restart.

The alternative composition, stm_1 `orElse` stm_2, combines two transactions such that if stm_1 performs a **retry** action, then this is caught and stm_2 is executed. If stm_1 succeeds, then stm_2 is not executed at all.

TVars storing any data modifiable by transactions can only be manipulated within the **STM** monad. Within the **STM** monad, only pure code and modifications of **TVars** are possible. No **IO** actions are allowed which guarantees a safe re-execution of transactions.

Finally, the **STM** monad provides exception handling, similar to the exception handling ghc provides for the **IO** monad. For details on *Concurrent Haskell Software Transactional Memory* see [HMPJH05]. In current ghc implementations the API has slightly changed. The **atomic** function is now called **atomically**, **catch** is called **catchSTM**. In addition, data invariants as proposed in [HPJ06] have been added with functions **always** :: STM a -> STM () and **alwaysSucceed** :: STM Bool -> STM (). We continue to use the original style API for brevity in this book.

37

2. Foundations

As a simple example, we show an STM implementation of the dining philosophers problem (see Section 2.2.2). Here, we let the philosophers eat using sticks. The sticks are represented by boolean `TVars`. A `True` value means the stick is laying on the table available to others.

```
155  type Stick = TVar Bool

156  takeStick :: Stick -> STM ()
157  takeStick s = do b <- readTVar s
158                   if b
159                     then writeTVar s False
160                     else retry

161  putStick :: Stick -> STM ()
162  putStick s = writeTVar s True
```

When trying to take a non-available stick, `takeStick` performs `retry` (line 160). The philosopher suspends until the value of the stick changes. Due to the two Boolean type constructors, the philosopher suspends exactly until its neighbor puts the stick back onto the table. Note that the efficiency of the `retry` mechanism depends on the `TVar` types of the transaction. Transactions on `TVar` types with one constructor may cause blocking and `TVar` types with more than two constructors may lead to immediate re-suspension.

```
163  phil :: Int -> Stick -> Stick -> IO ()
164  phil n l r = do
165    atomic $ do
166      takeStick l
167      takeStick r
168    putStrLn (show n++". Phil is eating.")
169    atomic $ do
170      putStick l
171      putStick r
172    phil n l r
```

By combining the two actions for taking the sticks as one atomic `STM` transaction, the program is deadlock free. Putting the sticks back on the table in one atomic action is not necessary but shorter than writing `atomic` twice. The code for starting n philosophers is presented for completeness. Lines 175–176 create a list of n TVars initialized with True by mapping the constant IO function `newTVar` on the list of the first n integers. The next lines (lines 177–178)

2.3. Software Transactional Memory

create all but the last philosopher threads by mapping an anonymous function with a three-tuple parameter over a list of such tuples created by zip3. Finally, line 179 creates the last philosopher thread initialized with left and right forks. The classic setting with five philosophers is started with the main function in line 180.

```
173   startPhils :: Int -> IO ()
174   startPhils n = do
175     sticks <- atomic $
176       mapM (const (newTVar True)) [1..n]
177     mapM_ (\(l,r,i)->forkIO (phil i l r))
178       (zip3 sticks (tail sticks) [1..n-1])[18]
179     phil n (last sticks) (head sticks)

180   main = startPhils 5
```

Software Transactional Memory described in [HMPJH05] is the main inspiration to this work. A concept of deadlock-free synchronization available in a pure functional language with a strong static type system proves to be a very valuable abstraction in concurrent programming. It has since its debut been well adopted by the Haskell programmer community and gone through a couple of improvements and evolution steps.

However, to our knowledge, there is no published work on combining strongly typed *Haskell Software Transactional Memory* and *distributed* programming. This combination is the main contribution of this work. It extends the STM abstraction to distributed systems and, thus, also to distributed fault tolerance which is a major benefit in itself. The following chapters describe in detail the implementation of our solution of *Robust Distributed Haskell Software Transactional Memory*.

---

[18]The Prelude function zip3 of type zip3 :: [a] -> [b] -> [c] -> [(a,b,c)] creates a list of tuples out of three lists.

Chapter 3
Using Distributed STM

The Distributed Software Transactional Memory library presented in this book gives the application programmer an abstraction to design complex distributed systems without worrying about an efficient and deadlock free communication.

We model a distributed system based on communication over the internet. Such a system consists of an arbitrary number of process nodes, each connected with the internet. The application programmer designs and creates the distributed system and transparently maintains a proper inter-process communication with the augmented Software Transactional Memory API that we supply with our library. The library hides the communication details from the application.

3.1. Library Interface Design

Concurrent Haskell applications benefit from the concise STM API, shown in Section 2.3.3. This API is, for many years, well established in the Haskell community. We want distributed system applications to be enabled to use a basically identical interface to make transitions between concurrent and distributed program development as easy as possible. Thus, reasoning about distributed systems becomes significantly less difficult. Application designers may easily test their concepts in a controlled concurrent environment before porting it to an open distributed setting, with only minimal changes required.

Therefore, our distributed API is mostly identical (lines 1–14) to the concurrent one. Note that we constrain the `TVar` handling functions with the class constraint `Dist`. For now we just assume that instances of class `Dist` ensure

3. Using Distributed STM

that transactional variables can be memory managed properly. Thus, large scale systems are feasible.

The functional programming language Erlang has a similar concept [Arm07] realizing both concurrent intra-process and distributed inter-process communication in message-passing style. Even concurrent Erlang programs do not synchronize on shared memory. Thus, distributed Erlang programs may be concurrently prototyped. In many other programming languages, concepts for concurrency and distribution are very different. Concurrent systems synchronize on shared memory using lock-based algorithms while their distributed counterparts synchronize using message-passing concepts. As a typical example, the imperative language Java offers concurrent libraries with different lock-based concepts and RMI as a message-passing distributed concept [Gar04].

We do augment the API, however, with functions explicitly necessary for distributed communication (lines 16–25). We also add dependability functionality, supplementing the possibilities of concurrent systems, to enable distributed robustness (see Section 3.4). We name this Haskell library *Distributed Software Transactional Memory* (*DSTM*[1]).

```
1    data STM a    -- abstract
2    instance Monad STM


3    -- Running STM computations
4    atomic  :: STM a -> IO a
5    retry   :: STM a
6    orElse  :: STM a -> STM a -> STM a


7    -- Transactional variables
8    data TVar a    -- abstract

9    newTVar    :: Dist a => a -> STM (TVar a)
10   readTVar   :: Dist a => TVar a -> STM a
11   writeTVar  :: Dist a => TVar a -> a -> STM ()


12   -- Exceptions
13   throw  :: Exception -> STM a
14   catch  :: STM a -> (Exception -> STM a) -> STM a
```

---

[1] In the literature we can find the acronym DSTM denoting also *Dynamic* STM. Throughout this book DSTM refers to *Distributed* STM.

3.1. Library Interface Design

```
15    -- Additional distributed interface
16    runDist          :: IO a -> IO a
17    registerTVar     :: Dist a =>
18                        TVar a -> String -> IO
19    deregisterTVar   :: String -> IO ()
20    lookupTVar       :: Dist a =>
21                        String -> String
22                        -> IO (Maybe (TVar a))
23    lookupWaitTVar   :: Dist a =>
24                        String -> Int -> String
25                        -> IO (Maybe (TVar a))
```

We model DSTM similar to the concurrent Haskell STM systems shown in Section 2.3.3, however, in a distributed system the transactional variable resources themselves may be distributed across the network. DSTM uses an implicit domain specific communication abstraction fully transparent to the application programmer. The abstraction hides the system node addresses from the application programmer. The distributed transactional variables carry the necessary communication information. Therefore, it is not necessary for the application to handle node addresses. In fact, it is not necessary for a node to know about other nodes at all, except for reasoning about system performance.

The inspiration for this communication abstraction is a process offering a shared resource, modeling this resource as a TVar. The TVar resources may be of any serializable type, hence, a type that can be encoded into and decoded from a universal representation which excludes pointer and function types. An often, also in this book, used universal representation is the String type. Explicitly, TVar types may be of type TVar, thus, also recursive TVar types are allowed. The library assures the serializability of the TVar itself. An application may send and receive easily TVars as values of other TVars. This enables the application programmer to set up a distributed system that synchronizes on distributed transactional variables by means of an abstract communication model.

In the *Dining Philosopher* example (see Sections 3.3 and B.1) the resources are sticks provided to eat the spaghetti. Sticks may be either available or occupied. Therefore, the sticks are modeled as boolean TVars. In the *Chat* example shown in Appendix B.2 the shared resource is a message box, consequently modeled as a TVar containing either a message or a new client's message TVar. The more complex *Bomberman* example in Appendix B.3 models a multitude of TVar resources like players, fields, and bombs.

3. Using Distributed STM

3.2. Distributed System Setup

Each node of a distributed system has to be initialized with the `runDist` function (line 16). It wraps the `main` function, given as its parameter, establishes inter-process communication and exception handling for the calling node, and, finally, terminates all process communication properly. This wrapper function also starts a helper thread, the *name server*.

The name server's functions allow the application programmer to start the inter-process communication (lines 17–25). The name server facilitates the initial distribution of `TVar`s and, hence implicitly, of initial network information. Thus, `TVar`s and not the processes themselves are initially exchanged to establish the transparent communication.

Every process node in the distributed system starts its own name server for an initial, named, `TVar` exchange. One process registers a `TVar` under a given name at its name server while another process may lookup a `TVar` with a given name at a name server with a known network address. Further, `TVar`s may be communicated as values of already known `TVar`s, realizing the fully transparent communication.

In a distributed transactional system at least one `TVar` is registered at a name server. This `TVar` is then either a shared resource or a *resources hub* for other `TVar`s used by other processes to exchange their `TVar`s. Each process node, participating in an arbitrary distributed system, at least either registers a `TVar` at its name server or looks up a registered `TVar` from another name server.

The `registerTVar` function (line 17) registers a `TVar` at its own name server. It is called with the `TVar` itself, and an arbitrary `String` name representation, the given name, for this `TVar`. The name server maintains a dictionary of all registered `TVar`s and their given name representations. The `deregisterTVar` function (line 19) removes an entry from the name server dictionary. The other participating system nodes can access registered `TVar`s calling `lookupTVar` (line 20) with the name server address and the given `TVar` name. The name server address is either its IP address or its domain name. The `lookupTVar` function returns `Just` the `TVar` previously registered under the given name or `Nothing` if the name is not registered at the called name server. For convenience, the interface also shows a lookup function variant, `lookupWaitTVar` (line 23), which does not immediately return `Nothing` if the requested `TVar` is not available. Instead, the functions returns either when the `TVar` becomes available or when a given timeout has been reached.

3.2. Distributed System Setup

An application programmer may design a distributed transactional system as shown in Figure 3.1. This sample system consists of three process nodes, each connected to the internet. Each node may reside on a separate computer with a separate physical internet connection or any combination of nodes may run on a single hardware sharing its resources.

In several DSTM library functions, the polymorphic TVar type variable is constrained by the Dist class. Therefore, the application programmer has to create Dist instances of every application-defined TVar data type used in the application. All basic Haskell data types like Bool and Int and standard constructor types like lists and tuples are already instantiated in the DSTM library.

The class Dist (lines 26–28) defines two functions that the library requires to properly memory manage distributed TVars and, hence, to prohibit memory leaks. It is not necessary to understand these functions in detail, yet. However, we need to understand how to build Dist instances of application-defined TVar data types. The instance functions need to descend any recursively defined TVar type and recursively call the instance function for any TVar occurrence. For non-recursive TVar types, we simply return ().

The class Dist itself is constrained by a self-defined class Serializable to guarantee serializability. The class Serializable provides the necessary functionality to convert between values of any serializable type and type String. Therefore, the application is required to create instances of class Serializable for all application defined TVar types.

```
26     class Serializable a => Dist a where
27         regTVars :: EnvAddr -> a -> IO ()
28         finTVars :: a -> IO ()
```

The following example TVar types show the idea. The TVar types AType, ATVarType and ATVarType2 define different TVar base types containing no, one, or two recursive TVars.

```
29     data AType      = Constructor1 SomeType
30     data ATVarType  = Constructor2 (TVar SomeType)
31     data ATVarType2 = Constructor3 (TVar SomeType)
32                                   (TVar SomeOtherType)

33     type TVar1 = TVar AType
34     type TVar2 = TVar ATVarType
35     type TVar3 = TVar ATVarType2
```

3. Using Distributed STM

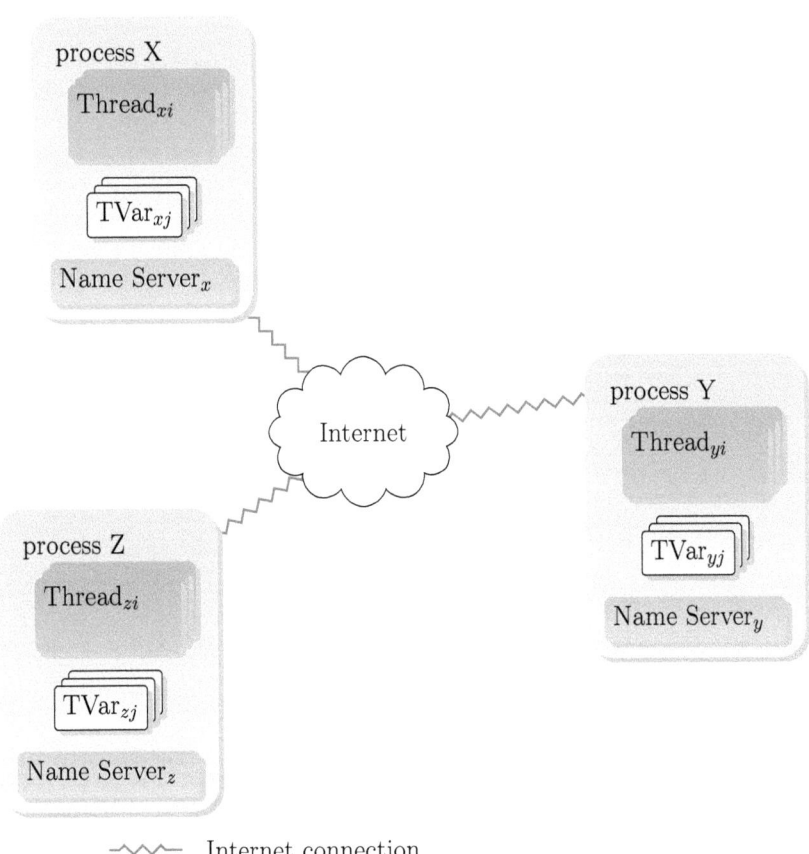

Figure 3.1.: Distributed system using the DSTM library

3.3. Introductory Example

An application, using these **TVars**, should declare the following instances to unwrap the **TVar** constructor and recursively call the respective class **Dist** function as with **ATVarType**.

```
36  instance Dist AType where
37    regTVars _ _ = return ()
38    finTVars _   = return ()

39  instance Dist ATVarType where
40    regTVars env (Constructor2 tVar) = regTVars env tVar
41    finTVars (Constructor2 tVar)     = finTVars tVar
```

In case of data constructors with multiple **TVars**, we bind the respective instance functions for each **TVar**.

```
42  instance Dist ATVarType2 where
43    regTVars env (Constructor3 tVar1 tVar2) =
44      regTVars env tVar1 >> regTVars env tVar2
45    finTVars (Constructor3 tVar1 tVar2) =
46      finTVars tVar1 >> finTVars tVar2
```

Additionally, the application needs to create the **Serializable** instances. However, it is not required to define any instance function because our library provides the necessary default definitions.

```
47  instance Serializable AType
48  instance Serializable ATVarType
49  instance Serializable ATVarType2
```

3.3. Introductory Example

We have shown a concise *concurrent* STM based implementation of the classic Dining Philosopher problem in Section 2.3.3. The DSTM library allows to implement a *distributed* version of the same problem. The resources, sticks modeled again as boolean **TVars**, are assumed to be distributed. Our intention to model the distributed API similarly to the concurrent one is reflected in the distributed Dining Philosopher example below.

3. Using Distributed STM

```
50  type Stick = TVar Bool

51  takeStick :: Stick -> Int -> STM ()
52  takeStick s = do b <- readTVar s
53                   if b
54                      then writeTVar s False
55                      else retry
56  putStick :: Stick -> STM ()
57  putStick s = writeTVar s True

58  phil :: Int -> Stick -> Stick -> IO ()
59  phil n l r = do
60    atomic $ do
61       takeStick l
62       takeStick r
63    putStrLn (show n ++ ". Phil is eating")
64    atomic $ do
65       putStick l
66       putStick r
67    phil n l r

68  startPhil = do
69    (arg:_) <- getArgs
70    let n = read arg
71    l <- atomic $ newTVar True
72    registerTVar l arg
73    (Just r) <- lookupWaitTVar "localhost" 60
74                  $ show ((n 'mod' 5) + 1)
75    phil n l r

76  main = runDist startPhil
```

Most parts of the distributed program are exactly identical to the concurrent version. Just the initialization is different. Each philosopher process runs now as a separate main program. Each philosopher process creates its left stick **TVar** (line 71), registers it (line 72) at its name server, and looks up its right stick **TVar** directly from the name server (lines 73–74) where it has been registered from the neighbor philosopher process. We show a pseudo distributed version running on a single node. Hence, we can use `"localhost"` as the name server address.

Note that both, the **TVar** type and the functions **takeStick**, **putStick** and **phil** (lines 50–67) are identical to the concurrent version shown in Section 2.3.3. The **main** function (line 76) calls the communication enabling **runDist** function with its `startPhil` (lines 68–75) argument as the, admittedly, rudimentary philosopher process setup.

The main difference for the application designer and the user is, however, that the code shown starts just one philosopher process instead of five philosopher threads in the concurrent example in Section 2.3.3. The complete distributed system then consists of five incarnations of the, identical, philosopher process. We start the system by starting the respective processes.

Albeit being the classic example, we believe that the Dining Philosopher's setting with a mutual resource, exchanged directly through the name server, is not the general DSTM program pattern. A distributed system, in general, initiates the first contact between processes through a registration or authentication process at a dedicated server. This server would be started before any other process. A typical example is the simple Chat system shown in Appendix B.2. It consists of one chat server and an arbitrary number of chat clients. Each client registers with the chat server. After the registration, the client may send and receive messages. The chat server maintains a list of all chat clients. It both registers new chat clients and distributes any messages received from one client to all other clients.

3.4. Robust Library Interface

In this section we augment the Haskell DSTM interface presented in Section 3.1 to enable the implementation of robust programs. The application requires some means to detect processes that have ceased to communicate. However, the inter-process communication is transparent to the application programmer while the known abstraction is the `TVar`. As a consequence, the application has no notion of processes, process availability, and process failure. Hence, established robustness mechanisms, like process linking in Erlang, make no sense on application level.

Instead, the DSTM library detects a failure within the inter-process runtime communication subsystem and translates it into a `TVar` failure that the application understands. Thus, we maintain the transparent communication abstraction also in the event of failing processes and yield a consistent interface.

3. Using Distributed STM

3.4.1. Design Pattern of a Robust DSTM Application

A typical interactive concurrent or distributed system design consists of endlessly looping threads performing a specific task within the system. Each thread synchronizes its critical sections with other threads performing other system tasks. In the context of this work, the running threads synchronize by controlling one or more TVars. The someThread function (lines 77–80) symbolizes such a looping thread.

```
77  someThread :: SomeTVars -> IO ()
78  someThread someTVars = do
79      ... <- atomic ... someTVars ...
80      someThread someTVars
```

A *robust* DSTM application catches exceptions, originating from *unavailable* TVars, and recovers from the fault leading to this exception. A TVar is unavailable if the application cannot read from or write to it. We define that a once unavailable TVar will remain unavailable forever. Each TVar represents a specific service, like a stick or a message box. Then, a robust application continues its execution refraining from using any unavailable TVar, thus, withdrawing the particular service. Additionally, it may replace any unavailable TVar with a new TVar to replace the particular service with an alternative or redundant one.

The example someRobustThread IO function (line 81) indicates the design pattern of robust DSTM applications. We use the IO catch function, shown in Section 2.1.4 and defined in the Control.Exception module, to execute an IO action while catching any exception thrown during the execution. Note that also STM exceptions thrown from within an atomic action may be caught.

```
81  someRobustThread :: SomeTVars -> IO ()
82  someRobustThread someTVars =
83                    Control.Exception.catch (do
84      ... <- atomic ... someTVars ...
85      someRobustThread someTVars)
86      (\e -> do
87          someTVars' <- recoverTVars someTVars e
88          someRobustThread someTVars')
```

A recovery function recoverTVars (line 87) analyzes someTVars used in the exception throwing transaction (line 84). The recovery function checks for unavailable TVars and creates available someTVars' used in further iterations

3.4. Robust Library Interface

of someRobustThread. At this point, we are not interested in exactly how the application specific recoverTVars function does this. However, we have to assure that the exception e (line 86) carries all error information about unavailable TVars that the recovery function needs for its analysis.

3.4.2. The DSTM Exception

The TVar type is an abstract type. The application cannot, and should not, access a TVar type constructor directly. Therefore, we design an access function to determine if, depending on a specific exception being thrown, a certain TVar has become unavailable. The TVar abstractly carries the necessary inter-process communication information. An unavailable TVar correlates to an inter-process communication problem. Hence, the specific exception, abstractly, has to carry information about inter-process communication problems. In general, exceptions do not carry the necessary information.

Therefore, the DSTM library defines such an application level exception, denoting one or more unavailable TVars. An attempt to read from or write to an unavailable TVar raises the exception. We use dynamically-typed exceptions as described in Section 2.1.5 to create our own DSTM library exception type. We name it SomeDistTVarException (line 89) and make it an abstract toplevel dynamic exception.

```
89  data SomeDistTVarException
```

Extensible dynamically-typed exceptions described in [Mar06] allow us to restrict caught exceptions by annotating the exception type (line 95) which itself is constrained by the Exception class. The catch function automatically propagates exceptions of unexpected types.

```
90  someRobustThread :: SomeTVars -> IO ()
91  someRobustThread someTVars =
92                     Control.Exception.catch (do
93     ... <- atomic ... someTVars ...
94     someRobustThread someTVars)
95     (\(e::SomeDistTVarException) -> do
96         someTVars' <- recoverTVars someTVars e
97         someRobustThread someTVars')
```

The abstract TVar data type hides the information on processes hosting TVars from the application. Consequently, the SomeDistTVarException type

3. Using Distributed STM

hides the details about unavailable processes, matching the `TVar` abstraction level. Unavailable processes result in unavailable `TVars`. However, one unavailable process may result in any number of unavailable `TVars`. Thus, a `SomeDistTVarException` thrown indicates at least one but possibly more unavailable `TVars`.

We define the predicate `isDistErrTVar` (line 98) as the access function to enable the application programmer to identify any unavailable `TVar`. The predicate tests if a `TVar` is affected by the caught abstract exception.

```
98    isDistErrTVar :: SomeDistTVarException -> TVar a -> Bool
```

Note that `isDistErrTVar` requires both the caught `TVar` exception and the `TVar` to be tested as parameters keeping it referentially transparent. The predicate *translates* the abstract error message into information the application can understand. The Chat application in Appendix B.2 shows how to implement easily a robust distributed system that continues to operate properly even when chat clients inadvertently disappear, rendering their communication `TVars` unavailable.

Having to use a predicate when catching an exception seems unusual. One would expect that the DSTM exception itself is sufficient to build a robust application. However, a characteristic transaction property is to use multiple `TVars`. Hence, it is not apparent from the caught exception which `TVars` are unavailable. We only know that at least one `TVar` is unavailable. A similar problem would be a calculation consisting of multiple division operations within a `catch` function. In case of a caught division-by-zero exception we do not know by the exception itself which of the divisors is zero. We had to test each divisor individually which, in this example, we would naturally have done before executing the calculation.

After catching a DSTM library exception the application should refrain from accessing the discriminated `TVars` by shutting down the services they provided and possibly replacing them by redundant or alternative services. The application may keep a log of unreachable `TVars`. However, in the current state of our implementation it does not make too much sense as we restrict our communication faults to be fatal. Any attempt to access an unreachable `TVar` will inevitably throw another exception. However, doing so is harmless as it will not cause any inconsistencies.

3.5. Complete API

We are now able to present the complete API of the Robust Distributed Software Transactional Memory library. It consists of the original interface for concurrent transactions as designed in [HMPJH05], our additions for distributed applications, and our additions to implement robustness in distributed applications.

Note that we have adapted the dynamically-typed exceptions also for the STM exception functions throw and catch (lines 111–112).

```
99    data STM a   -- abstract
100   instance Monad STM

101   -- Running STM computations
102   atomic  :: STM a -> IO a
103   retry   :: STM a
104   orElse  :: STM a -> STM a -> STM a

105   -- Transactional variables
106   data TVar a  -- abstract

107   newTVar   :: Dist a => a -> STM (TVar a)
108   readTVar  :: Dist a => TVar a -> STM a
109   writeTVar :: Dist a => TVar a -> a -> STM ()


110   -- Exceptions
111   throw :: SomeException -> STM a
112   catch :: STM a -> (SomeException -> STM a) -> STM a

113   -- Additional distributed interface
114   class Serializable a => Dist a where
115     regTVars :: EnvAddr -> a -> IO ()
116     finTVars :: a -> IO ()

117   runDist         :: IO a -> IO a
118   registerTVar    :: Dist a => TVar a -> String -> IO
119   deregisterTVar  :: String -> IO ()
120   lookupTVar      :: Dist a => String -> String
121                         -> IO (Maybe (TVar a))
122   lookupWaitTVar  :: Dist a => String -> Int -> String
123                         -> IO (Maybe (TVar a))
```

53

3. Using Distributed STM

```
124    -- Additional robustness interface
125    data SomeDistTVarException    -- abstract

126    isDistErrTVar :: SomeDistTVarException -> TVar a -> Bool
```

Chapter 4

Implementing Software Transactional Memory for Distributed Haskell

With this book we present a lightweight Haskell library implementation extending Concurrent Haskell with functions to enable distributed programming using the Software Transactional Memory abstraction described in Section 2.3.

In Section 4.1 we motivate the abstract types **TVar**, as distributed mutable synchronization variables, and **STM** monad, as stateful enclosure for distributed transactions.

The STM communications protocol we introduce in Section 4.2 implements distributed transactions. We refine this protocol in the remainder of this book, especially when introducing robustness.

We transparently integrate distributed communication into the STM protocol in Section 4.3 and present an efficient solution for an STM inherent synchronization problem in Section 4.4.

4.1. Transaction Paradigm

The application, *using* transactional memory, and the library, *implementing* transactional memory, view a transaction differently (see Figure 4.1). The application sees a transaction as an, atomically executed, sequence of **TVar** actions, implicitly synchronized with other potentially conflicting transactions. We call it the *transaction program*.

4. Implementing Software Transactional Memory for Distributed Haskell

The library view consists of two parts. One is the same transaction program the application sees. The other is a *transaction protocol*, a sequence of predefined actions, actually implementing the transactional synchronization. We will look at the transaction protocol in detail in Section 4.2.

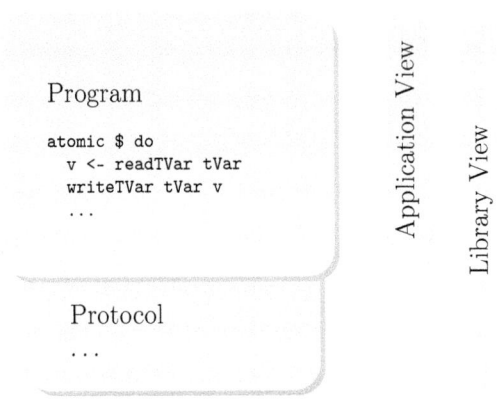

Figure 4.1.: Transaction Views

A key concept of the concurrent implementation in [HMPJH05] is that all, atomically executed, transactions are confined to an STM monad. This is the guarantee on type system level that transaction programs can only perform library controlled operations on TVars, namely creating, reading, and writing them. Thus, we preclude any unsolicited TVar access, provided the application refrains from using *unsafe* functions, like unsafePerformIO, interfering with referential transparency.

The original concurrent approach presents a low-level implementation with abstract STM and TVar types. The high-level STM approach [HK05] implements these abstract classes in Concurrent Haskell. We model the STM monad and the TVar type based on the latter implementation such that they can be used in a distributed system.

4.1.1. Transaction Monad

We define the STM monad as an extension of the IO monad with a state used for collecting information about the execution of a transaction. The STM data

4.1. Transaction Paradigm

type (line 1), instantiated to a monad (lines 7–22), is defined similar to other IO monad extensions like the GUI monad defined in TclHaskell [Dor98]. Note that we use **newtype** instead of **data** to define the STM monad. A **newtype** declaration renames a data type creating a distinct new type. It can be used like a **data** declaration but is limited to one unary constructor.

```
1 newtype STM a = STM (STMState -> IO (STMResult a))
```

The type STMState is the state carried through the STM monad used to collect information about the execution of a transaction in a log. We discuss its concrete realization further along with the implementation. The data type STMResult models the possible results of a transaction.

```
2 data STMResult a =
3       Success STMState a
4     | Retry STMState
5     | Exception STMState
6                 Control.Exception.SomeException
```

The STMResult constructor names already imply their meaning. A transaction can be executed successfully returning the new state and the resulting value (line 3). It can result in a **retry** request from the application, thus, simply returning the new state (line 4). Finally, the result may be a transactional exception, thrown within the STM monad, returning the new state plus the thrown exception (line 5) using the *Extensible Dynamically-Typed Hierarchy of Exceptions* described in [Mar06]. An unsuccessful transaction is implicitly restarted immediately.

A transaction, yielding a **Retry** result, denotes that the application decided that a program continuation does not make sense because of a resource conflict. An application may decide that a transaction, reading a certain **TVar** value, prohibits further execution, thus, calling **retry**. An immediately repeated execution would deterministically yield the same result, thus, implement busy waiting. Therefore, we do not immediately restart the transaction but suspend the thread executing it. We resume this thread when any one or more of its read **TVars** is modified by another thread, hence, changing the resource situation. Note that the changed situation may not be sufficient, hence, the conflict may still exist.

The application may throw an exception within a transaction. This – transactional – exception may be caught within the transaction itself. If it is not caught, the transaction yields the `Exception` result and re-throws the transactional exception as an `IO` exception.

We overload the bind operator (line 9) and the `return` function (line 22) for the STM monad instance. The latter simply returns a successful STM result keeping the STM state unchanged. Note that the right-hand side `return` is the IO `return` function. The bind operator first applies the first STM transaction to the current state, yielding the intermediate IO result (line 11). We simply return a `Retry` or `Exception` result, ignoring the second STM transaction. In case of a successful intermediate result, we feed its value to the second STM transaction (line 14) which we apply to the intermediate result state, yielding the final result (line 15).

```
7   instance Monad STM where
8   -- (>>=)   :: STM a -> (a -> STM b) -> STM b
9   (STM trans1) >>= f =
10    STM (\st -> do
11              stmRes <- trans1 st
12              case stmRes of
13                Success newSt v ->
14                  let (STM trans2) = f v
15                  in trans2 newSt
16                Retry newSt ->
17                  return (Retry newSt)
18                Exception newSt e ->
19                  return (Exception newSt e)
20          )
21   --return :: a -> STM a
22   return x = STM (\st -> return (Success st x))
```

We start the `STM` monad with the `runSTM` function applied to the initial state to unwrap the `IO` result from its monadic value.

```
23   runSTM :: STM a -> STMState -> IO (STMResult a)
24   runSTM (STM stm) state = stm state
```

Our `STM` monad obeys the three monad laws. We show a semi-formal proof in Appendix C.

4.1.2. Transactional Variables

The transaction information, we log in the STM state, is based on attributes of the transactional resources, the `TVars`, referenced in the transaction.

4.1. Transaction Paradigm

Besides the TVar value and an identifier, there are further attributes. If a transaction program calls retry, it creates a dependency between transaction and TVar. A *dependent* transaction has suspended itself in response to an inadequate value of a read TVar. At some later point in time, one of the read TVars is updated which in turn resumes this transaction. Thus, the transaction depends on the set of all read TVars. Each TVar collects its dependent transactions in a *wait queue*. We use this wait queue to resume suspended transactions once the TVar is finally modified. In addition, the transaction protocol requires that the TVars, being synchronized, are locked. We describe the protocol in detail in Section 4.2.

Concurrent Approach

Like the STM monad, we base also our TVar implementation on the lightweight concurrent programming approach. Thus, we first discuss briefly the concurrent approach where TVars provide the following:

- Storage for the TVar value itself
- A unique identifier to reference the TVar
- A lock to guard access to its value
- A wait queue of *dependent* transactions

The concurrent approach models TVars as a record of the above attributes. The TVar value is stored in a tuple of the value itself and a version number (line 26). The version number increments with every modification. Hence, we define two TVar values to be identical iff their version number and the TVar identifier are identical.

The unique global TVar identifier (line 27) is generated from a global Integer type[1] variable (lines 30–36) and the lock value is the single () value (line 28).

Concurrent Haskell offers shared mutable variables (Section 2.1.3) for synchronization. We suspend transactions when the application calls retry using a *retry-variable* which we implement as an MVar on a single () value (line 25). Each transaction uses its own retry-variable.

---

[1] Haskell Integer type values can hold infinitely large values by design. In reality, they are limited by the physical memory available at run-time.

4. Implementing Software Transactional Memory for Distributed Haskell

```
25 type RetryVarData = MVar ()
```

Before suspending itself, the transaction adds its retry-variable to the wait queue of all **TVars** being read in this transaction. Thus, the read **TVars** can resume the transaction at some later point in time. Each **TVar** uses its wait queue to resume all dependent transactions when its value is being modified.

```
26 data TVar a = TVar (MVar (a, VersionID))   -- value
27                   TVarID                    -- unique
28                   (MVar ())                 -- lock
29                   (MVar [RetryVarData])     -- wait q
```

All attributes except for the unique identifier are concurrently mutable. Thus, they are stored in **MVars**.

Whenever our implementation uses unique identifiers, they are generated from a conceptually infinite, global[2] counter (line 33) by the **uniqueId** function (lines 36,36) returning the current count and replacing it with its increment.

```
30 type TVarID    = Integer
31 type RetryVarID = Integer
32 type VersionID = Integer

33 gUniqueId :: MVar TVarID
34 gUniqueId = unsafePerformIO (newMVar 1)
35 uniqueId :: IO TVarID
36 uniqueId = modifyMVar gUniqueId (\i -> return (i+1, i))
```

Distributed Approach

In a distributed environment, we maintain the concurrent **TVar** attributes and generalize the concurrent **TVar** structure. Mutable variables are defined in a shared memory as it exists in concurrent systems. In general, memory cannot be shared among processes. Therefore, a global mutable variable is bound to its process. Thus, we define two **TVar** variants for the distributed approach:

- A *host* **TVar**, managing all **TVar** data, and

- A *link* **TVar**, maintaining a link to its host **TVar**

---

[2]Global variables in a concurrent program can be declared using the potentially unsafe **unsafePerformIO** function as described in [Mar02].

4.1. Transaction Paradigm

The *host* `TVar` is a resource of the process defining it. This is the original `TVar` containing the real value, lock, and wait queue mutable data. It is hosted by the process the resource is located in. There is exactly one host `TVar` for every `TVar` throughout the distributed system. Multiple occurrences of the host `TVar` may exist in the host process. They are, however, only pointer references of the shared mutable objects.

The *link* `TVar` is implemented as a reference link (line 41) to the host `TVar` resource residing in a different or the same process. It can be thought of being a remote proxy of the host `TVar`. For each `TVar` there can be any number of link `TVars` in every process of the distributed system.

```
37  data TVar a = TVar (MVar (a, VersionID))  -- value
38                     TVarID                  -- unique
39                    (MVar ())                -- lock
40                    (MVar [RetryVar])        -- wait q
41              | LinkTVar VarLink             -- host
```

The distributed host `TVar` is almost identical to the concurrent version. The difference is the distributed design of the wait queue of retry-variables (line 40). A `RetryVar` is defined as part of a transaction. Transactions and, hence, `RetryVars` may exist in the process defining it as well as in other processes. Therefore, we define `RetryVars` similarly to `TVars` as a *host* and a *link* variant. The *host* `RetryVar` contains the real retry-variable data (line 42). The *link* `RetryVar` is the proxy for the host `RetryVar` (line 44). Both variants contain also a unique identifier to allow referencing the retry-variable.

```
42  data RetryVar = RetryVar RetryVarData   -- retry var
43                           RetryVarID     -- unique id
44                | LinkRetryVar VarLink    -- host addr
45  \begin{lstlisting}[name=diststm]
46  data VarLink = VarLink EnvAddr TVarID
47  data EnvAddr = EnvAddr PortID IPAddr
```

The reference link variant type `VarLink` of both `TVar` (line 41) and `RetryVar` (line 44) denotes an identifier being unique throughout the whole distributed system. It consists of three, arbitrarily ordered, components:

- Host process IP address or domain name

- Host process communication port

- Unique identifier within the host process

61

4. Implementing Software Transactional Memory for Distributed Haskell

We summarize IP address and port as the network environment address `EnvAddr`. Its particular component order allows to use partial functions for a given `PortID`. We provide full `TVar` and `RetryVar` transparency with their *host* and *link* variants. All STM interface functions accept a generic `TVar` and decide how to deal with the request by pattern matching its constructor.

As an example, the API function `readTVar` will, besides modifying the transaction state, read the `TVar` value by calling `coreReadTVar` (line 48) to transparently read the `TVar` value independently of its origin. In case of a `TVar` hosted in the calling process, *getHostTVal* directly reads the value from the shared mutable variable v. Otherwise, *getLinkTVal* asks the linked process for the value and returns it.

```
48  coreReadTVar :: (Dist a) => TVar a -> IO (a,VersionID)
49  coreReadTVar (TVar v _ _ _)     = getHostTVal v
50  coreReadTVar (LinkTVar env tId) = getLinkTVal env tId
```

Figure 4.2 shows the different kinds of distributed `TVar`s. There is a `TVar`

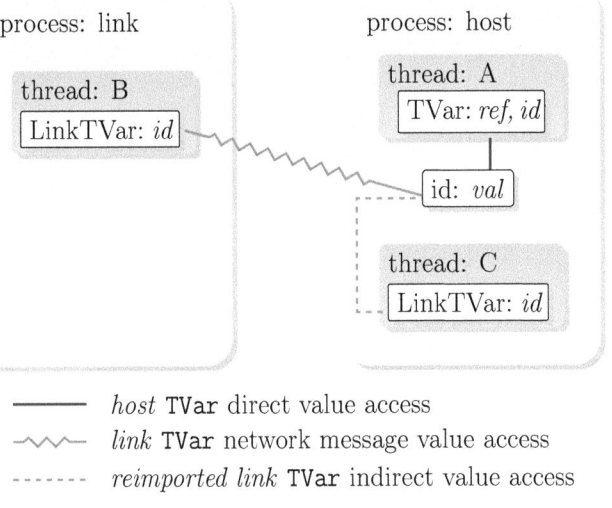

— *host* `TVar` direct value access
⁓ *link* `TVar` network message value access
----- *reimported link* `TVar` indirect value access

Figure 4.2.: Distributed TVar Types

defined in process *host*. Hence, the `TVar` value is stored in that process. Thread

A accesses the host variant of this TVar and its value directly. Thread *B*, in process *link*, accesses the link variant of this TVar. The process *link* proxy in turn accesses the TVar value by exchanging network messages with the *host* process. Link variables can be created from host variables but not vice versa. Once a host variable is converted to a link variable, there is no way back. Thread *C*, in process *host*, accesses another link variant of this TVar. We call this a *reimported* link TVar. Reimported TVars may result from TVars containing TVars as their value. We will apply special optimizations to reimported TVars in Section 5.5.2 to avoid relatively costly network messages. Note that the name server does not host any variables itself and, therefore, knows only link TVars.

4.2. STM Protocol

In general, a protocol is a description of actions. However, we extend the protocol notion also to the described actions themselves. Thus, the *STM protocol*[3] represents the sequence of steps necessary to synchronize software transactions. The protocol depends on the transaction program. It is, thus, generated by a protocol itself. Hence, the STM protocol, also called *transaction protocol*, consists of two parts, a *creation protocol* and an *execution protocol*. The creation protocol dynamically generates the execution protocol based on the transaction program. The creation protocol buffers intermediate results in a *transaction log*. The execution protocol eventually uses the logged information.

Software Transactional Memory provides an API to define *atomic* transactions as described in Section 2.3. An atomic transaction, the transaction program, is any combination of the single STM actions newTVar, readTvar, writeTVar, retry and throw with the STM action combinators (>>=), orElse and catch enclosed by the atomic function transforming a compound STM action into a single IO action.

The behavior of atomic transactions reminds of sandboxes as used in Java run-time systems to securely run applets in a safe environment [GMPS97]. Web browsers use sandboxes to restrict insecure web server communication to tightly controlled channels [RBP09]. Here, an atomic transaction works as the sandbox for STM operations which it both executes and examines.

---

[3]There are other unrelated notions of the term *STM protocol* in the literature as well. It can denote *Synchronous Transport Mode* in telecommunications networking. There are also references to *Simple TCP/IP Messaging*.

4. *Implementing Software Transactional Memory for Distributed Haskell*

4.2.1. Synchronizing Transactions

From an implementation perspective, a transaction runs its **STM** actions, the transaction program, first in monadic isolation, then checks if this isolated view is still consistent with the outside view, and possibly re-executes the isolated **STM** actions until the transaction eventually succeeds. The result is an **IO** action, generated out of the **STM** actions, synchronized with any other potentially conflicting action. The synchronization is a two-step process, performed by the execution protocol.

The first step, called *validation*, verifies if the transaction views a consistent system state. The view is consistent, if for all **TVar**s both the version, read in the transaction program, and the corresponding version, read by the transaction protocol, are identical.

After a successful validation, the second synchronization step of the execution protocol, called **commit**, performs all **TVar** write actions defined in the transaction program. No write action is directly executed in the transaction program itself. However, all actions are logged for later use. An unsuccessful validation resets the protocol and runs the transaction program again.

The state has a transaction log to reflect the transaction up to the current point. There are accumulation actions collecting and updating **TVar** information in the state of each transaction. Executing protocols has an **IO** effect by executing the accumulated actions on **TVar**s. They depend on the, at that time, current transactional state of type **STMState**.

4.2.2. Transaction State

Now, we can define a coarse version of the **STMState** record. Like **TVar**s and **RetryVar**s, each transaction is also uniquely identified (line 52). Each transaction uses a mutable **RetryVar** (line 53) to suspend itself after a **retry** call. The STM protocol later resumes this particular transaction using its **RetryVar**. The **initialState** function sets both values (lines 62, 63) that are never changed throughout the lifetime of this transaction. Two transaction log entries conclude the **STMState** record elements. One collects information needed to validate a transaction, the other to commit the transaction.

In Chapter 5 we detail the information both logs contain exactly. For now, we assume a *validate log* (line 54) containing *validate*, *extend wait queue*, *lock* and *unlock* **IO** actions and a *commit log* (line 55) containing *commit* and *notify* **IO** actions. Both logs initialize to the empty list. Note that the *validate* action

4.2. STM Protocol

returns a boolean value, denoting TVar validity.

The STM protocol constitutes critical sections which we synchronize using the logged lock actions. We avoid deadlocks by applying a strict total order to the lock actions and hence to the validate log. Therefore, the validate log is a sorted dictionary[4]. We choose the distributed system global unique TVar identifier VarLink as the key type (line 56) to establish the strict total order of the validate log actions, ignoring duplicate entries.

The order of the commit log actions is the order of their creation, hence no sorting of entries is necessary. However, newer entries must override older entries. We implement this by simply adding newer entries to the head of the action log list and reverting it prior to execution.

```
51  data STMState = STMState {
52                  stmId         :: TVarID,
53                  stmRetryVar   :: RetryVar,
54                  stmValidLog   :: [ValidLog],
55                  stmCommitLog  :: [CommitLog]}

56  type ValidLog  = (VarLink, (IO Bool, IO (), ...))
57  type CommitLog = (IO (), IO ())

58  initialState :: IO STMState
59  initialState = do
60    atomicId <- uniqueId
61    retryVar <- newRetryVar
62    return (STMState {stmId         = atomicId,
63                      stmRetryVar   = retryVar,
64                      stmValidLog   = [],
65                      stmCommitLog  = []})

66  newRetryVar :: IO RetryVar
67  newRetryVar = do
68    retryMVar <- newEmptyMVar
69    newID     <- uniqueId
70    return (RetryVar retryMVar newID)
```

The protocols work transparently with both host and link TVars. Host TVars update their mutable data directly. Link TVars initiate updates through messages exchanged between the link TVar client process and the host TVar server

---

[4] A dictionary is a key-value pair map. We use the key to look up an associated value like in a dictionary. We implement mostly lists because of the very small number of expected entries.

4. Implementing Software Transactional Memory for Distributed Haskell

process (see Section 4.3.1). The `coreReadTVar IO` action in line 48 is an example of such a transparent `TVar` action. We have defined similar transparent `IO` functions for the other logged actions.

4.2.3. Controlling Transactions

Before we look closer at the individual protocols, we give an overview of the implementation of atomic transactions themselves. The `atomic` function executes the whole transaction, which we named the transaction program, by running the `STM` monad on the initial state (line 74). The returned result is an `IO` action.

The remainder of the `atomic` function, which we named the transaction protocol[5], defines a two-step operation. Step one checks the consistency of the isolated monadic view. Step two executes the resulting `IO` action, iff the view is consistent, and restarts the transaction otherwise. We call checking the consistency of an isolated view *validating* the transaction and executing the `IO` action *committing* the transaction.

```
71  atomic :: STM a -> IO a
72  atomic stmAction = do
73    iState <- initialState
74    stmResult <- runSTM stmAction iState
75    case stmResult of
76      Retry newState         -> ...
77      Exception newState e   -> ...
78      Success newState res   -> do
79        valid <- startTrans newState
80        if valid
81          then do
82            commitTrans newState
83            endTrans newState
84            return res
85          else do
86            endTrans newState
87            atomic stmAction
```

Thus, the transaction protocol within the `atomic` function, conceptually, is a two-phase *validate* and *commit* protocol. In Chapter 6 we will see that it is

---
[5]Imbs and Raynal describe an STM protocol in [IR08] where they call the final sub-protocol *try_to_commit*, thus avoiding duplicate notions of *atomic*. We keep calling the final sub-protocol at the end of the transaction, *transaction protocol*. When we refer to the `atomic` function construct including the enclosed `STM` actions we use the terms *transaction program* or *transaction* for short.

4.2. STM Protocol

necessary, however, to expand this *validate-commit* protocol in order to gain robustness.

A first version of the `atomic` function implementation (lines 71–87) shows the two-phase approach. We run the isolated `STM` monad on the initial state (line 74) and evaluate the result. In case of a successful sandboxed transaction (line 78) we first validate it calling `startTrans` (line 79) and then either commit a valid transaction with `commitTrans` (line 82) or restart an invalid transaction from scratch (line 87).

Note that `startTrans` first locks all involved `TVars` and then checks for transaction validity while `endTrans` unlocks the `TVars` again. Hence, we always use these two function as a pair. The `atomic` function eventually terminates and returns the transaction result (line 84).

Transactions may either be successful or return a `Retry` (line 89) or an `Exception` (line 106) result. Executing `retry` temporarily suspends the transaction to avoid busy waiting loops of invalid transactions, if resources are not available. Raising an exception with `throw` prematurely exits the transaction.

```
88  retry   :: STM a
89  retry = STM (\state -> return (Retry state))

90  atomic :: STM a -> IO a
91  atomic stmAction = do
92      ...
93      Retry newState -> do
94          valid <- startTrans rState
95          if valid
96              then do
97                  retryTrans newState
98                  endTrans newState
99                  suspend (stmRetryVar newState)
100             else endTrans newState
101         atomic stmAction
102     ...

103 suspend :: RetryVar -> IO ()
104 suspend (RetryVar retryMVar _) = takeMVar retryMVar
```

The `retry` function simply returns the `Retry` result (line 89) eventually yielding `Retry` as the compound transaction result when evaluated in `atomic` (lines 76, 93). A retrying transaction also starts by validating the locked `TVars` (line 94). While a valid successful transaction would be committed at this

67

4. Implementing Software Transactional Memory for Distributed Haskell

point, a valid retrying transaction suspends on its own **stmRetryVar** (line 99). Note that we always suspend on a host **RetryVar** (line 104) containing the real retry-variable data. A link **RetryVar** should never be returned by a transaction. Before the suspension we enable the read **TVars** collected in the transaction state to resume this transaction at some later point with the **retryTrans** function in line 97. Again, **endTrans** unlocks all involved TVars. Note that this is done before the suspension, as well. We restart an invalid retrying transaction immediately and a valid one after it resumes (line 101).

```
105  throw :: SomeException -> STM a
106  throw e = STM (\st -> return (Exception st e))

107  atomic :: STM a -> IO a
108  atomic stmAction = do
109    ...
110      Exception newState e -> do
111        valid <- startTrans newState
112        if valid
113          then do
114            endTrans newState
115            Control.Exception.throw e
116          else do
117            endTrans newState
118            atomic stmAction
119    ...
```

Similar to **retry**, the **throw** function returns the **Exception** result (line 106) eventually yielding **Exception e** as the compound transaction result of an **atomic** evaluation (lines 77, 110) with e being of type **SomeException**, an extensible dynamic type. Validation of the transaction result with locked **TVars** (line 111) selects between restarting an invalid transaction (line 118) and propagating the exception e of a valid transaction into the I/O world (line 115), thus, terminating the transaction. Again, **endTrans** unlocks all involved **TVars**. Note that this is done before the exception propagation.

Thus, **startTrans** initiates the transaction protocol sequence and represents the validate protocol by additionally cumulating and returning the boolean validation result. The functions **commitTrans**, **retryTrans**, and **endTrans** represent the commit protocol, sequentially executing the respective **IO** actions that are logged by the transaction program. We will give a concrete implementation description in Chapter 5.

4.2. STM Protocol

Transaction Composition

The functions `catch`, (`>>=`), and `orElse` are essentially STM action combinators and, therefore, modify the transaction state in respective ways.

```
120  catch :: STM a -> (SomeException -> STM a) -> STM a
121  catch (STM stm) eHandler = STM (\stmState -> do
122      res <- stm stmState
123      case res of
124        Exception _ e -> do
125                         let (STM stmEx) = eHandler e
126                         stmEx stmState
127        _             -> return res)
```

The STM `catch` function works similarly to its `Control.Exception` module `IO` sibling. It returns the result of a given transaction unless this transaction calls `throw` to throw an exception. In this case `catch` discards the transaction and returns the possibly successful result of the alternative transaction which has been given the exception as its parameter. Thus, the application programmer has the choice to handle exceptions within the STM world or to have them propagated to the IO world.

Note that the concurrent STM paper [HMPJH05], in its original version, proposed a somewhat inconsistent semantics which the authors repaired in a later update to the paper and their implementation. Originally, all STM actions, performed before throwing an STM exception, might be possibly committed if the exception is caught by an STM `catch` call. However, if the application catches the exception outside the `atomic` transaction with an IO `catch` call, the complete transaction is always discarded. Our implementation keeps the semantics of both STM `catch` and IO `catch` consistent, like the updated concurrent implementation.

The (`>>=`) function is the regular monadic bind operator sequencing STM actions as defined in Section 4.1.1.

```
128  orElse :: STM a -> STM a -> STM a
129  orElse (STM stm1) (STM stm2) =
130     STM (\(stmState@STMState{stmCommitLog = saved})
131          -> do
132             stm1Res <- stm1 stmState
133             case stm1Res of
134               Retry newState
135                 -> stm2 newState{stmCommitLog = saved}
136               _ -> return stm1Res)
```

69

4. Implementing Software Transactional Memory for Distributed Haskell

The orElse function is an alternative composition of two transactions whose result depends on the actual suspension state of the two transactions. If the first transaction succeeds or throws an exception, it simply becomes the compound result (lines 132, 136). If it suspends, the second transaction becomes the result (line 135).

We discard any commit information collected during the partial execution of the first transaction when starting the execution of the second transaction. However, it is not sufficient to initialize the commit log with the empty list as we still need the information of STM sequences preceding the compound orElse action. Therefore, we save the commit log (line 130) before beginning the execution of the first transaction and set the commit log to that saved state (line 135) before the start of the second.

In order to handle nested orElse calls correctly, we stack the saved logs. We do not need to build our own stack, we simply utilize the run-time function stack. Every orElse instance pushes the saved outer commit log onto the stack and pops it automatically when it is not needed anymore.

Contrasting the commit log behavior, we cumulate all validation entries from both transactions because validating the current and resuming other transactions always depends on both executed transaction alternatives. We split the transaction state log into a commit and a validate part for the sole reason of easily separating the two information logs when executing an orElse function. This log splitting causes us to take extra precautions when adding robustness to Distributed Software Transactional Memory as we will see in Section 6.3.8.

TVar actions

The function newTVar simply creates and returns a new empty mutable host TVar initialized to the given value and a default version identifier, a TVar identifier unique to the current node, an unlocked lock, and an empty wait queue of dependent transactions.

```
137 newTVar   :: Dist a => a -> STM (TVar a)
138 newTVar val = STM (\stmState -> do
139   ref  <- newMVar (val, 1)
140   tId  <- uniqueId
141   lock <- newMVar ()
142   wQ   <- newMVar []
143   return (Success stmState (TVar ref tId lock wQ)))
```

4.2. STM Protocol

We show here a first version of readTVar and the completed writeTVar function emphasizing the modifications of the transaction logs. We define both the logs and the readTVar function completely in Chapter 5.

For now, we assume that the validate log (updated in lines 149 and 157) contains TVar lock and unlock information (provided by the tVar parameter in lines 150 and 158), validation information, and information on TVar wait queues (provided by TVar version identifier vId and the transaction stmRetryVar in line 151).

```
144   readTVar   :: Dist a => TVar a -> STM a
145   readTVar tVar = STM (\st -> do
146     (val, vId) <- coreReadTVar tVar
147     ...
148     let newSt = st{
149       stmValidLog = insertValidLog
150                       tVar
151                       (Just (vId, (stmRetryVar st)))
152                       (stmValidLog st)}
153     return (Success newSt val))
```

The commit log (updated in line 161) contains TVar commit (provided by the value parameter val in line 163) and wait queue notification information (provided by the tVar in line 162).

```
154   writeTVar  :: Dist a => TVar a -> a -> STM ()
155   writeTVar tVar val = STM (\st ->
156     let newSt = st{
157       stmValidLog  = insertValidLog
158                        tVar
159                        Nothing
160                        (stmValidLog st),
161       stmCommitLog = insertCommitLog
162                        tVar
163                        val
164                        (stmCommitLog st)}
165     in return (Success newSt ()))
```

We keep the logs always sorted by their key, the unique TVar identifier. The functions insertValidLogs and insertCommitLogs insert a new log element into the log in the order of its key. Note that only lock and unlock information must be sorted to prevent deadlocks within the transaction protocol. For simplicity, however, we keep all log entries sorted.

4. Implementing Software Transactional Memory for Distributed Haskell

Protocol Structure

We use the transaction log for buffering and creating the transaction protocol. Now, we abstract from the log structure and describe the transaction protocol in detail. We distinguish a *creation protocol* and an *execution protocol*. The creation protocol dynamically generates the execution protocol based on the transaction program. We divide each protocol into sub-protocols. Each STM API function performs a specific operation, thus, executes either a creating or executing sub-protocol.

Table 4.1 gives an overview of which `STM` function performs an execution or creation sub-protocol which we then examine in detail. Note that the implementations of the protocols, we associate with the `atomic`, `retry` and `throw` functions, are all integrated into the `atomic` implementation. They are selected by the transaction result constructor, `Success`, `Retry`, and `Exception`, respectively. However, we list their STM protocols separately to emphasize the protocol structure.

API	EXECUTION	CREATION
	PROTOCOLS	
atomic	✗	–
retry	✗	–
throw	✗	–
catch	–	(✗)
(>>=)	–	(✗)
orElse	–	(✗)
newTVar	(✗)	–
readTVar	✗	✗
writeTVar	–	✗

Table 4.1.: API with STM Protocol (Direct ✗ and Indirect (✗) Log Modification)

4.2.4. Execution Protocols

We first look at the API protocol execution details shown in Table 4.2 with their respective action sequences being executed and the possible action results.

4.2. STM Protocol

API	Protocol	Execute	Result
atomic (Success)	lock validate commit unlock notify	[lock TVar] [read TVar] [write TVar] [unlock TVar] [notify TVar]	[confirm] [value/version] — — (*)
(*)	awake wait q	[awake RetryVar]	—
retry (Retry)	lock validate extend wait q unlock suspend	[lock TVar] [read TVar] [extend TVar wait q] [unlock TVar] —	[confirm] [value/version] — — —
throw (Exception)	lock validate unlock throw IO	[lock TVar] [read TVar] [unlock TVar] —	[confirm] [value/version] — —
readTVar	lock read unlock	lock TVar read TVar unlock TVar	*confirm* *value/version* —
newTVar	create	*allocate and init TVar*	new TVar

Table 4.2.: STM Execution Protocols

atomic

The atomic protocol commits valid transactions and notifies dependent transactions. It restarts invalid transactions. A valid transaction has, throughout its monadic run, a consistent view of the world represented by all TVars that are read in this transaction. A transaction is valid iff all read TVars are valid. A read TVar is valid iff no other transaction has modified it before starting the validation protocol which checks the TVar version identifier.

The concurrent lightweight Haskell implementation checks that the value at the time it is read is pointer-equal to its value at the time of validation. In our distributed implementation, each TVar modification increments its version identifier. Thus, an identical version identifier is equivalent to an unmodified TVar. The validate-commit sequence is a critical section that may be interrupted by other transaction threads. Hence, we protect it from concurrent

4. Implementing Software Transactional Memory for Distributed Haskell

access by the totally ordered `TVar` locks. The first sequence of actions performs lock operations on all `TVar`s accessed in this transaction program. The protocol waits for the confirmation of each lock operation.

One could argue that it is more efficient to only lock all read `TVar`s for validation and separately lock all `TVar`s to be written only when committing. However, there would be a possible performance advantage only on invalid transactions and it is the goal of the optimistic STM approach to avoid those as much as possible. More importantly, such an approach could introduce a deadlock if the read lock can be accessed while the write lock cannot. Of course, this could be algorithmically solved but then there would hardly be any performance improvement left.

Then the exclusive validate and tentative commit sequences take place. A validate sequence performs a read operation returning the actual `TVar` value. The mutable `TVar` value component includes both the value content and the version identifier, however, our implementation does not transmit unnecessary validation data as we will see in Section 5.4. A commit sequence actually writes the new value to the `TVar` making the change permanent.

The critical section ends with a sequence of unlock operations on all involved `TVar`s. The final sequence of action is a notification of each committed `TVar`. In turn each notified `TVar` executes the awake-protocol on its wait queue of `RetryVar`s to resume its dependent transactions.

retry

This protocol extends the wait queue of all read `TVar`s with the valid transaction `RetryVar`. Invalid transactions are restarted. Validation and wait queue extension sequences form a critical section like the **atomic** validate-commit sequence and therefore are encapsulated in lock and unlock sequences. The final protocol action suspends the transaction.

throw

The **throw** protocol raises an exception to leave the current valid transaction context. Invalid transactions are restarted. The validation sequence forms a critical section by itself. If the transaction is valid, the exception is raised outside of the critical section.

4.2. STM Protocol

readTVar

The read action itself forms a critical section. Thus, the readTVar protocol is a lock encapsulated read action. Other than with the transaction terminating protocols, this is not to validate transaction consistency but to prevent distributed race conditions. We understand these race conditions better when we look at inter-process communication in Section 4.3.1.

newTVar

We list newTVar for completeness although it does not use the transaction log and, thus, not exactly fits our definition of an STM protocol. It allocates and initializes the mutable object TVar and returns it.

4.2.5. Creation Protocols

The execution sub-protocols are created by accumulating the necessary information in transaction log entries. We call this accumulation the creation protocol. Table 4.3 shows the items each STM action logs for each sub-protocol. The creation protocol executed within a transaction program is based on the sequence of readTVar and writeTVar functions.

This sequence depends, naturally, on the readTVar and writeTVar functions themselves and on their composition with the catch, (>>=), and orElse functions. The combinator functions combine two STM actions. Hence, in our implementation, they combine both logged sub-protocols, either by selecting one of the two or by accumulating both. Table 4.4 shows how the STM combinator functions combine the respective protocols.

readTVar

The readTVar function expands the validation type protocols to be executed in atomic with actions for this particular TVar. The extended protocols are *validate* to ensure consistency of this read TVar during the transaction, *lock* and *unlock* to include this TVar into the critical section of the transaction, and *extend wait queue* to have other transactions possibly resume the current transaction when they update this TVar.

4. Implementing Software Transactional Memory for Distributed Haskell

writeTVar

Similar to readTVar, writeTVar expands the commit type protocols executed in atomic with actions for this particular TVar. The extended protocols are *commit* to actually write the given TVar value when the transaction succeeds, *lock* and *unlock* to include this TVar into the critical section of the transaction, and *notify* to initiate resuming all dependent transactions of this TVar.

API	CREATION PROTOCOL	LOG ITEM
readTVar	validate lock unlock extend wait queue	read TVar value lock TVar unlock TVar extend TVar wait queue
writeTVar	commit lock unlock notify	write TVar value lock TVar unlock TVar notify TVar wait queue

Table 4.3.: STM Creation Protocols

catch

The catch function is an alternative composition of two transactions returning one of them as its result. The selection depends on the exception status of the first transaction. Therefore, catch selects one of the two respective log sets accordingly as the resulting log set.

(>>=)

The (>>=) function is the sequential monadic composition which cumulates two transactions and, therefore, also combines both log sets to cumulated resulting log sets of the composition.

orElse

The orElse function is an alternative composition of two transactions whose result depends on the actual suspension state of the two transactions. If the

4.2. STM Protocol

API	CREATION PROTOCOL	LOG COMBINATION
catch	all protocols	select
(>>=)	all protocols	cumulate
orElse	validate	cumulate
	lock	cumulate
	unlock	cumulate
	extend wait queue	cumulate
	commit	select
	notify	select

Table 4.4.: STM Protocol Combination

first transaction succeeds, its result simply becomes the compound result. If the first transaction suspends, the second transaction result becomes the compound result. If the second transaction also suspends, the compound transaction suspends. As a result, we require a more sophisticated protocol creation.

Because of the latter case we create the validation protocol such that it cumulatively validates all read TVars of both alternatives. It also cumulates the lock and unlock protocols. Likewise, we cumulate both wait queue creation protocol sets. Thus, resuming the compound transaction is independent of the retrying transaction alternative.

The resulting commit and notification protocols, in contradiction, become the respective protocols of either alternative transaction to correctly commit the compound transaction. If both alternatives suspend, the compound protocols are possibly incorrect, however, they are discarded and rebuild from scratch when the transaction resumes and restarts.

As a side note, the different handling of validate and commit logs in orElse alternatives is the reason why we split the transaction state log into a commit and a validate part, covering the sub-protocols shown in Table 4.5. Alternatively, inserting new elements into one common log for all protocol items seems to be more efficient than the two insertions we use in writeTVar (line 154). However, it is more efficient to use a split log, if the majority of application programs frequently use the orElse STM composition which we believe is quite a safe assumption.

4. Implementing Software Transactional Memory for Distributed Haskell

Log	Protocol
validate	validate
	lock
	unlock
	extend wait queue
commit	commit
	notify

Table 4.5.: STM protocol logs

4.3. Distributed Communication

The TVar access in our implementation occurs highly transparent. As much as possible, we use generic functions accepting generic TVars as parameters. At the core of the implementation we determine a host or link access using pattern matching on the TVar constructors to actually modify the TVar elements. In case of a host TVar, we mutate the respective TVar elements using the mutable variable functions performing IO actions. In case of a link TVar, we mutate its host TVar using network message communication.

4.3.1. Network Messaging

Conceptually, our Distributed STM library distinguishes *unidirectional* messages (telling the host TVar to perform a certain action like saving a given value) and *bidirectional* messages (in addition to telling the TVar to perform a certain action also asking for a feedback like reading a value). If the message is to read the TVar value, the feedback, naturally, is the read value. A lock message feeds back a confirmation message, because the client has to be sure the lock action is finished before continuing with the protocol. Bidirectional messages implement synchronous communication. The client side is synchronized with the server action. Unidirectional messages perform asynchronous communication, both client and server sides continue to work asynchronously.

The two most used transport layer protocols (see Section 2.2.4) are the *user datagram protocol* (UDP) and the *transmission control protocol* (TCP). We choose TCP for our STM communication because of the reliable communication it offers. TCP is a connection based protocol. It is initiated by a client process

4.3. Distributed Communication

requesting a connection from a server process. The server process itself is prepared to receive and respond to such requests.

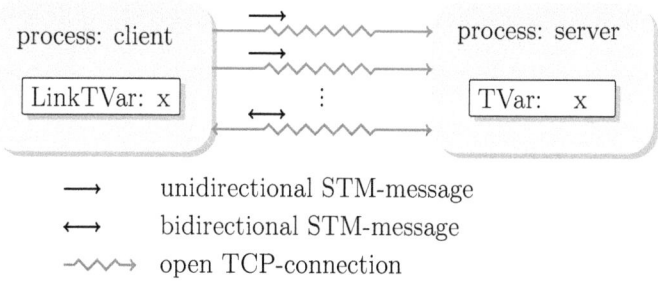

Figure 4.3.: Generic TCP Communication

STM interface functions send messages to the server process node hosting a link TVar (see Figure 4.3). In our first approach we open a TCP connection for every STM message being sent. Then we send the message and close the connection. So, at any time there are as many open TCP connections as there are messages being transmitted. This behavior is identical both for bidirectional and unidirectional messages. Note that TCP connections are always bidirectional to ensure a reliable communication. Conceptually, however, we still distinguish unidirectional and bidirectional connections.

The implementation is simple but causes a considerable amount of system processing overhead. Therefore, we discuss in Chapter 5 STM protocol performance improvements.

Receiving STM Messages

Each link **TVar** targets the process node hosting the linked **TVar** with messages. Therefore, each node provides a TCP server thread to receive messages and to perform the actions on the **TVar** requested by the message. Actually, only process nodes which have exported at least one **TVar** at some point need to be able to react on messages. However, we start a TCP server thread as part of the initialization performed by **runDist** in each process node. This is not a performance drain because the socket communication interface suspends until

79

4. Implementing Software Transactional Memory for Distributed Haskell

new messages arrive at the port. A socket is an I/O channel bound to a given TCP port of the IP network connection.

```
166  runDist :: IO () -> IO ()
167  runDist nodeMain = do
168    socket <- listenOn (Portnumber 60001)
169    forkIO (nodeReceiver socket)
170    nodeMain
```

The initialization wrapper function `runDist` binds a socket to an available and well known port (line 168) and forks a thread listening on this port (line 169). Any port number that is not reserved by the system can be used. Line 168 shows a simplified version. In our implementation we do not use a fixed port number. Instead, we initially try using port 60001. In case this port is already in use we increment the port number until we detect an unused port and use this port for the current process.

```
171  nodeReceiver :: Socket -> IO ()
172  nodeReceiver socket = do
173    (h,_,_) <- accept socket
174    readMsg h
175    hClose h
176    nodeReceiver socket
```

The `nodeReceiver` thread is our STM protocol internet message receiver thread. We start the `nodeReceiver` concurrently to the actual application program main function (line 170) of that process node.

The `accept` function prepares a handle (line 173) from which we read the incoming message (line 174). In addition, `accept` prepares an arbitrary available TCP port through which the actual communication is routed by the operating system. This arbitrary port is occupied during the whole communication session whereas the well known port is again ready to receive further messages. Finally, we close the handle which makes the arbitrary port available again.

In this book we describe low-level internet communication as needed to understand our design decisions. A very comprehensive description of all levels of internet communication protocols can be found in [KR07] for more detailed information.

Haskell uses the predefined functions `show` (`Show a => show :: a -> String`) of class `Show` and `read` (`Read a => read :: String -> a`) as a specialized version of a class `Read` function for conversions between `String` and

4.3. Distributed Communication

other data types. However, the `show` and `read` functions may be used from an application to interact with the user. Hence, the application may change their default behavior.

The DSTM library also requires a `String` conversion functionality for sending and receiving STM messages. In order to be independent of possible application specific modifications of the conversion functions, we define a class `Serializable`. The instance functions `toString` and `fromString` functions define encoding and decoding of serializable types to and from `String`.

```
177  class (Read a, Show a) => Serializable a where
178    toString :: a -> String
179    toString = show
180    fromString :: String -> a
181    fromString = read
```

We default `toString` to `show` and `fromString` to `read`. Thus, `show` and `read` may be changed for any type as long as the corresponding `Serializable` function is also defined to retain the default behavior.

```
182  readMsg :: Handle -> IO ()
183  readMsg h = do
184    str <- hGetLine h
185    handleMsg h (fromString str)
```

The call to `hGetLine` suspends the `nodeReceiver` thread until a message arrives (line 184). We then parse this message of type `STMMessage` using `fromString` and execute the requested remote procedure (lines 185, 189).

```
186  data STMMessage = RemReadTVar TVarID
187                  | RemWriteTVar TVarID String
188                  ...
```

We define a message for every sub-protocol of the STM protocol. For conciseness we focus on read and write sub-protocols as examples of the complete protocol to discuss the implementation ideas. Each message is an alternative of the `STMMessage` data type (line 186) with its constructor denoting the STM protocol and parameters as needed for that command. The `TVar` read message requires the unique identifier of the `TVar` to be read, the `TVar` write message requires the identifier and the value to be written.

Note that the actual inter-process message transmission is beyond the influence of the Haskell type system. The operating system adds an untyped

4. Implementing Software Transactional Memory for Distributed Haskell

arbitrary chunk of data as payload to the TCP message. We usually interpret this untyped data as being of type String by default and use the Haskell type system to transform our genuine data to and from String. We can build bijective transformations between any monomorphic type, like TVarID and String. However, we can build only injective transformations to String for polymorphic types like the data to be written. Therefore, at this point, we keep this data in String format within STMMessage. Fortunately, the polymorphic Haskell type system helps us solving this problem elegantly.

```
189  handleMsg :: Handle -> STMMessage -> IO ()
190  handleMsg h msg = do
191    case msg of
192      RemReadTVar id            -> readAction h id
193      RemWriteTVar id valStr -> writeAction id valStr
194      ...


195  readAction :: Handle -> TVarID -> IO ()
196  readAction h id = do
197    valStr <- readTVarFromId id
198    hPutStrLn h valStr


199  writeAction :: TVarID -> String -> IO ()
200  writeAction id valStr =
201    writeTVarFromId id valStr
```

Parsing the STM message selects the corresponding remote procedure by matching its pattern, like readAction (line 192) or writeAction (line 193). We use the link TVar identifier id as the unique key into a dictionary of TVar actions. The readAction function retrieves the TVar value in String representation (line 197) and writes it to the handle creating a TCP reply message (line 198) the client process is waiting for. Similarly, writeAction takes a value in String representation and stores it as the TVar value of the identified TVar (line 201). The problem left at this point is to properly retrieve the TVar information with only its identifier given.

The Haskell type system allows us to build recursive data structures like lists or trees containing homogeneous values only. However, the polymorphic TVars used in a distributed STM system, in general, require heterogenous data structures. What seems like another problem, at first, actually evokes the solution to the former two. We model a dictionary of a record of any *action*

4.3. Distributed Communication

needed to operate on the TVar instead of the TVar itself. The type signatures of these actions are then identical for any TVar. Line 204 shows a draft version of the TVarActions record. It is the type of the value in a global dictionary implemented as a Map (line 202) which is an efficient size balanced binary tree implementation in module Data.Map.

```
202  gActions    :: MVar (Map TVarID TVarActions)
203  gActions    = unsafePerformIO (newMVar empty)

204  data TVarActions = TVarActions {
205                       remRead   :: IO String,
206                       remWrite  :: String -> IO (),
207                       ...}
```

We define a polymorphic insertTVarAct function to create and insert into the global map all necessary TVar actions for a specific TVar. So, each instance of that function selects the type correct instance of the overloaded functions toString and fromString. The fromString function in line 217 transforms the given String value into the value type defined by the tVarRef MVar referenced in line 218. In Section 4.3.4 we will see that we create these TVar access functions just when they are needed.

```
208  insertTVarAct :: Dist a => TVar a -> IO ()
209  insertTVarAct (TVar tVarRef _ _ _) = do
210    actions <- takeMVar gActions
211    let tVarActs = TVarActions {
212        remRead   = do
213                     val <- readMVar tVarRef
214                     return (toString val),
215        remWrite  = \str -> do
216                     (_,vId) <- takeMVar tVarRef
217                     let val = fromString str
218                     putMVar tVarRef (val, vId + 1),
219        ...
220      }
221    putMVar gActions (insert tVarId tVarActs actions)
```

Now, we can straightforward retrieve the proper TVar action from the TVar actions dictionary using the TVar identifier key (lines 225, 229).

```
222  readTVarFromId :: TVarID -> IO String
223  readTVarFromId tVarId = do
224    map <- readMVar gActions
225    remRead (map ! tVarId)
```

83

4. Implementing Software Transactional Memory for Distributed Haskell

```
226 writeTVarFromId :: TVarID -> String -> IO ()
227 writeTVarFromId tVarId str = do
228   map <- readMVar gActions
229   remWrite (map ! tVarId) str
```

Sending STM Messages

We send unidirectional messages to a `TVar` by opening a TCP connection to the server process node hosting that `TVar` (line 232). Link `TVars` always carry their host process `EnvAddr` address information. Then we write the `String` converted message to the access handle, yielded on opening, and close the connection.

```
230 remPutMsg :: EnvAddr -> STMMessage -> IO ()
231 remPutMsg env msg = do
232   h <- connectTo (ipAddr env) (portId env)
233   hPutStrLn h (toString msg)
234   hClose h
```

Bidirectional messages start out like unidirectional ones. After writing the message we flush the socket and read it, suspending on the socket until a reply from the server, written to the socket (line 198), is available. Finally the connection is closed as well.

```
235 remGetMsg :: EnvAddr -> STMMessage -> IO String
236 remGetMsg env msg = do
237   h <- connectTo (ipAddr env) (portId env)
238   hPutStrLn h (toString msg)
239   hFlush h
240   answer <- hGetLine h
241   hClose h
242   return answer
```

4.3.2. Communicating Mutable Variables

Both `TVars` and `RetryVars` consist of two variant definitions (see lines 37–41 and 42–44). The first variant defines data types for a polymorphic mutable transactional variable and a monomorphic mutable retry variable, respectively. A mutable variable is bound to the process it is defined in. It is meaningful only in the context of that process and should not be transferred to other processes.

4.3. Distributed Communication

However, we need to have logical instances of both mutable variables potentially in all processes being part of the distributed system. Therefore, we define a String *equivalent*[6] identifier as the second variant of each type that can be communicated and works as a proxy of the real mutable variable. The identifier is a unique key allowing us to refer to the process where the real variable resides and to the variable itself at any time from any process.

When we need to transfer either mutable variable to another process, we always communicate its proxy variant. We transparently communicate RetryVars implicitly to implement the STM protocol as described in Section 4.3.3. Note that other than RetryVars the application programmer explicitly communicates TVars as values written to other TVars. A TVar is a polymorphic variable capable of holding values of any type including other TVars. When the application writes a TVar value into another TVar residing in a different process, our library transparently converts the TVar value into its proxy variant and communicates that to the other process.

We encode any data into String when building and sending a TCP message and decode it from String when we receive a TCP message. Haskell defines the Show and Read type classes to simplify conversions to and from String.

```
243  instance Show (TVar a) where
244    show (TVar _ tId _ _) =
245      show (LinkTVar (VarLink gMyEnv⁷ tId))
246    show (LinkTVar link) = "(" ++ show link ++ ")"

247  instance Read (TVar a) where
248    readsPrec i str =
249      map (\(x,s)->(LinkTVar x,s)) (readsPrec i str)
```

We overloaded the show and readsPrec functions to perform the conversions. lines 243 – 249 define the TVar conversion functions. Note that we encapsulate the showed link TVar in brackets (line 246) to ensure proper reading of application defined TVar data types. The RetryVar versions are similar. We define a show function for both the host and the link TVar variant where the host version calls the link version. Therefore, we convert the host TVar into its link variant initialized with the local process environment description (line 245). The link version simply unwraps the constructor and uses the derived function.

---

[6]We refer to any type that can be converted to and from String as String *equivalent*. Any monomorphic type that is an instance of the Read and Show classes is String equivalent. Note that functions and constructor class instances like IO action types are not String equivalent.

[7]We initialize the global variable gMyEnv with the current process environment.

4. Implementing Software Transactional Memory for Distributed Haskell

The predefined read function which we call to decode TCP messages calls the function readsPrec :: Int -> String -> [(a,String)] taking the input string to parse and a precedence level number responsible for parsing the correct number of parentheses. The result is a possibly empty list of successful parses of the input as a tuple of the parsed value and the remaining string. The read function extracts the parsed value out of a successfully parsed string.

```
250 instance Serializable a => Serializable (TVar a)
```

By making TVar a an instance of Serializable we make sure that toString and fromString can be used to encode and decode TVars with the default behavior of show and read as defined above.

4.3.3. Retry Variables

In this book we have discussed isolated parts of the retry command implementation covering a different aspect each time. Now, we want to look at the complete picture.

Each transaction consists of a retry variable which simply is a concurrent mutable variable of type MVar (). The retry command results in suspending the actual transaction on its RetryVar. The RetryVar in our distributed implementation also has a link alternative to allow communicating itself across the network. An attempt to suspend on a link retry variable would be an implementation error.

Each TVar maintains a list of dependent transactions. The transactions are represented by their RetryVars. In this book we also call the dependency list a *wait queue* in concordance with the lightweight concurrent implementation in [HMPJH05]. A transaction becomes dependent on a TVar if the transaction reads this TVar before suspending itself. Maintaining the dependency list follows our two-step protocol. Throughout a transaction we collect information to extend the wait queues of the read TVars, either as a queue extending IO action for each host TVar or as a RetryVar for each link TVar. On terminating a transaction with a retry command we either execute the collected actions or communicate the collected RetryVar to the link TVars and have the hosting processes extend the TVar wait queues. Note that for link TVar targets the communicated retry variables are always host retry variables converted to their link variant.

4.3. Distributed Communication

Whenever another transaction commits writeTVar commands it afterwards maps a notification function over the dependent transaction list of each committed TVar resuming these transactions. In general, a transaction depends on more than one TVar. In order to prevent multiple resume actions, we just tentatively resume the transaction (lines 251–253).

```
251  resumeRetryVarAct :: MVar () -> IO ()
252  resumeRetryVarAct retryMVar =
253     tryPutMVar⁸ retryMVar () >> return ()
```

The *notify* sub-protocol notifies all dependent transactions in a TVar's wait queue. The protocol is always executed in the process hosting a certain TVar, independent of the TVar type. Thus, in case of a link TVar, the protocol itself is triggered by a network message.

In general, a wait queue consists of both host and link RetryVars. We resume host RetryVar transactions directly and communicate the notification message to the link RetryVars.

In Figure 4.4 we show two processes concurrently running a couple of transactions. In a possible scenario transaction A in process I might notify host TVar 1 because it has just committed a new value to it. Then, the transaction notifies the transactions in the wait queue of host TVar 1 by sending RetryVar notifications. Notification messages go to link RetryVars 2 and 3, thus, resuming transactions D and E in process II. Also, the collected notification action on host RetryVar 4 is executed, thus, resuming transaction B in process I. In another scenario transaction C in process II notifies the same logical TVar, being link TVar 1 in process II, by sending a notification message to the host TVar 1 which in turn executes the same notifications as in the first scenario.

4.3.4. Distributed Garbage Collection

We have introduced a TVarActions record data structure instance managed in a global map. The record consists of IO actions to remotely access a TVar given its unique identifier only instead of the TVar itself. A server process hosting a TVar calls one of these actions when a client process performs an operation on a link TVar by sending an action message with the link TVar identifier to the server process.

---

⁸Multiple applications of tryPutMVar alter the MVar state still only once. It is a non-blocking version of putMVar.

4. *Implementing Software Transactional Memory for Distributed Haskell*

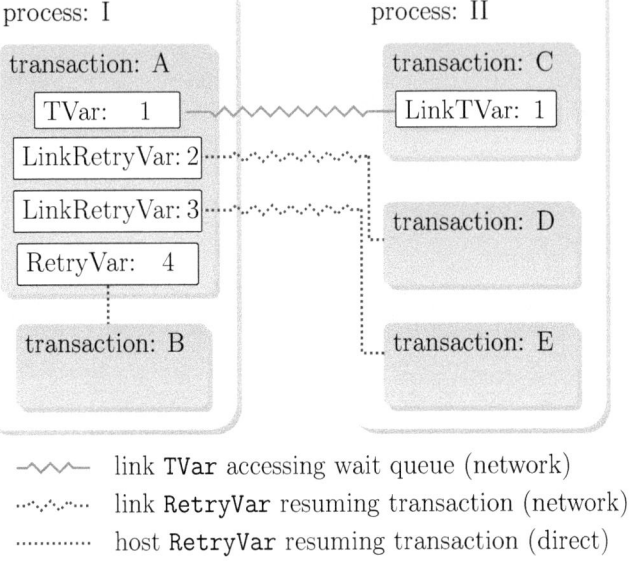

  ⟿⟵ link `TVar` accessing wait queue (network)
  ⋯⋅⋯⋅⋯ link `RetryVar` resuming transaction (network)
  ⋯⋯⋯⋯ host `RetryVar` resuming transaction (direct)

Figure 4.4.: Resuming Suspended Transactions

The application explicitly creates a mutable `TVar` with a `newTVar` call. The run time system implicitly deletes the `TVar` when it is no longer used. This means that there are no more references to it and the garbage collector reallocates its heap space. In a first attempt, we could call `insertTVarAct` (line 208) right from `newTVar`, thus, making sure that any `TVar` could be operated properly. As a result, however, the `IO` action record for any new `TVar` would never become garbage collected as the actions themselves reference that `TVar`. This would result in a memory leak[9] problem for applications creating many `TVar`s and running for a long time thus reducing the scalability of our library.

Therefore, the distributed STM library manages the global `IO` action record. The idea is to add the actions for a new `TVar` when they are needed for the first time, keep track of its usage, and remove the action record when it is not

---

[9]A memory leak is a memory allocation that is never deallocated, even when the memory is not used any longer. The result is an application accumulating, over time, more resources than necessary and eventually more than available.

4.3. Distributed Communication

needed any longer throughout the distributed system. Thus, we remove the last reference to the TVar explicitly and the garbage collector properly deallocates the unused TVar.

We need TVar access functions to access host TVars through their link TVar proxies. The application generates link TVars by registering host TVars at a name server in an initial program phase. In general, the application programmer creates a link TVar by making a TVar the value of another TVar hosted in a different process. In Section 4.3.2 we have shown how we communicate TVars to other processes as string messages. We create the access functions for a particular TVar when we communicate it for the first time, keep track of all host and link TVars subsequently communicated across process boundaries, and delete the access function record for a TVar when its last communicated proxy becomes garbage. The first communication of a TVar always uses a host variant generated by the application with a newTVar call. All succeeding communications may use either host or link TVars.

In order to keep track of the TVar communication, we add a target process environment list to the preliminarily defined global TVar action map (line 254) and implement two new functions, regTVars to register a TVar with its target destination on cross-process-communications and finTVars to deregister the target when the link TVar becomes garbage itself. We use an EnvAddr parameter of the final insertTVarAct version (lines 255–261) to manage the target list. The map insertWith function sets the first environment on a newly inserted host TVar (line 261) and adds possible consecutive target environments on previously inserted TVars (line 260).

```
254  gActions  ::  MVar (Map TVarID (TVarActions, [EnvAddr]))

255  insertTVarAct  ::  Dist a => TVar a -> EnvAddr -> IO ()
256  insertTVarAct (TVar ... tVarId ...) fstDest =
257    let tVarActs = ... in
258    modifyMVar_ gActions $
259      return . Data.Map.insertWith
260        (\_ (acts, envs) -> (acts, (fstDest:envs)))
261        tVarId (tVarActs, [fstDest])
```

Calling regTVars with a *host* TVar and a target environment generates the TVar access functions and initializes the target list with the first target. Consecutive calls of regTVars with the same host TVar keep the access functions unchanged but collect the new, possibly identical, target environments (line 264). Calling regTVars with a *link* TVar just adds the target environment in its host

4. Implementing Software Transactional Memory for Distributed Haskell

TVar action list using the network messaging mechanism defined for the STM protocol (line 266). Multiple occurrences of the same target environment are allowed.

```
262  regTVars   :: EnvAddr -> TVar a -> IO ()
263  regTVars destEnv tVar@(TVar _ _ _ _) =
264     insertTVarAct tVar dstEnv
265  regTVars dstEnv (LinkTVar (VarLink tEnv tVarId)) =
266     remPutMsg tEnv (RemAddEnvToAct tVarId dstEnv)
```

Haskell enables access to its garbage collector with *finalizer* functions that can be attached to any object. When such an object becomes garbage collected, the run-time system calls the attached finalizer function. We use this mechanism to remove environments from the TVar target lists. Calling finTVars with a link TVar attaches a finalizer to that TVar (line 270). Whenever a link TVar in any process becomes garbage, we use its finalizer function to remove one instance of this process environment from the host TVar target list by sending the appropriate network message (line 273). Removing the last target environment of a host TVar action target list removes its access functions which in turn deletes their references to the TVar. Eventually the host TVar itself is garbage collected. Host TVars do not need finalizers (line 268) because all references to them are already removed when they are garbage collected.

```
267  finTVars :: TVar a -> IO ()
268  finTVars (TVar _ _ _ _) = return ()
269  finTVars tVar@(LinkTVar linkTVar) =
270     addFinalizer tVar (finalizeLinkTVar linkTVar)

271  finalizeLinkTVar :: LinkTVar -> IO ()
272  finalizeLinkTVar (VarLink tEnv tVarId) =
273     remPutMsg tEnv (RemDelEnvFromAct tVarId gMyEnv)
```

The message constructors RemAddEnvToAct and RemDelEnvFromAct augment the STMMessage type with messages to add and delete target environments. Both take the TVar TVarID and EnvAddr as parameters. We also define the respective server side functions (lines 274 and 275) updating the global TVar action map. The implementation is straight forward and therefore not shown here.

```
274  addEnvToTVarActions  :: TVarID -> EnvAddr -> IO ()

275  delEnvFromTVarActions :: TVarID -> EnvAddr -> IO ()
```

4.3. Distributed Communication

We register the destination environment of all TVars leaving the current process encapsulated in an STM protocol message being sent. We add a finalizer to each received TVar encapsulated in a protocol message. In both cases the message may contain TVar values that possibly contain further TVars. We encode and decode the encapsulated TVars using the overloaded toString and fromString functions (see Section 4.3.2) when communicating any TVar.

Ideally, we would take advantage of the same overloading mechanism by calling regTVars and finTVars when encoding and decoding TVars using toString and fromString. However, both toString and fromString are pure functions. We cannot safely call the IO functions regTVars and finTVars within these pure functions.

We solve this dilemma by introducing a new class Dist (lines 276–278), making TVar an instance of Dist (lines 279–286), and constraining the TVar value parsing functions by the Dist class which in turn is constrained by the class Serializable. As the polymorphic TVar value can be of any type in an arbitrary application, we implement instances of these methods for every Haskell type like Haskell did for predefined classes. The Distributed STM library defines instances for all standard types and compositions to do nothing. The application programmer has to make all application defined data types, eventually becoming a TVar value, an instance of Dist as shown in Section 3.2.

```
276  class Serializable a => Dist a where
277    finTVars :: a -> IO ()
278    regTVars :: EnvAddr -> a -> IO ()

279  instance Dist a => Dist (TVar a) where
280    regTVars destEnv tVar@(TVar _ _ _ _) =
281      insertTVarAct tVar destEnv
282    regTVars dstEnv (LinkTVar (VarLink tEnv tVarId))=
283      remPutMsg tEnv (RemAddEnvToAct tVarId dstEnv)
284    finTVars (TVar _ _ _ _) = return ()
285    finTVars tVar@(LinkTVar linkTVar) =
286      addFinalizer tVar (finalizeLinkTVar linkTVar)
```

Host TVars fulfill proxy requests through the actions in the global TVar action map. Thus, we add the register and deregister calls to the remote access functions defined in insertTVarAct and to the read and commit functions shown in detail in Section 4.4. Note that we add the destination environment as a parameter to the remRead function and thus to the STM protocol message not shown here.

4. Implementing Software Transactional Memory for Distributed Haskell

```
287  insertTVarAct :: Dist a => TVar a -> EnvAddr -> IO ()
288  insertTVarAct (TVar tVarRef tVarId ...) fstDest =
289    let tVarActs = TVarActions {
290          remRead  = \destEnv -> do
291                       v'@(v,_) <- readMVar tVarRef
292                       regTVars destEnv v
293                       return (toString v'),
294          remWrite = \str -> do
295                       (_,vId) <- takeMVar tVarRef
296                       let val = fromString str
297                       putMVar tVarRef (val, vId+1)
298                       finTVars val,
299        ...} in
300    modifyMVar_ gActions ...
```

Lines 287–300 show the shortened final version of **insertTVarAct**.

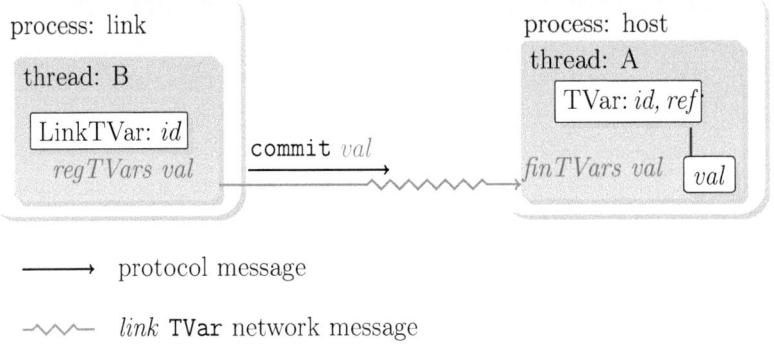

⟶ protocol message

⟿ *link* **TVar** network message

Figure 4.5.: Registering TVar Actions Committing Link TVar

An STM protocol message to be send to another process potentially contains an arbitrary **TVar** data structure to be registered either if a link **TVar** is committed (Figure 4.5) or if a host **TVar** fulfills a read request from a link **TVar** (Figure 4.6). A received message from another process possibly contains a **TVar** structure to be prepared for finalization either if a link **TVar** is read (Figure 4.6) or if a host **TVar** fulfills a commit request (Figure 4.5) from a link **TVar**.

92

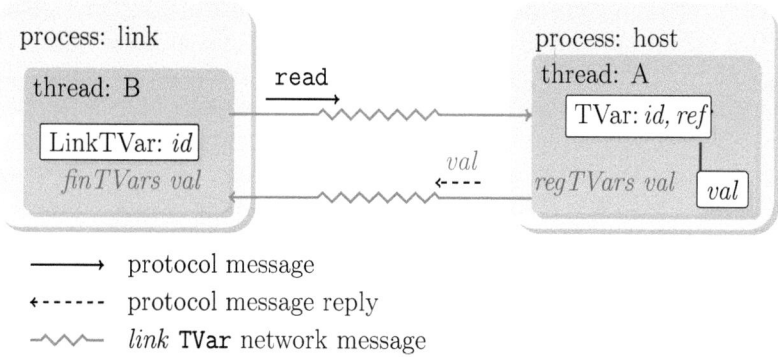

Figure 4.6.: Registering TVar Actions Reading Link TVar

4.4. Intra-Transaction State

The readTVar function, within a transaction program, reads the current TVar value. In general, this is the last committed TVar value. However, it may also be a yet uncommitted value, provided by writeTVar preceding the readTVar function within the same transaction program. A properly formed program like the following example might first write a TVar, then read the same TVar, and finally react on the read result.

```
301  writeRead :: TVar Bool -> IO Bool
302  writeRead tVar =
303     atomic $ do
304        writeTVar tVar True
305        b <- readTVar tVar
306        if b then return b else retry

307  main = do
308     atomic (newTVar False) >>= writeRead >>= print
```

An STM library updating TVars solely on committing the complete transaction might indefinitely suspend the above transaction in line 306 because the writeTVar action in line 304 is not committed before the readTVar action in line 305 takes place. This dilemma exists because the STM protocol intentionally does not synchronize application-level TVar writing and library level TVar committing.

93

4. Implementing Software Transactional Memory for Distributed Haskell

We cannot simply execute the commit action prematurely as this would violate the STM protocol. Instead, we mimic an application-level `TVar` writing command neutralizing its effect to the library. In [HK05] the proposed solution is to additionally log discard actions and execute those to revert the commit actions. However, this solution renders highly inefficient in a distributed scenario as each action potentially involves expensive network messages. We found a solution not requiring additional messages. We describe this solution in Section 5.5 after having optimized our log data structure.

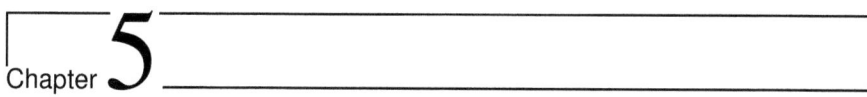

Chapter 5

Implementing Efficient Transactional Communication

The Distributed STM implementation in Chapter 4 is fully operational. A big flaw so far, however, is that most practical distributed applications with a significant amount of TVars will perform very poorly using this approach as we see in the benchmark analysis in Section 5.6.

In this chapter we first analyze the implementation in Section 5.1 and show that the communication strategy is mainly responsible for this performance lack.

Therefore, we discuss several approaches towards a better communication efficiency. Besides accelerating Distributed STM based application programs by reducing system computation overhead dramatically, we also relieve internet communication in general from unnecessary communication thus improving the performance of other internet users.

We discuss two different measures to significantly reduce the amount of TCP connections in Sections 5.2 and 5.3.

In Section 5.4 we discuss another performance improvement idea optimizing the STM protocol itself. The effect is orthogonal to the aforementioned improvements thus accumulating the benefit. We use this new structure in Section 5.5 to provide correct intra-transaction TVar values.

5. *Implementing Efficient Transactional Communication*

5.1. Individual Line

The distributed communication of the STM protocol described in Section 4.3 simply opens, uses, and closes a new TCP connection for every single STM protocol step as shown in Figure 4.3. This single message approach makes support for distributed real-time applications virtually impossible and reduces the potential advantages of others. Our performance improvements enable the use of much more demanding applications. We still cannot accommodate most practical real-time requirements guaranteeing precise sub-second reaction times. However, soft real-time applications can be executed with acceptable performance. We use the term *soft real-time* to denote requirements for interactive applications like online games. Soft real-time reaction times are not exactly defined, however, they should be acceptable for human operators. We show an example at the end of this chapter.

The first tests of our library described in Chapter 4 used by `TVar` communication rich applications yield very disappointing results. The performance is in fact so poor that a practical usage seems rarely possible. Our analysis quickly determines network messaging as being the main performance barrier. Depending on the application, the STM protocol easily generates hundreds of `TVar` accesses per second. In a distributed STM system using this individual line approach many of those result in single TCP messages. Measured round-trip-times (RTT) of less than 100 microseconds in local area networks (LAN) up to a few hundred milliseconds in wide area networks (WAN) ([DdMY05]) explain the poor results.

We need to understand the basic functionality of TCP communication to be able to solve the performance problem. In this book we do not have room for an in-depth description of the many technical details in layered network communication. A very profound explanation of the different computer networking layers can be found in [KR07]. However, to follow the following ideas for improvement it is important to understand that establishing an internet TCP connection between two process nodes requires quite a bit of system resources both on each host computer and the internet infrastructure itself.

The TCP protocol causes client and server processes to create a connection with a so called *three-way handshake*. The client sends a message to the server which replies with an acknowledgement message which the client in turn acknowledges also. During this TCP handshake protocol both the server and the client create a new socket connected to an unused local TCP port and use

5.2. Dedicated Line

this port for subsequent information exchange. Similarly, both processes end the connection by exchanging another handshake sequence and free the used resources. The communication system overhead increases at least linearly with the amount of individual TCP connection open-use-close cycles. Therefore, our first goal is to reduce the amount of the connection cycles used in our distributed STM protocol.

5.2. Dedicated Line

In Chapter 4 we have seen that the TCP based, inter-process communication used in our STM protocol consists of both asynchronous unidirectional messages like writing a `TVar` and synchronous bidirectional messages like reading a `TVar`. We call the sending process a (TCP) client and the receiving process a (TCP) server. In general, process nodes being part of a distributed application work both as client and server.

Therefore, it should be possible to organize the communication with exactly two TCP connections between every process node, one for each communication direction. The idea is for a client process to open a TCP connection for its first message to a server, to use it, and to keep it open until the program terminates. The next message to the same node then uses the already established connection.

Thus, we create at most $p(p-1)$ conceptually unidirectional *dedicated lines* for p process nodes in a distributed system. This is the minimal number of TCP connections for a totally connected distributed system. Note that with this dedicated line approach the number of connections depends only on the number of processes in a distributed system. It does neither depend on the message protocol nor on the application program. Thus, we cannot determine how many connection cycles we save exactly. Almost any reduction rate is possible depending on the application program. Closely coupled highly communicative distributed systems like soft real-time games may save close to a hundred percent of their connection cycles. We discuss benchmark results in Section 5.6.

Figure 5.1 shows a client and a server process connected through two dedicated TCP connection lines, one for each communication direction. We send unidirectional messages similar to the individual line approach but always use the same line. No synchronization is needed. Bidirectional messages, however, require process synchronization through their reply message. The run-time

97

5. Implementing Efficient Transactional Communication

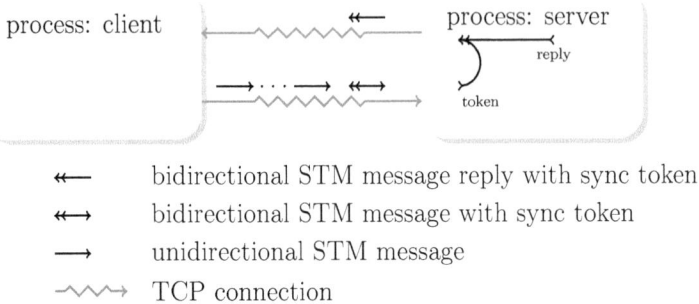

- ←   bidirectional STM message reply with sync token
- ←→   bidirectional STM message with sync token
- →   unidirectional STM message
- ∿   TCP connection

Figure 5.1.: Dedicated Line TCP Communication

system socket interface provides this synchronization in our single message approach by suspending the client thread until the reply is available. Note that we cannot use the same dedicated line for sending the reply because it is for unidirectional use and must not be blocked to be able to send further messages. An example message sequence might consist of reading a **TVar** to validate some transaction followed by writing another **TVar** to commit another transaction. If we waited for the reply to the first message, the second transaction would be blocked unnecessarily. Instead, we send the reply using the dedicated line for the reverse direction.

The client process in this example subsequently sends a bidirectional and two unidirectional messages to the server process. The server then sends a reply message to the conceptually bidirectional message back to the client process. In order to synchronize the client process with the server the client adds a unique token to every new bidirectional message. The server receives that message and adds the received token to its reply message. The client suspends the thread after sending the message until the token is received back by the client receiver thread.

In our dedicated line implementation we define a **STMMessageSC** type, divided into unidirectional **Standard** (line 2) and bidirectional **Certified** (line 5) messages, and add a new unidirectional reply message variant **RemReply** (line 6). The certified message includes a unique token of type **MsgID** which the reply message returns along with the string reply.

```
1 type MsgID = ID
```

5.2. Dedicated Line

```
2   data STMMessageSC = Standard STMMsg
3                    | Certified ReplyMsg
4                                MsgID
5                                EnvAddr

6   data STMMsg = RemReply MsgID String
7               | RemWriteTVar ID String
8               | ...

9   data ReplyMsg = RemReadTVar ID EnvAddr
10                | ...
```

We replace the run-time synchronizing mechanism with a lightweight synchronization using process global dictionaries of *pending replies*. The dictionaries collect all received but not yet read reply strings in a synchronization buffer. We realize the buffer with mutable variables of type MVar using the message identifier token as the key (line 11).

```
11  gPendReplies :: MVar [(MsgID, (MVar String))]
12  gPendReplies = unsafePerformIO (newMVar [])
```

A thread, sending a bidirectional message by calling remGetMsg (line 13), generates a new reply MVar buffer with a unique message identifier token as the key (line 15), sends the message (lines 17, 17), and synchronizes with the newly generated reply MVar (line 18). Note that we suspend the sending thread on the reply buffer itself (line 29).

```
13  remGetMsgSC :: EnvAddr -> ReplyMsg -> IO String
14  remGetMsgSC env msg = do
15    msgId <- newReply
16    h <- connectTo (ipAddr env) (portId env)
17    hPutStrLn h (toString (Certified msg msgId gMyEnv))[1]
18    answer <- takeReply msgId
19    return answer

20  newReply :: IO MsgID
21  newReply = do
22    msgId <- uniqueId
23    buffer <- newEmptyMVar
24    modifyMVar_ gPendReplies (return . ((msgId, buffer):))
25    return msgId
```

---

[1]Write access to a dedicated line handle is a critical section and thus lock protected in our implementation which is not shown here for readability.

5. Implementing Efficient Transactional Communication

```
26 takeReply :: MsgID -> IO String
27 takeReply msgId = do
28   replyBuffer <- lookupReply msgId
29   reply <- takeMVar (fromJust replyBuffer)
30   modifyMVar_ gPendReplies
31     (return . filter ((/= msgId).fst))
32   return reply



33 lookupReply :: MsgID -> IO (Maybe (MVar String))
34 lookupReply msgId =
35   readMVar gPendReplies >>= return . lookup msgId
```

The sending process then, upon receiving back the token, resumes the suspended thread and the sender removes the buffer **MVar** from the pending reply dictionary. The message server of the sending client process receives a reply and releases the corresponding buffer **MVar** by filling it with the response **String** (line 44). The suspended sender thread continues safely synchronized with the remote process. Note that no suspension at all takes place if the reply message arrives before the sender reads it.

```
36 handleMsgSC :: Handle -> STMMessageSC -> IO ()
37 handleMsgSC h msg = do
38   case msg of
39     Standard RemReply -> putReply
40     ...



41 putReply :: MsgID -> String -> IO ()
42 putReply msgId replyStr = do
43   replies <- readMVar gPendReplies
44   putMVar (fromJust (lookup msgId replies)) replyStr
```

Application programs using the dedicated line library achieve a significantly better performance than identical programs using the single message approach library as we will see from the benchmark tests we show in Section 5.6. The former library features the minimum number of totally required TCP connections. However, we pay a price for the dramatic reduction of socket run-time system overhead by adding a lightweight synchronization overhead by managing buffer **MVars**.

5.3. Line Stack

The dedicated line synchronization overhead cannot be neglected. Therefore, we improve this messaging strategy further. We already efficiently communicate asynchronous unidirectional messages with the dedicated line approach described in Section 5.2 but there is a synchronization overhead on bidirectional messages.

Thus, we keep the unidirectional dedicated lines to now communicate unidirectional messages only. Their maximum number is still $p(p-1)$ when connecting p processes in a distributed system. Additionally, we open bidirectional TCP connections for the bidirectional STM protocol messages. Our goal is to both use the efficient built-in socket synchronization and to reduce the managing overhead for TCP connections as much as possible. Our idea is to allow each client process to open as many *exclusive* bidirectional TCP connections to a server process as it needs to use in parallel and to keep every connection open for later reuse.

Each bidirectional connection in use communicates exactly one bidirectional message at a time using the built-in synchronization. We reuse existing connections as much as possible. There is little additional system overhead in a startup phase when adding more bidirectional connections to fulfill the STM protocol needs of parallel communication. Note that our implementation transparently creates exactly the number of maximal required parallel bidirectional connections. There is some managing overhead in our library to control the usage of the open connections. Luckily, this overhead is much smaller than both the system overhead in the single message approach and the synchronization overhead in the pure dedicated line approach as Section 5.6 shows.

In Figure 5.2 we show a client process sending multiple sequential unidirectional messages to a server process using a single dedicated line TCP connection. There are also multiple exclusive TCP connections shown, each occupied with just one bidirectional message at a time.

We implement a simple stack to collect open bidirectional connections. The bidirectional message sending function (line 45) uses an augmented connection function to manage the stacked communication lines (line 47) and a higher-order bidirectional communication function `recvTCP` (line 54) to access the line. Whenever a thread sends a bidirectional message, it pops an already open TCP connection from the stack (line 50), uses it exclusively for message and reply (line 51), and pushes the still open connection back onto the stack

5. Implementing Efficient Transactional Communication

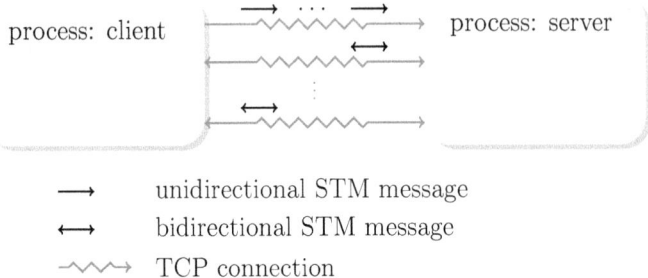

→ unidirectional STM message
↔ bidirectional STM message
⇝ TCP connection

Figure 5.2.: Stacked TCP Communication

(line 52) for further usage.

```
45  remGetMsg :: EnvAddr -> ReplyMsg -> IO String
46  remGetMsg env msg = connectExclTo env (recvTCP msg)


47  connectExclTo :: EnvAddr -> (Handle -> IO String)
48                -> IO String
49  connectExclTo env retTcp = do
50    h <- popTcpHandle env
51    answer <- tcp h
52    pushTcpHandle h env
53    return answer


54  recvTCP :: ReplyMsg -> Handle -> IO String
55  recvTCP msg h = do
56    hPutStrLn h (toString msg)
57    hFlush h
58    hGetLine h
```

Each target process requires a separate stack of open bidirectional TCP connections. Therefore we implement a process global dictionary of stacks with the target environment address as the key (line 59).

When popping a connection the stack is typically already filled (line 65) and we replace the target stack with its tail and return its head, being the handle to the next available exclusive bidirectional communication line. If there is no stack yet for a specific target or the stack is empty (line 69), we open a new connection returning its handle.

5.4. Line Bundle

Pushing a connection either replaces an existing stack with itself extended by the now available and still open connection (line 76) or creates a new stack with its first now available open connection (line 78).

```
59  gTCPStacks :: MVar [(EnvAddr, [Handle])]
60  gTCPStacks = unsafePerformIO (newMVar [])

61  popTcpHandle :: EnvAddr -> IO Handle
62  popTcpHandle env = do
63    tcps <- takeMVar gTCPStacks
64    case lookup env tcps of
65      Just (h:hs) -> do
66        putMVar gTCPStacks $
67          (env,hs) : filter ((/= env) . fst) tcps
68        return h
69      _ -> do
70        putMVar gTCPStacks tcps
71        connectTo (ipAddr env) (portId env)

72  pushTcpHandle :: Handle -> EnvAddr -> IO ()
73  pushTcpHandle h env = do
74    tcps <- takeMVar gTCPStacks
75    case lookup env tcpConns of
76      Just hs -> putMVar gTCPStacks $
77        (env,h:hs) : filter ((/= env) . fst) tcps
78      Nothing -> putMVar gTCPStacks ((env,[h]) : tcps)
```

A distributed system with p process nodes creates at most $p(p-1)$ unidirectional connections. Additionally, the number of bidirectional connections is $p(p-1)maxpar$, where $maxpar$ is the maximal number of parallel bidirectional messages to the same target process. For practical applications this line stack approach also creates significantly fewer connections than the naive single connection approach. However, we utilize more TCP connections than the dedicated line approach for the benefit of reducing the high-level synchronization effort. The benchmark section in this chapter shows the line-up of all optimizations.

5.4. Line Bundle

We have optimized the TCP communication of STM messages between process nodes in a Distributed STM system, hence, the internet protocol *transport* layer

5. Implementing Efficient Transactional Communication

(see Table 5.1). Analyzing the *application* layer, the STM protocol itself, there is even more room for improvement.

LAYER	PROTOCOL
Application	STM
Transport	TCP
Internet	IP
Network Link	Ethernet, WLAN, ...

Table 5.1.: Distributed STM Internet Protocol Layers

Our goal is to reduce the amount of STM messages. The fewer messages we send the faster the communication will be, in addition to the transport layer improvements. The STM execution protocol (Table 4.2) shows that all sub-protocols consist of either sequences of single TVar actions or sequences of collections of TVar actions. Additionally, we sort lock- and unlock action lists by TVar to prevent deadlocks in lock/unlock sequences. We keep all other action lists in their application given order.

Executing these distributed system actions either mutates process global structures or translates into messages, depending on the TVar type. If a certain transaction operates on l link TVars executing s protocol steps, we send sl messages, one for each link TVar in each step.

Our idea is to bundle together as many of the STM protocol messages as possible and to send a bundle of few large TCP messages rather than many small ones. Obviously, we can bundle all non-sequential messages to the *same* TVar. In addition, and much more effective, we can bundle all non-sequential messages to *any* TVar located in the *same* target process. Obeying the STM protocol we can bundle only conceptually independent messages. Protocol sequences, of course, have to stay sequential.

The example in Table 5.2 shows an unbundled partial atomic protocol sequence executed at the end of a transaction as described in Section 4.2.4. We assume all TVars are hosted in processes disjunct to the transaction process. Then each unbundled protocol item represents a TCP message sent to the respective process. In this example we lock TVar1 and TVar4 hosted in process 1 and TVar1 and TVar3 of process 3. The other protocol sequences are described similarly. Note that atomic locks all TVars either read or written in a transaction and that the commit sequence does not have to be sorted. The validate

5.4. Line Bundle

sequence did not have to be sorted either, however, we collect lock and validate information in the same log dictionary hence the validate data is also sorted.

API	Protocol	Execute
atomic	lock	lock TVar1P1
		lock TVar4P1
		lock TVar1P3
		lock TVar3P3
		...
	validate	read TVar1P1 value
		read TVar4P1 value
		read TVar3P3 value
		...
	commit	write TVar1P1 value
		write TVar3P3 value
		write TVar1P3 value
		...
	unlock	...
	notify	...
	...	

Table 5.2.: Unbundled STM protocol messages

Using our bundling approach we join some of the protocol messages in Table 5.2 and send them as one bundle to the respective process without altering the protocol. Table 5.3 shows the same partial sequence using message bundling. In the example we send *one* message to process 1 to lock both TVar1 and TVar4 and another message to process 3 to lock TVar1 and TVar3. Note that process bundling requires the primary key for the strictly ordered locks to be the process identifier. Similarly, we bundle the other protocol items resulting into fewer line items and thus fewer messages.

To get an idea of the optimization potential, we assume a transaction with s protocol steps using l link TVars evenly distributed on p processes. Then this transaction would ideally send only sp messages instead of sl messages before, with l usually being significantly larger than p. The fewer messages a transaction sends, the longer they become. However, the length of a network message can only be an integral multiple of a defined minimum length, the

105

5. Implementing Efficient Transactional Communication

API	Protocol	Execute
atomic	lock	lock {TVar1P1, TVar4P1} lock {TVar1P3, TVar3P3} ...
	validate	validate {TVar1P1, TVar4P1} validate TVar3P3 ...
	commit	write TVar1P1 value write {TVar3P3, TVar1P3} value ...
	unlock	...
	notify	...
	...	

Table 5.3.: Bundled STM protocol messages

Ethernet frame length in the context of this work. Therefore, it is efficient to bundle messages that are short in relation to the frame length which the DSTM messages are, in general.

Note that this is only an estimate. The exact number of messages and their lengths depend on the application program. In a worst-case scenario the amount of bundle messages is identical to the individual message approaches, when all link TVars are hosted on different process nodes. Likewise, the length of a bundled message is identical to the cumulated length of the individual messages, when the cumulated unused portion of the frames of the individual messages is not large enough to save frames with the bundled message.

STM message bundling works with any TCP connection approach. Figure 5.3 shows a client process sending one bundle message consisting of two STM messages to two TVars hosted by the same server process (a). The server unbundles the message and applies each STM message to its respective target TVar (b).

In order to implement the bundling approach, we not only need to augment the functionality to receive messages from simply executing remote procedures on TVars to managing more complex transaction data. We also need to adapt the log type structure itself. The logs described in Chapter 4 collect IO actions for any protocol step. Unfortunately, we can only execute IO actions as they are. It is neither possible to access the information they include nor to send

5.4. Line Bundle

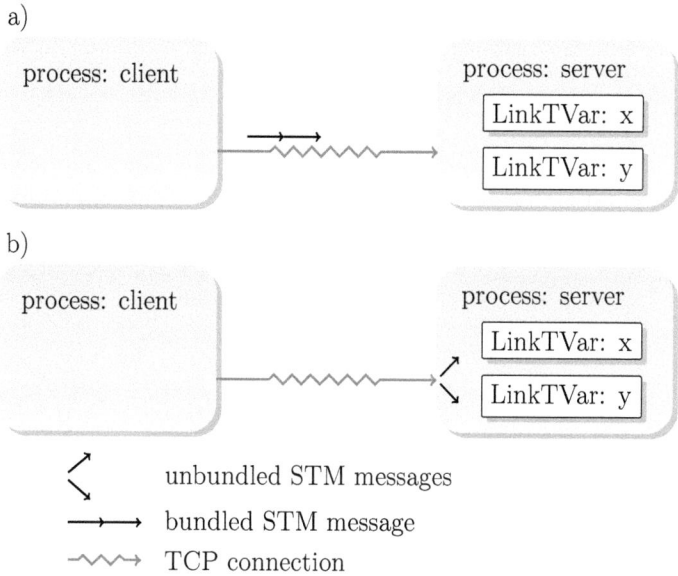

Figure 5.3.: Bundled STM Messages

5. Implementing Efficient Transactional Communication

them across the network. Therefore, we collect a different kind of information and modify the types of the transaction logs.

5.4.1. Logging Transactions using Bundle Logs

To accommodate the line bundle message structure, we define logs consisting of either `IO` action entries for host `TVars` or `String` equivalent value entries for link `TVars`. The action entries are executable monadic host `TVar IO` actions. The `String` equivalent values are STM protocol messages, readily formatted to be send to the `TVar` hosting process where the corresponding `TVar IO` action is created and executed.

The two log dictionaries are always sorted by the process node identifier `EnvAddr`. Each dictionary contains either host or link `TVar` data accumulating and updating the STM protocol in each transaction while scanning the application program transactional functions.

```
309  type ValidLog        = (EnvAddr, ValidLogBundle)
310  type ValidLogBundle  = Either HostVLogBundle
311                                LinkVLogBundle

312  type CommitLog       = (EnvAddr, CommitLogBundle)
313  type CommitLogBundle = Either HostCLogBundle
314                                LinkCLogBundle
```

Ideally, we kept all information in one dictionary to minimize the sorting effort. As we have seen in Section 4.2.5, an efficient management of the `orElse` function requires splitting the log. As a downside we need to sort two dictionaries. However, we do not require a total order on the commit log. We split the `VarLink` key into the process environment as its primary key and the `TVar` identifier as its secondary key. We sort both logs by their primary keys to enable message bundling and additionally sort the validate log by its secondary key to keep the total lock and unlock order.

We keep the logs always sorted when inserting new elements to save on additional complexity in transaction management. Although the insert sort complexity of $\mathcal{O}(n^2)$ is worse than that of a best comparison sort of $\mathcal{O}(n \log n)$, the performance can even be better for a small number of items n. As efficient transactions are short, this should be a safe assumption. Each insert sorting step is simple, thus, cheap to implement. In addition just `writeTVar` commands insert into the commit dictionary log shortening the performance lag further.

5.4. Line Bundle

Host TVar Logs

The host `TVar` log parts contain essentially the same information as the former coarse definition. We use record structures for better readability and build a tuple of a lock action record dictionary and a validation action record for the validation log containing all actions required for the first transaction protocol phase for host `TVar` entries. Note that we join consecutive validation actions by binding them accordingly. The lock information needs to be globally ordered and, thus, cannot be consolidated.

```
315  type HostVLogBundle = ([(ID, LockActs)], ValidActs)
316  data LockActs = LockActs {lockAct   :: IO (),
317                            unLockAct :: IO () }
318  data ValidActs = ValidActs {validAct   :: IO Bool,
319                              extWaitQAct :: IO () }
```

The `LockActs` record simply collects `TVar` lock and unlock actions. The `ValidActs` record consists of a boolean validation action and an action extending the `TVar` wait queues with the current transaction `RetryVar` to resume the possibly suspended transaction by an application `retry` call.

The commit log defined for the second STM protocol phase manages information to commit transactions finally and to notify dependent transactions to resume. The commit action writes a new value into the `TVar`. The notify action maps the `TVar` wait queue resuming each transaction suspended on its `RetryVar`.

```
320  type HostCLogBundle = [(ID, CommitActs)]
321  data CommitActs = CommitActs {commitAct :: IO (),
322                                notifyAct :: IO () }
```

Note that we make the log a dictionary over the `TVar` identifier and not simply accumulate the actions to be able to access individual `TVar` commit actions. The reason is the proper handling of intra-transaction `TVar` values as we show in Section 5.5.

Link TVar Logs

We define a `String` equivalent validate log maintaining information for link TVars. In addition to the key process node identifier `EnvAddr` used for addressing the bundle message we always need to include the `TVar` identifier (line 324)

109

5. Implementing Efficient Transactional Communication

in the message. The message receiving process builds lock and unlock protocols just from the link `TVar` identifier with no additional information needed.

```
323  type LinkVLogBundle = [ValidRemVal]
324  type ValidRemVal    = [(ID, MaybeRead)]
325  type MaybeRead      = Maybe (VersionID, RetryVar)
```

Protocols for transactions with link `TVar`s being read require additionally the `VersionID` at the time of reading and the transaction `RetryVar` needed to extend the wait queue (line 325). We have shown how to communicate retry variables in Section 4.3.2. Note that we use a `Maybe` type as only read `TVar`s contribute to a complete validate log entry while written `TVar`s only require logging the `TVar` identifiers enabling the lock protocols generation. However, we will augment the `ValidRemVal` type (line 324) for our robustness implementation in Chapter 6.

```
326  type LinkCLogBundle = ([(ID, String)], IO() )
```

We define the link `TVar` commit log as a `String` type holding the converted new `TVar` value given in a `writeTVar` command (line 326). The conversion is necessary to transmit the data as a network message. Like the host bundle information, also the link commit data is a dictionary to be able to access individual commit `String`s. Additionally, we collect an `IO` action which we naturally cannot send across the network. This is the registration action we execute when sending the bundle commit message. In Section 4.3.4 we have described how the registration of link `TVar`s works.

5.4.2. Collecting Bundle Logs

The transaction logs buffer information extracted from the transaction program. We build the transaction logs while executing the STM transaction in monadic isolation according to the STM collection protocol. Both, `readTVar` and `writeTVar` call the `insertValidLog` and `insertCommitLog` functions to build the logs.

The `insertWith` helper function (line 327) inserts a new value with its key into a given dictionary. If the key already exists, its value is altered using the given update function.

5.4. Line Bundle

```
327  insertWith :: Ord a =>
328                 (b -> b -> b) -> a -> b -> [(a, b)]
329                 -> [(a, b)]
330  insertWith _ key new [] = [(key, new)]
331  insertWith upd key new ((k, old) : kvs)
332    | key == k = (k, upd new old) : kvs
333    | key > k = (k, old) : insertWith upd key new kvs
334    | otherwise = (key, new) : (k, old) : kvs
```

Both, `insertValidLog` and `insertCommitLog` insert a new entry into their respective log structures calling `insertWith` with an update function for existing keys (lines 338 and 346), the bundle key (lines 339 and 347), a singleton log generator for the actual log data (lines 340 and 348), and the log itself (lines 341 and 349).

```
335  insertValidLog :: TVar a -> MaybeRead -> [ValidLog]
336                    -> [ValidLog]
337  insertValidLog tVar versIdRetryVar validLog =
338    insertWith updateVLog
339              (tVarEnv tVar)
340              (singletonVLog tVar versIdRetryVar)
341              validLog

342  insertCommitLog :: Dist a =>
343                     TVar a -> a -> [CommitLog]
344                     -> [CommitLog]
345  insertCommitLog tVar value commitLog =
346    insertWith updateCLog
347              (tVarEnv tVar)
348              (singletonCLog tVar value)
349              commitLog
```

The helper function `tVarEnv` (line 350) extracts the process environment from a given `TVar` used as the primary log key and as the address for link log messages. Host `TVar`s yield the current process environment `gMyEnv`.

```
350  tVarEnv :: TVar a -> EnvAddr
351  tVarEnv (TVar _ _ _ _) = gMyEnv
352  tVarEnv (LinkTVar (VarLink env _)) = env
```

In the remainder of this section, we show the, rather technical, detailed implementation of the singleton and update functions for both host and link `TVar` patterns. At the end of a transaction program, the completely collected logs

5. Implementing Efficient Transactional Communication

consist of dictionaries sorted by the process environment. There is at most one set of *host* bundle actions dictionaries and zero or more sets of *link* bundle String equivalent dictionaries, one for each target environment.

```
353  singletonVLog :: TVar a -> MaybeRead -> ValidLog
354  singletonVLog (TVar ref tId lock waitQ)
355                (Just (versionId, retryVar)) = Left
356    ([(tId, LockActs {lockAct   = takeMVar lock,
357                      unLockAct = putMVar lock ()})],
358     ValidActs {
359       validAct    = readMVar ref >>=
360                     return . (== versionId) . snd,
361       extWaitQAct = modifyMVar_ waitQ insertRetry })
362       where insertRetry =
363             return . (insertRetryLog retryVar)
```

We create lock and unlock actions for a host `TVar` lock directly. The boolean validation action is a comparison of the given `versionId` at the time of reading the `TVar` with the version number at the time of executing this validation action. The wait queue extending action inserts the dependent transaction `retryVar`. Note that we have changed the wait queue to a `retryVar` dictionary bundle (see Section 5.4.4) to gain additional communication performance and thus call an `insertRetryLog` function (line 363) to bundle the retry log messages as well.

```
364  singletonVLog (TVar _ tId lock _)
365                Nothing = Left
366    ([(tId, LockActs {lockAct   = takeMVar lock,
367                      unLockAct = putMVar lock ()})],
368     ValidActs {validAct    = return True,
369                extWaitQAct = return () })
```

The `Nothing` pattern indicates a host `TVar` write access. There are no transaction dependencies. Thus, we do generate lock actions but neutral validation actions.

```
370  singletonVLog (LinkTVar (VarLink env tId))
371                (Just (versionId, retryVar))
372    | env == gMyEnv = Left
373      ([(tId, LockActs {
374          lockAct   = lockTVarFromId tId,
375          unLockAct = unLockTVarFromId tId})],
```

112

5.4. Line Bundle

```
376        ValidActs {
377          validAct   =
378            validateTVarFromId (tId, versionId),
379          extWaitQAct =
380            extWaitQFromId (tId, retryVar) })
381     | otherwise = Right
382       [(tId, Just (versionId, retryVar))]
```

We differentiate between link **TVars** and reimported **TVars** by analyzing their process environment address (line 372). Reimported **TVars** reside in the current process but we have lost the direct access by communicating the **TVar** across the network at some point. However, we can access their mutable variables through the access functions we have generated with remote controlling **TVars** in mind (see Section 4.3.1). With the access functions, we generate efficient log actions requiring no network communication as with host **TVars**. For real link **TVars** we generate the String equivalent log data later to be sent in a network message (lines 381–382).

Note that we collect (line 382) and later send the bundled version identifiers of the read **TVars** to their host processes for validation. The alternative solution of requesting all potentially necessary version identifiers for a validation in the process that executes the transaction would evaluate more strictly and hence require possibly more remote **TVar** accesses.

```
383  singletonVLog (LinkTVar (VarLink env tId))
384                  Nothing
385     | env == gMyEnv = Left
386       ([(tId, LockActs {
387             lockAct    = lockTVarFromId tId,
388             unLockAct  = unLockTVarFromId tId})],
389          ValidActs {validAct   = return True,
390                     extWaitQAct = return () })
391     | otherwise = Right [(tId, Nothing)]
```

We also differentiate between reimported (line 385) and link **TVar** (line 391) write accesses not creating transaction dependencies. We then either generate lock and neutral validation actions or a singleton **String** equivalent log entry. In the latter case the **TVar** identifier is sufficient to remotely generate the lock actions.

The **updateVLog** function creates a new value out of the value to be entered and the value already existing in the dictionary if both entries have an identical key. Our primary key for either transaction log and the **retryVar** log is the

5. Implementing Efficient Transactional Communication

process environment of type `EnvAddr`. The primary key update function combines either the actions or the `String` equivalent values of two log entries for, identical or different, `TVar`s hosted in the *same* process. Thus, we define the `updateVlog` function on two host bundle entries and on two link bundle entries. Note that reimported `TVar`s also generate a host bundle entry. Mixed entries would indicate a programming error in building our dictionaries. Further note that we match the first argument on singleton list patterns only, suggesting that a list is not needed and the update function should convert the type. However, we then needed to parametrize `insertWith` with another constructor function for the singleton result which is why we stay with our solution.

```
393  updateVLog :: ValidLogBundle -> ValidLogBundle
394                 -> ValidLogBundle
395  updateVLog (Left ([(tId, lock)], val))
396             (Left (locks, vals)) = Left
397    (insertWith const tId lock locks,
398     ValidActs {
399       validAct    = validAct val >>+ validAct vals,
400       extWaitQAct =
401         extWaitQAct val >> extWaitQAct vals })
402  updateVLog (Right [(tId, rwVal)])
403             (Right rwVals) =
404    Right (insertWith mergeRVal tId rwVal rwVals)
```

With host bundles we insert new lock actions into the existing lock dictionary using `insertWith` on the secondary key, the `TVar` identifier (line 397). Note that the secondary key update function `const` just overwrites old lock information with the new data. We combine the boolean validate actions (line 399) using the lazy logical-and helper function (`>>+`) defined in line 405 yielding a lazy bound boolean validation action. Likewise, we bind the `TVar` wait queue extending actions (line 401).

```
405  (>>+) :: IO Bool -> IO Bool -> IO Bool
406  b1 >>+ b2 = do
407    b <- b1
408    if b then b2 else return False
```

To combine the link `TVar` data, we insert the new entry into the existing dictionary using the secondary key (line 404). We update values for identical keys with the `mergeRVal` helper function, defined in line 409, overwriting `Nothing` but preserving existing log data.

5.4. Line Bundle

```
409  mergeRVal :: MaybeRead -> MaybeRead -> MaybeRead
410  mergeRVal Nothing m  = m
411  mergeRVal (Just r) _ = Just r
```

The `singletonCLog` function creating a new commit log entry is called from `writeTVar` calls to prepare committing a transaction.

```
412  singletonCLog :: Dist a => TVar a -> a -> CommitLog
413  singletonCLog (TVar ref tId _ waitQ) val = Left
414      [(tId, CommitActs {
415               commitAct = modifyMVar_ ref updVal,
416               notifyAct = swapMVar waitQ [] >>=
417                           mapM_ coreNotify })]
418     where updVal = return . (,) val . (+1) . snd
```

We create commit and notify actions for host **TVars**. The commit action, when called, writes the new value into the **TVar** and increments its version identifier by one. The notify action maps a notification of dependent transactions (see Section 5.4.4) over the wait queue log emptying the log afterwards.

```
419  singletonCLog (LinkTVar (VarLink env tId)) val
420      | env == gMyEnv = Left
421        [(tId, CommitActs {
422                 commitAct =
423                   writeTVarFromId (tId, toString val),
424                 notifyAct = notifyFromId tId })]
425      | otherwise     = Right ([(tId, toString val)],
426                               regTVars env val)
```

Like with validation log entries, we also differentiate between committing reimported (line 420) and link **TVars** (line 425). Again, we create efficient log actions using **TVar** access functions for reimported **TVars** and **String** equivalent log data for link **TVars** to allow for network message creation. We also generate a **TVar** registration action which we execute just when communicating the message. Note that `regTVars` analyses the given value for possibly enclosed host or link **TVars**.

```
427  updateCLog :: CommitLogBundle -> CommitLogBundle
428                 -> CommitLogBundle
429  updateCLog (Left [(tId, comNfyAct)])
430             (Left comNfys) = Left
431      (insertWith const tId comNfyAct comNfys)
432  updateCLog (Right ([(tId, val)], reg))
433             (Right (idStrs, regs)) = Right
434      (insertWith const tId val idStrs, regs >> reg)
```

115

5. Implementing Efficient Transactional Communication

Like its validate counterpart, the commit log update function also combines either the actions or the `String` equivalent values of two log entries for `TVars` hosted in the *same* process. Both, for host (line 431) and link bundles (line 433), we insert the new entries into the commit dictionary using `insertWith` on the secondary key, the `TVar` identifier. Again, identical keys replace existing entries which, for commit logs however, is necessary as we want to keep and later commit the most recent `writeTvar` entry. Finally, we bind the registration actions for link bundles to one compound registration action.

5.4.3. Executing Bundle Logs

In Section 4.2 we have introduced the STM protocol implementation using the functions `startTrans`, `commitTrans`, `retryTrans` and `endTrans`. Now, as an example, we show a first version of `startTrans` operating on the validation bundle log data. In Chapter 6 we show the full transaction control version for a robust Distributed Software Transactional Memory implementation.

We map a start function over all collected validation bundles (line 437) folding the boolean result to the common validation result of that transaction.

```
435  startTrans :: StmState -> IO Bool
436  startTrans st =
437    foldr startAction (return True) (stmValidLog st)


438  startAction :: ValidLog -> IO Bool -> IO Bool
439  startAction (_, Left (locks, valids)) isValid = do
440    mapM_ (lockAct.snd) locks
441    isValid >>+ validAct valids
442  startAction (env, (Right vBundle)) isValid = do
443    answer <- remGetMsg env (RemStartTrans vBundle)
444    return (fromString answer) >>+ isValid
```

We directly lock (line 440) and validate (line 441) host process bundle `TVars`. Note that we fold the result using the lazy logical-and operator (`>>+`). For link process bundles we send a start message to the respective bundle process (line 443) and also lazily fold the message result (line 444).

The `handleMsg` function interprets the incoming STM protocol messages. We show the `RemStartTrans` message calling the `startLinkTVars` function (lines 449, 450) with a reply message generating function as an additional parameter. We execute the action and call this higher order function in a new

5.4. Line Bundle

thread (line 455). Thus, the parsing thread finishes each action asynchronously. Synchronizing it with the next message would violate the STM protocol and easily produce deadlocks. We safely synchronize actually locking the TVars with the reply message in the independent thread.

```
445  handleMsg :: Handle -> RemMessage -> IO ()
446  handleMsg h msg =
447    case msg of
448      RemStartTrans idVRVars ->
449        startLinkTVars idVRVars
450                      (hPutStrLn h . toString)
451      ...


452  startLinkTVars :: LinkVLogBundle -> (Bool -> IO ())
453                                   -> IO ()
454  startLinkTVars idVRVars notifyCaller = do
455    forkIO (lockValid idVRVars >>= notifyCaller)
456    return ()
```

After locking (line 459) the link TVars each link process unbundles the message and folds the validation results of its TVars to report back the compound validation result (line 460). As we collect lock and validation data in the same validate log, we provide a folding function for TVars not to be validated (line 470) as well. Again, the TVar access functions perform locking and validating an individual TVar.

```
457  lockValid :: [ValidRemVal] -> IO Bool
458  lockValid idVRVars = do
459    mapM_ lockId idVRVars
460    foldr validateId (return True) idVRVars

461  lockId :: ValidRemVal -> IO ()
462  lockId (tVarId, _) = do
463    map <- readMVar gActions
464    remLock (fst (map ! tVarId))

465  validateId :: ValidRemVal -> IO Bool -> IO Bool
466  validateId (tId, (Just (vId,_),_)) isValid = do
467    map <- readMVar gActions
468    answer <- remValidate (fst (map ! tId)) vId
469    return (fromString answer) >>+ isValid
470  validateId (_, (Nothing,_)) isValid = isValid
```

5. Implementing Efficient Transactional Communication

Note that a possible host bundle and each link bundle execute a process individual sequence of lock and validation actions rather than the distributed system as a whole executing a sequence of first locking all `TVars` used in a transaction and then validating them. Both operations execute a correct STM protocol because validating is a non-blocking operation and locking is validation state neutral. However, each solution implements a different schedule. Our bundled sequentialization significantly reduces the amount of network messages.

5.4.4. Logging Retry Variables

A transaction suspends itself on its `RetryVar`. In Section 4.1.2 we have seen that the host `TVar` data type contains a wait queue collecting the `RetryVars` of all dependent transactions. Transactions insert a *host* `RetryVar` into a `TVar` residing in the same process or a *link* `RetryVar`, communicated within the distributed system, otherwise. In our communication-efficient bundle approach, we change the wait queue into a wait queue *dictionary* with the `RetryVar` process environment as key. We call the wait queue dictionary a *retry log* which we implement similarly to validate and commit logs.

```
471  type RetryLog        = (EnvAddr, RetryLogBundle)
472  type RetryLogBundle  = Either (IO ()) [VarID]
```

The `insertRetryLog` function inserts a new `retryVar` into the retry log using an update function (line 475), the bundle key (line 476), a singleton log generator (line 477), and the log itself (line 478).

```
473  insertRetryLog :: RetryVar -> [RetryLog] -> [RetryLog]
474  insertRetryLog retryVar waitQ =
475      insertWith updateRLog
476               (retryVarEnv retryVar)
477               (singletonRLog retryVar)
478               waitQ
```

The helper function `retryVarEnv` simply extracts the process environment from the `retryVar`.

```
479  retryVarEnv :: RetryVar -> EnvAddr
480  retryVarEnv (RetryVar _ _) = gMyEnv
481  retryVarEnv (LinkRetryVar (VarLink env _)) = env
```

The singleton log creator function `singletonRLog`, like the other log functions, distinguishes between a host TVar (line 484), a reimported link TVar (line 486), and a link TVar (line 487) case. Note that we *try* to resume a transaction on a suspended `RetryVar` because a transaction might depend on multiple TVars. Multiple `tryPutMVar` rather than `putMVar` calls do not block on full `MVar`s and, thus, conform to the STM protocol.

```
482  singletonRLog :: RetryVar -> RetryLogBundle
483  singletonRLog (RetryVar retryMVar _) =
484    Left (tryPutMVar retryMVar () >> return ())
485  singletonRLog (LinkRetryVar (VarLink env rVarId))
486    | env == gMyEnv = Left (resumeFromId rVarId)
487    | otherwise     = Right [rVarId]


488  updateRLog :: RetryLogBundle -> RetryLogBundle
489                -> RetryLogBundle
490  updateRLog (Left resume) (Left resumes) =
491    Left (resumes >> resume)
492  updateRLog (Right [rVarId]) (Right rVarIds) =
493    Right (rVarId:rVarIds)
```

The `updateRLog` function simply either binds host resume actions or concatenates link `RetryVar` identifiers, respectively.

Having defined the retry log, we can now show the implementation of the `coreNotify` function used to create notification actions in the commit log (line 417) generator. Note that we create a notification *action* both for a possible host retry log bundle and for each link retry log bundles. The reason is that either `RetryLog` is part of a *host* TVar wait queue.

```
494  coreNotify :: RetryLog -> IO ()
495  coreNotify (_, Left resumeAct) = resumeAct
496  coreNotify (env, Right retryVarIds) =
497    remPutMsg env (RemResume retryVarIds)
```

5.5. Reading Uncommitted TVar Values

In Section 4.4 we have shown that it is not sufficient to return the last committed TVar value to an application `readTVar` action if it is preceded by an intra-transaction `writeTVar` action.

119

5. Implementing Efficient Transactional Communication

Our highly efficient distributed solution to this problem is to keep a record of all intra-transaction `writeTVar` actions which we access when reading a `TVar`. If such a record exists, we read and return to the application program the pre-committed recorded value. Otherwise, we read and return the regular `TVar` value. Luckily, we already have implemented such a record, namely the transaction `CommitLog` (see Section 5.4.1). It includes commit information for either host or link `TVars`.

In Section 4.2.3 we have shown how the `readTVar` and `writeTVar` functions update the transaction state. This is all `writeTVar` does and, hence, it is already completely defined. The `readTVar` function, however, distinguishes between reading a precommitted value and a committed one and in either case between reading a host `TVar` residing in the current process and a link `TVar` hosted in another process.

```
498  readTVar    :: Dist a => TVar a -> STM a
499  readTVar tVar = STM (\st -> do
500    (val, vId) <-
501      readIntraTransTVar tVar (stmCommitLog stmState)
502    let newSt = st{stmValidLog = sortedValidateLogs
503                  tVar
504                  (Just (vId, (stmRetryVar st)))
505                  (stmValidLog st)}
506    return (Success newSt val))
```

The read result is a tuple of the value itself and its version number (line 500) determined in the main reading function `readIntraTransTVar`. Essential to reading the correct value is to look up the `TVar` in the current transaction commit log (line 511). The keys of our transaction logs are of type `VarLink`, representing the process environment, and `TVar ID` for both link and host `TVars` determined by the `tVarToLink` helper function.

```
507  readIntraTransTVar :: Dist a =>
508                        TVar a -> [CommitLog]
509                        -> IO (a, VersionID)
510  readIntraTransTVar  tVar commitLog =
511    case lookup env commitLog of
512      Nothing -> coreReadTVar tVar
513      Just (Left commitActs) ->
514        case lookup tId commitActs of
515          Just acts -> readHost tVar $ commitAct acts
516          Nothing   -> coreReadTVar tVar
```

5.5. Reading Uncommitted TVar Values

```
517      Just (Right (strVals, _)) ->
518        case lookup tId strVals of
519          Just v -> coreReadTVar tVar >>=
520            return . ((,) (fromString v)) . snd
521          Nothing -> coreReadTVar tVar
522    where VarLink env tId = tVarToLink tVar

523  tVarToLink :: TVar a -> VarLink
524  tVarToLink (TVar _ tId _ _) = VarLink gMyEnv tId
525  tVarToLink (LinkTVar link) = link
```

We first look up the bundle with the primary key. There are three possible results: An empty commit log yielding **Nothing** (line 512), a host (line 513) and a link **TVar** commit log dictionary (line 517).

Then we look up either dictionary with the secondary key, the **TVar** identifier, to get its actual intra-transaction non-committed host (line 515) or link (line 519) **TVar** value or **Nothing** (lines 516, 521) if there has not yet been a **writeTVar** call prior to this **readTVar** call in the current transaction. The following subsections detail these three cases.

5.5.1. Empty Commit Log

If the commit log recorded no preceding **writeTVar** action for the **TVar** to be read, we simply read the regular **TVar** value calling the polymorphic **coreReadTVar** function. It either simply reads the mutable variable of a host **TVar** (line 527) or it requests the value from a link **TVar** by using the distributed STM communication (line 529). Note that we add finalizer functions to link **TVars** received within the read value (line 532).

```
526  coreReadTVar :: Dist a => TVar a -> IO (a,VersionID)
527  coreReadTVar (TVar tVarRef _ _ _) =
528    readMVar tVarRef
529  coreReadTVar (LinkTVar (VarLink tEnv tId)) = do
530    reply <- remGetMsg tEnv (RemReadTVar tId gMyEnv)
531    let vv@(v,_) = fromString reply
532    finTVars v
533    return (vv)
```

5. Implementing Efficient Transactional Communication

5.5.2. Host TVar

If the commit log recorded at least one preceding `writeTVar` action for the host `TVar` to be read, `readIntraTransTVar` looks up the bound commit IO action of all preceding writes. As we cannot safely log the polymorphic values themselves, we record the value committing actions. The `readHost` function executes this action yielding the correct not yet committed `TVar` value, however, requiring some special considerations.

```
534  readHost :: forall a . Serializable a =>
535           TVar a -> IO () -> IO (a, VersionID)
536  readHost (TVar tVarRef _ lock _) commit = do
537    takeMVar lock
538    orig@(_, origVersion) <- readMVar tVarRef
539    commit
540    (modV, _) <- swapMVar tVarRef orig
541    putMVar lock ()
542    return (modV, origVersion)
543  readHost (LinkTVar (VarLink _ tId)) commit = do
544    lockTVarFromId tId
545    origStr <- readTVarValFromId tId
546    let (_::a, origVersion) = fromString origStr
547    commit
548    (modV, _::VersionID) <-
549      liftM fromString (swapTVarValFromId tId origStr)
550    unLockTVarFromId tId
551    return (modV, origVersion)
```

Reimported link TVar

A host `TVar` might also be referenced as a link `TVar` from within its host process. We refer to such a `TVar` as a reimported link `TVar` (see Section 4.1.2) as it has been send to another process and received back later. Thus, we define `readHost` both on host `TVar`s (line 536) and on reimported link `TVar`s (line 543) and implement an identical protocol using different access routines. While the host TVar accesses its mutable components directly, the reimported link TVar utilizes the access actions stored in the global actions map (see Section 4.3.1).

Reverse Commit

Reverting host `TVar` commit actions is challenging: We cannot log polymorphic `TVar` values and we do not want to log expensive discard actions. Instead, we

5.5. Reading Uncommitted TVar Values

use the local **TVar** value as a buffer, copy it (lines 538, 545), commit to that local buffer (lines 539, 547), swap the saved copy back to the buffer (lines 540, 549), and return the pre-committed value. Modifying the **TVar** value is a critical section. Therefore, we lock protect the complete algorithm.

Version Identifier Count

We return the *application level* written, yet *library level* uncommitted **TVar** value to the application. However, we must not reflect this operation in any transaction log. Therefore, we return the version identifier value of the last *committed* value, counting the number of changes to the **TVar**, in order for **readTVar** to correctly record the validation log (line 504).

Note the use of the overloaded **fromString** function in line 546. Reading a link **TVar** value always yields a **String** value. Link **TVar** communication requires **String** converted values. For efficiency we omit the network communication for reimported link **TVars** and use the monomorphic access routines. However, **readTVar** is polymorphic in the read **TVar** value type. We declare **readHost** to be polymorphic also in the **TVar** value type variable **a** and the - ignored - value to be of type **a** and hence select the proper **fromString** function to convert the version identifier. Using the type variable within the function body requires the existential type definition **forall a** (line 534).

5.5.3. Link TVar

If the commit log recorded at least one preceding **writeTVar** action for the link **TVar** to be read, **readIntraTransTVar** yields the **String** converted value of the last[2] preceding write action. Therefore, we first read the last committed link **TVar** value and version identifier count using the **coreReadTVar** function. Then we replace the value with the not yet committed **String** log value converted into the **TVar** value data type using the overloaded **fromString** function (line 520) while keeping the committed version identifier count.

This way we achieve intra-transaction read actions of link **TVars** requiring only one expensive distributed communication like any regular **readTVar** action would require also.

---

[2] We overwrite old values with new ones when logging write actions for existing **TVars**.

5. *Implementing Efficient Transactional Communication*

5.6. Benchmark Tests

Throughout this chapter, we have claimed various communication enhancements to our Distributed Software Transactional Memory library. With this section we now substantiate our promises. We have tested our library with the applications shown in Appendix B, each highlighting a different aspect of distributed programming. Many test applications are not well suited to judge the performance of a distributed library solution as they generate relatively little synchronization communication. We present here a distributed interactive *bomberman* game application which we let intensely synchronize atomic transactions. We describe the bomberman test application in detail in Section B.3.

```
W W W W W W W W W W
W     @             W
W         W W W
W       W W W W
W         W W W
W   X X W W                 o: player
W X X X X       .@          @: opponent
W   X X         .           .: bomb
W               o           X: explosion
W W                 W       W: wall element
```

Figure 5.4.: Bomberman Game Screen Shot

Figure 5.4 shows the screen of one bomberman player in the middle of a game. A player moves around a field and drops bombs which explode with a delay destroying existing walls and opponents. We use settings like game layout, key-strokes, input rate, number of players, and the test equipment itself that demonstrate realistically the capacity of our library.

Our goal with these benchmark tests is to realistically compare the performance of the different library implementations. Therefore, we define a resource hungry bomberman application. We gain reproducible and comparable results by running the applications, autonomously reading the commands from a file, subsequently with all libraries used. We show comparisons of the four distributed library variants described in this chapter together with results of a similar concurrent application with players modeled as threads rather than process nodes using both the lightweight concurrent STM library in [HK05] and the [Mar10] STM library.

5.6. Benchmark Tests

We build applications from the following STM libraries:

Individual One IP connection per STM protocol step (see Section 5.1)

Dedicated Two dedicated IP connections between nodes (see Section 5.2)

Stack A stack of IP connections between nodes (see Section 5.3)

Bundle A stack of bundled IP connections between nodes (see Section 5.4)

Concurrent Median of concurrent STM libraries as benchmark

The concurrent library benchmarks show results without any network communication involved. Our concurrent results are a mean value of applications using three different STM libraries. We use two different lightweight libraries, for which we can generate all benchmark data, and the highly efficient ghc implementation, for which we can only measure the execution time. Also, there are inevitable differences between the concurrent and distributed implementation of the application program. Therefore, the concurrent values cannot be quantitatively compared exactly with the other results. They are still shown for reference, however.

We benchmark our library applying two different use cases:

Soft Real-time Executing player commands at individual clock speeds skipping out-of-sync commands

Burst Executing all player commands consecutively as fast as possible

Internet round-trip response times vary by a large order of magnitude depending on the network infrastructure. We execute the above test scenarios both on our university local area network and on our personal computer alone[3] only *simulating* a real distributed environment. The latter is both easier to realize and generates more reproducible results.

LAN Each player application running on its own LAN connected computer

Virtual Each player application running as a separate process on the same computer

---

[3] We run all tests on 1.8 GHz Intel Core Duo type machines which we, however, do not emphasize as we focus on the relative performance of all tests rather than on hardware dependent absolute benchmark numbers.

5. Implementing Efficient Transactional Communication

We have performed all benchmark tests shown here with a designated master player and two regular players each performing automated commands read from a file. Each bomberman application synchronizes on TVars for the game field, its player, a repaint flag, link TVar lists of all players including its own, and all repaint flags including its own. The master player hosts game field and TVar lists.

Soft Real-time Test

The soft real-time test conditions are a realistic gaming situation. We run a network game where three individual players, users of the bomberman application, type their play commands and react on the commands of the other players. In order to get comparable and repeatable results, we predefine the user interaction as a gaming scenario. All user play commands and the time interval between them is determined. However, a command is skipped, if the previous one cannot be executed in time. Note that the network game itself is not exactly determined because the network nodes themselves naturally interact with other nodes non-deterministically. The soft real-time test shows how many user commands can be executed with applications using the different library implementations.

The diagram in Figure 5.5 shows groups of relative results of virtual network soft real-time test runs. Each column group describes the test results for an application using the respective library. All values are average results of multiple test runs.

The first two columns of each group show the amount of invalid and total transactions for each run in relation to each other. All transaction and invalid transaction numbers are relative to the maximum number of transactions which, in Figure 5.5, is reached with the bundle library solution. All TCP message numbers are relative to the maximum which in this test is the dedicated line solution. The next column shows the throughput. As a soft real-time throughput test we set a keystroke speed rate for each player. If the player is not able to process the keystroke in time before the next clocked keystroke occurs, succeeding commands are dropped until the player is in time again. The throughput is the percentage of successfully executed keystrokes. All throughput values are relative to the theoretical maximum of a complete execution with no skipped commands. The last column of the distributed tests represents the number of TCP messages. The concurrent test, obviously, uses no TCP connection at all and the number of transactions is evaluated using just the lightweight concur-

5.6. Benchmark Tests

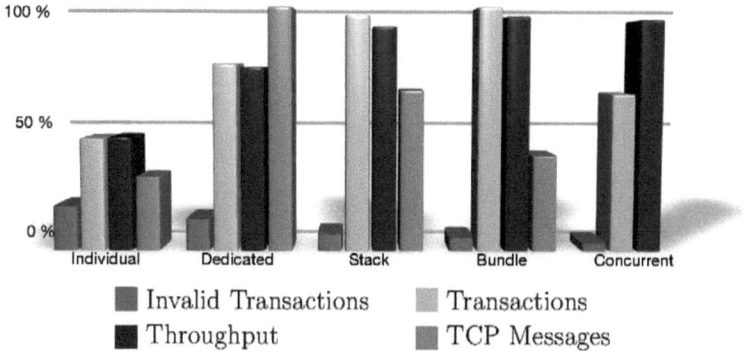

Figure 5.5.: Virtual Network Bomberman Soft Real-time Benchmark

rent library. All TCP connections actually are *localhost*-connections simulating a real distributed test.

The throughput is rising from left to right supporting our intuition. All test runs need the same execution *real*-time. Higher throughput correlates with more transactions[4] and less conflicting, thus invalid, transactions as we can see. The individual-line library performs so poorly that there are only a few TCP messages. The dedicated-line approach produces the most TCP messages as it performs significantly better than the simple one and we also count the bidirectional replies as separate messages. The stack-line solution really establishes more TCP connections, either uni- or bidirectional, due to its higher performance. Finally, we see that the bundle approach significantly reduces the amount of TCP messages while still improving the throughput.

Figure 5.6 compares the computing time of virtual and local area network tests. We see that real network TCP communication takes more computing time than simulated localhost communication. Note that we show accumulated processing times. Although the LAN run requires more computing resources than the virtual network run, each individual LAN node requires less. The performance distribution between the different libraries of virtual and real distributed tests is comparable.

---

[4]The concurrent test inherently differs slightly due to its adapted implementation.

5. Implementing Efficient Transactional Communication

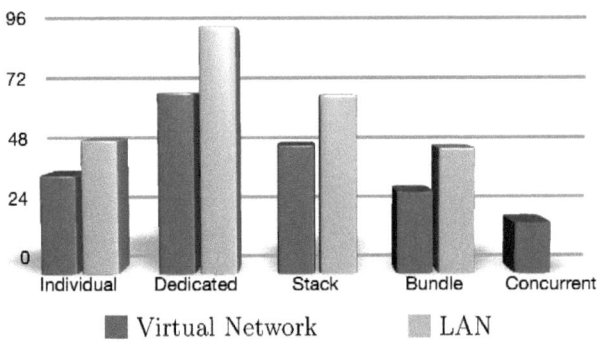

Figure 5.6.: Bomberman Soft Real-time Computing Times in s

Burst-mode Test

While the soft real-time test scenario shows a realistic gaming situation, the burst-mode test runs all predefined user commands as fast as possible without a predefined delay between them. The next command is executed as soon as the previous one is finished. Thus, the test shows how fast a set of user commands can be executed with applications using the different library implementations.

Figure 5.7 shows the test results of the burst mode tests where we run the same configurations as with the soft real-time tests in Figure 5.5 but never drop a keystroke. Instead we execute all filed commands independent of their execution time. Therefore, we show the total execution time relative to its maximum which here is the individual line result rather than the throughput which is always at its maximum. From left to right we see a significant reduction in total execution time similar to the soft real-time tests. None of the distributed versions comes close to the concurrent version benchmark results. Conceptually, the amount of valid and invalid transactions should be the same in all distributed tests each processing the same input sequences. The fluctuations reflect the random transaction conflicts depending on the execution speed of the filed commands in each node.

Figure 5.8 shows again a faster simulated localhost communication and a comparable performance distribution between the different libraries with virtual and local area network runs.

5.6. Benchmark Tests

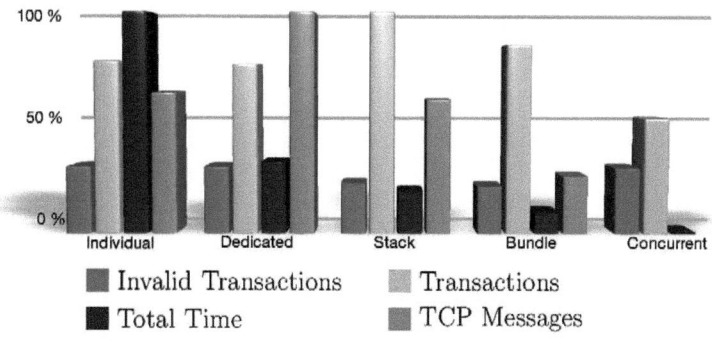

Figure 5.7.: Virtual Network Bomberman Burst Benchmark

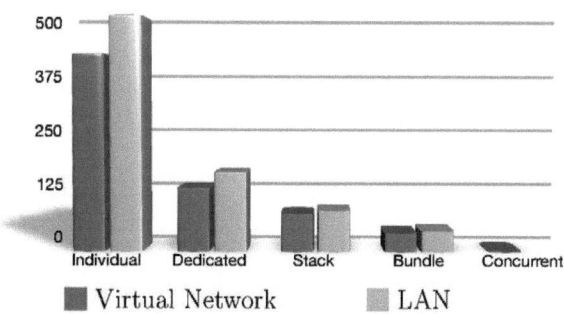

Figure 5.8.: Bomberman Burst Execution Times in s

5. Implementing Efficient Transactional Communication

Benchmark Conclusion

The bomberman test application has a high synchronization need. Each player repeatedly performs its next move, interacts with other moves, and displays all moves. Each of these steps requires synchronization. We intentionally designed an application using many `TVar`s to maximize synchronization effort and synchronization conflicts. Many practical network applications with a significant amount of user interaction, like a chat program, use only a few synchronization variables. Therefore, the bomberman example is, in our view, well suited to judge the relative performance of the different DSTM libraries.

Our tests support our ideas of communication performance enhancements described in this chapter. A communication line stack using bundled messages yield significantly better results than previous attempts.

Chapter 6

Implementing Robustness

There are systems that are distributed by their nature simply because their resources are distributed among multiple network nodes, like the ATM network of a bank as we have advertised in Chapter 2. Other systems, like a file server cluster, are explicitly designed as a distributed system to gain benefits such as load balancing, reliability, or tolerance against faults.

Our Distributed Software Transactional Memory library as described in the previous chapters, however, is not yet very reliable. If, in a distributed application using our library, only one of the nodes, supplying distributed TVars, terminates, all other nodes, using any of those TVars, will very likely also terminate or be blocked indefinitely.

We begin this chapter defining the dependability terms employed in this book in Section 6.1 to describe the robustness of our library and define the scope of Distributed STM robustness.

In Section 6.2 we analyze possible library errors leading to a more detailed characterization of software transactions.

Section 6.3 details the fundamental changes in our DSTM implementation to gain system robustness. We augment the protocol itself leading to adapted basic data structures and algorithms.

We conclude this chapter with a discussion of caveats in distributed and especially robust transaction synchronization in Section 6.4.

6. Implementing Robustness

6.1. Dependability

There are numerous terms to describe a program that does not behave as the user, the developer, or both expect it to do. There are errors, faults, failures, bugs. Applications might be robust, fault tolerant, reliable.

Avizienis, Laprie, Randell, and Landwehr have established a taxonomy of dependable computing [ALRL04]. Their root term is *dependability* defined as the *ability to avoid service failures that are more frequent and more severe than is acceptable*. The taxonomy subsumes coping with mostly hardware problems in the early computer days to a combination of development, physical, and interaction issues nowadays. We focus on the effects of unusual behavior to the user of either an application or service. We assume that the application or service is correctly specified and developed.

The authors describe dependability in terms of its *attributes, threats*, and *means* to attain it. Dependability is threatened by faults, errors, and failures and attained by means like fault tolerance. For a discussion on the various dependability attributes like reliability and integrity and different means we refer to the literature.

We follow the notion of a fundamental chain of dependability threats [ALR02] where *faults* activate *error* states which propagate a *failure* which in turn may cause other faults as shown in figure 6.1. A failure occurs when the system delivers an incorrect service which is what a user of the system will notice from the outside. As an example, a mail server fault, caused by an electrical energy spike activates an error state in the server program, which propagates the mail service failure of that service. In turn, this failure causes a fault in a client trying to deliver a mail to the server, activates a mail not delivered error, and propagates the mail sending failure.

$$\ldots \to \text{fault} \xrightarrow{activation} \text{error} \xrightarrow{propagation} \text{failure} \xrightarrow{causation} \text{fault} \to \ldots$$

Figure 6.1.: Chain of dependability threads [ALR02]

A *fault tolerant* system breaks the chain of dependability and avoids failure if one or more faults exist by first detecting the error state and then recovering the system by transforming it into a regular system state again. We use redundant system parts, independent in regards to the faults, to recover from those faults. Already *von Neumann* showed that reliable machines can be con-

6.1. Dependability

structed from unreliable components [vN56]. A well known example of fault tolerance through redundancy is implemented in RAID[1] systems with highly adjustable *robustness* properties. We use the term robustness in this chapter rather than dependability as it is defined as *dependability with respect to external faults* which more specifically describes our intent as we will see in the following sections.

6.1.1. Fault Tolerance in a Distributed Library

In regards to robustness the notion of a *partial failure* is characteristic to distributed systems [TVS01]. While already one fault possibly propagates a total failure of all services in sequential and concurrent systems, a fault tolerant distributed system potentially successfully recovers from a partial failure and continues to deliver its services. In the example above another mail server supplied by a different power source may take over the service from the failed server.

It is impossible to prohibit or circumvent *every* possible fault. Therefore, we cannot avoid every possible error state and system failure. More so, we can only build a system or a library that is tolerant against faults that we have conceived during its design and development phase. In this book, we restrict our library to cope with only one but comprehensive and common fault class – the *permanent failure of a system process*.

We assume that a once terminated or dead process will remain terminated forever excluding temporarily inactive processes and fluctuating communication. Also, we do not distinguish between communication and process termination faults. A process that cannot be communicated with is pronounced dead, and will, by assumption, never resume its service.

With these restrictions in mind, we design and implement a fault tolerant Distributed Software Transactional Memory library that in turn enables the application programmer to design a fault tolerant distributed system taking advantage of our DSTM library. Note that the library on its own does not ensure a fault tolerant system. It is the application that has to implement the specific means. However, without a fault tolerant library this would be an impossible task for the application programmer.

Achieving a fault tolerant distributed system thus becomes a two-step approach. The library provides error detection and recovery in its domain of

---
[1] Redundant Array of Independent Disks

6. Implementing Robustness

distributed transactions. The application programmer then implements proper system recovery based on that error detection information.

6.1.2. System Levels

If the run-time system detects an error state within a program it throws an exception which cascades from the run-time system all the way up to the application-level until it is caught at some level. Figure 6.2 shows the run-time, library, and application-levels and examples of known variables used for communication. The run-time communicates using sockets, our library protocol communicates locks and other variables described in this book, and the application knows TVars and the DSTM API to use them.

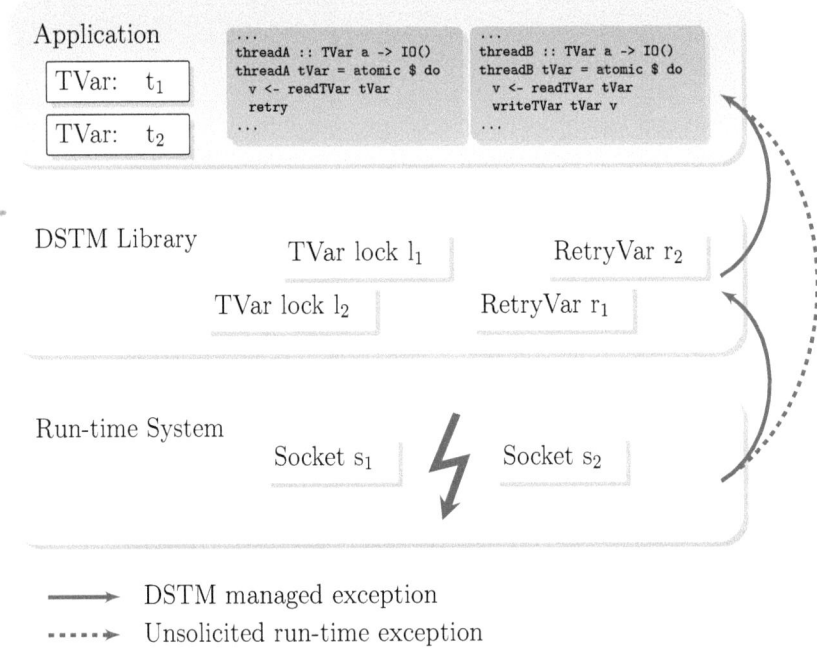

Figure 6.2.: DSTM Error Propagation

The inter-process communication is transparent to the application programmer while the known abstraction is the TVar. Therefore, the library detects TVars hosted in unavailable processes, independent of the fault activating that error, and propagates the application-level failure of a TVar that has become *unavailabe*. From an application program point of view, a TVar is unavailable if it cannot be read from or written to. An attempt to do so without any precautions from our library would let the run-time system propagate a low-level failure when trying to communicate with the process hosting the unavailable TVar. Haskell propagates failures within the program using exceptions (see Section 2.1.4). While the application program could catch a low-level exception it could not make any sense of it. The application programmer could not deduce the fault by the low-level exception and had no means to prohibit a system failure. Therefore, we translate all run-time system exceptions occurring during transactions into a DSTM library generated exception.

A run-time-level system fault results in an exception which we catch inside our library thus hiding it from the application. Within the library we fully recover from that fault at the price of causing a TVar access fault instead. This fault then activates the error state that throws an application-level TVar access exception. A fault tolerant application is then able to catch the TVar exception and to recover itself by suitable means as circumventing and replacing faulty TVars.

6.2. Transaction Failure

We have shown that it is necessary to translate run-time-level system faults within transactions into library-level TVar faults. Run-time system errors can be activated from a number of faults on all sub-application internet protocol layers like a physical network cable problem or a remote process termination. Table 6.1 summarizes the dependability threads on each layer. Note that the application layer shown describes the DSTM library-level. The application-program layer is on top and not shown here. The DSTM library replaces any run-time exception within a transaction with a library exception. The inevitable result of a fault while executing a transaction, however, is the transaction failure.

6. *Implementing Robustness*

LAYER	PROTOCOL	FAULT	ERROR	FAILURE
Application	STM	TVar	Library	
Transport	TCP	Socket		Transaction
Internet	IP	Process	Run-time	
Network Link	Ethernet, ...	Network		

Table 6.1.: Internet Protocol Layer Dependability

6.2.1. Error Detection

Haskell throws exceptions to signal error states. We base all communication within our DSTM library on TCP connections. The name suggests physical point-to-point connections which immediately propagate failures if they are disconnected. However, TCP is a connection-*oriented* protocol indicating that the communication is reliable. Thus, TCP guarantees an uncorrupted, gapless, sequential data transfer without duplication [KR07]. If TCP cannot fulfill this guarantee an exception is generated.

Therefore, the following holds in regards to TCP protocol error detection

- Faulty TCP communication activates socket errors when
  - creating a socket
  - reading from or writing to a socket
- Open TCP connections do not activate any errors on
  - termination of a process connected through a socket
  - failure of physical communication to socket connected process

At first sight one could argue that the latter category of faults would not lead to immediate errors and, hence, should not raise (activate) errors. However, as we will see in Section 6.2.2, there are transaction states leading to potential deadlocks if linked processes fail to communicate. As a suddenly terminated or unaccessible process cannot trigger any more messages communicating this event, the only way to detect such potentially faulty connections is to query the process from the outside by probing the potentially terminating process with a message on a regular basis (see Section 6.3.6). Note that the behavior of DSTM-based applications running on a *single* network node simulating a multiple node networked system is different. The run-time system may throw

6.2. Transaction Failure

an exception on termination of a linked process even if there is no active TCP communication. In this uncommon case no further error detection is necessary.

6.2.2. Fault Scenarios

Any fault related to a link TVar safely activates a library error the application then uses for its recovery. However, a proper recovery of the library itself depends on the transaction state when the fault occurs. Therefore, we analyze the different fault scenarios within a transaction.

Transactions maintain a consistent system state. The transaction protocol either commits or aborts the transaction completely. Thus, all participating TVars either all commit or all abort. With the recovery means shown in this chapter, we ensure consistency also under the influence of any permanent fault during a transaction.

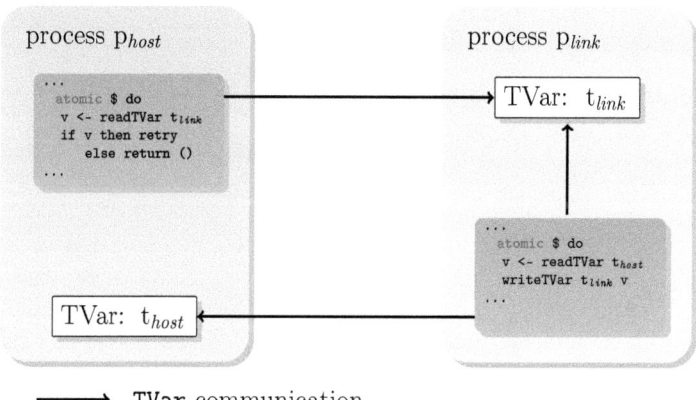

Figure 6.3.: Conceptual Transaction Example

The setting in Figure 6.3 shows two processes p_{host} and p_{link} atomically reading link TVars t_{link} and t_{host}, respectively. Additionally, p_{link} also writes t_{link}. We observe the situation from the *host process perspective* and analyze the possible three scenarios. We call the host transaction either active (Section 6.2.3), inactive (Section 6.2.4), or reactive (Section 6.2.5).

6. Implementing Robustness

6.2.3. Active Transaction

Every transaction has exactly one active part, we call the active transaction, and zero or more reactive parts. The active transaction protocol controls itself and all of its reactive transactions with its Two-Phase Commit protocol. We have shown the DSTM protocols in Section 4.2.3 for reference.

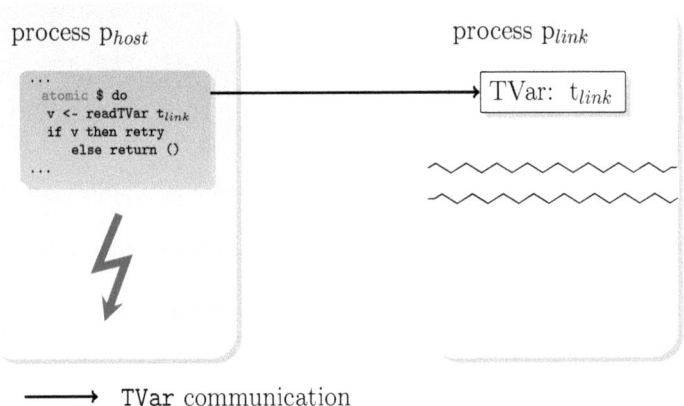

⟶ TVar communication

Figure 6.4.: Active Transaction Fault

If the linked process terminates during the protocol execution, as indicated by the sliced link process in Figure 6.4, the host process throws an exception, indicated by a lightning symbol, on the next access of a link TVar. We catch this exception while executing the DSTM protocol, detect the fault, and recover from it depending on the current protocol phase (see Table 6.2).

Fault	Error Detection	Recovery
Validation	TVar access	Abort (Revert locks)
Committment	TVar access	Continue (Skip faulty TVars)

Table 6.2.: Active Transaction Recovery

Validation If an exception occurs while validating any TVar read in the transaction, we have started to lock all involved TVars and possibly already

138

6.2. Transaction Failure

started to query the `TVars` if they are still valid. We have not changed any `TVar` value yet. Therefore, we can safely abort the transaction. In order to undo the started transaction we unlock all locked `TVars`.

Commitment If a fault occurs after the transaction has decided to commit all `TVars`, we cannot revert the transaction any more. It is impossible to undo a commit action which potentially launches a missile. The decision for committing a transaction marks the *point of no return* for that transaction. Therefore, the transaction simply continues while skipping the faulty `TVars`. Note that system consistency is still preserved as we assume `TVar` faults to be permanent by definition. Dealing with fluctuating faults would be much harder and is not part of this work.

6.2.4. Inactive Transaction

An active transaction becomes inactive when the executing thread suspends itself following the `retry` protocol. The inactive transaction waits to be resumed by another thread updating a dependent `TVar`, like t_{link} in Figure 6.5.

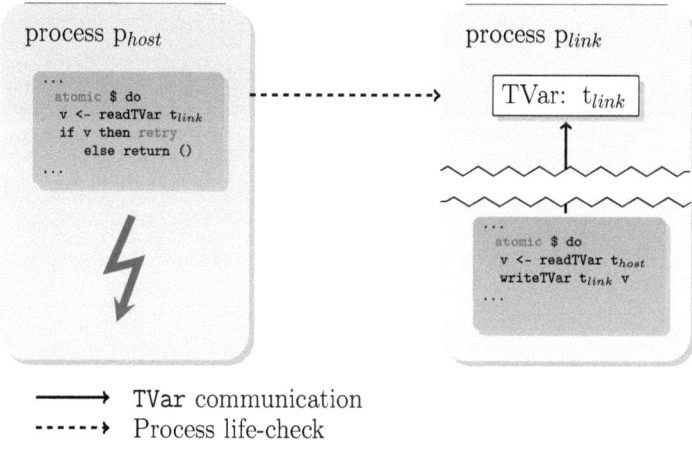

Figure 6.5.: Inactive Transaction Fault

If a fault terminates the process, hosting a dependent link `TVar`, the inactive transaction might never be resumed. Unfortunately, in general, no exception is

6. Implementing Robustness

raised in the host process. Therefore, we provoke an exception by periodically polling all processes that are hosting dependent TVars (like t_{link} in Figure 6.5). Yet, we are not interested in a reply. The target processes simply ignore the poll message for the purpose of efficiency. However, if a poll message causes a communication fault, the run-time system of the calling process throws a low-level exception which we catch and deduce an inactive transaction fault. We then recover from it by restarting the transaction just as if the dependent and now inaccessible TVar had been modified (see Table 6.3). We call the polling mechanism a *life-check*.

Fault	Error Detection	Recovery
Retry	Life-check	Restart

Table 6.3.: Inactive Transaction Recovery

Note that periodically sending messages to other processes reduces the efficiency of the DSTM protocol. Therefore, we start polling when a transaction suspends and stop again when the transaction successfully resumes. We show the details of this life-check mechanism in Section 6.3.6.

6.2.5. Reactive Transaction

A reactive transaction executes the remote-controlled protocol of an active transaction in another process. Thus, the reactive transaction controls hosted TVars (like t_{host}) that are part of the transaction as shown in Figure 6.6. An active transaction controls zero or more reactive transactions. Remember that we regard the transaction scenarios from the p_{host} perspective. From a p_{link} perspective, Figure 6.6 would show an active transaction scenario.

Just like inactive transactions also reactive transactions have no built-in mechanism to detect a fault within the transaction. A terminating active transaction process (like p_{link} in Figure 6.6), in general, would cause an eventual deadlock without further precautions in the reactive transaction process, as a host TVar in the middle of a transaction is locked but will never be unlocked again.

Fortunately, we can solve the error detection problem. We take advantage of the same life-check mechanism that we use for inactive transactions. Again, we send as few polling messages as possible. Therefore, the TVar hosting process

6.2. Transaction Failure

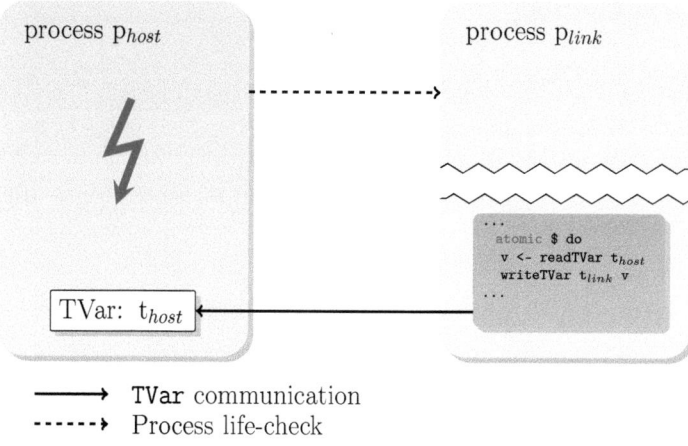

→ TVar communication
┈► Process life-check

Figure 6.6.: Reactive Transaction Fault

keeps track of all active transactions and we send a life-check message only if there are pending transactions. When we catch a life-check exception surveying a process terminated within the execution of a transaction, we perform a recovery process for the hosted TVars. We show the details of this life-check mechanism in Section 6.3.6.

Fault	Error Detection	Recovery
Validation	Life-check	Abort ?
Committment	Life-check	Continue ?

Table 6.4.: Naive Reactive Transaction Recovery Attempt

A naive recovery would probably assume a similar approach as used in the active transaction scenario. Depending on the faulty transaction phase, we would either abort or continue the transaction like Table 6.4 shows. Comparing the control flow of the two scenarios in detail, however, we see the problem of such an assumption and the modifications necessary to enable a proper recovery of reactive transactions.

6. Implementing Robustness

Transaction Control

An active transaction is in control. It controls itself and any number of reactive transactions and is often called the transaction *coordinator*. The coordinator determines a validation dependent commit and, thus, the *point of no return* of the current transaction. As a result, it knows exactly the phase each reactive transaction is in. Therefore, the recovery process described in Section 6.2.3 is valid for active transactions.

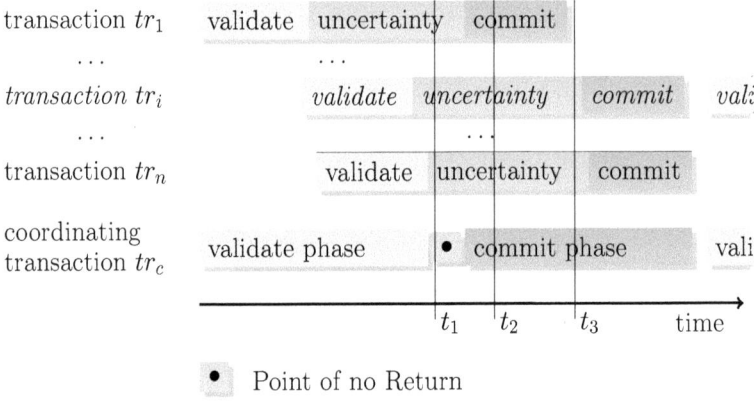

• Point of no Return

Figure 6.7.: Two-Phase Protocol Time Line

Figure 6.7 illustrates the time line of a transaction consisting of the coordinating active transaction tr_c executing the Two-Phase DSTM protocol and a set TR of n remotely controlled reactive transactions $tr_i \in TR$, that is, $TR = \{tr_1, \ldots, tr_n\}$. The coordinating transaction tr_c consecutively validates each reactive transaction $tr_i \in TR$ and cumulates the result. In case of a positive validation of all reactive transactions, as shown here, tr_c passes the point of no return and then consecutively commits each reactive transaction. In case of a negative validation of at least one tr_i, the coordinator tr_c hence replaces the commit phase with an abort phase.

The start and execution of each validation and each commit step take up some time. As indicated, only the active transaction tr_c knows the complete control flow. Oppositely, each tr_i executed in a process like p_{host} in Figure 6.6

6.2. Transaction Failure

only sees and executes the commands necessary for its own current reactive transaction part. A reactive transaction tr_i cannot track the commit decision and hence the point of no return yielding a period of *uncertainty*. Thus, the naive recovery approach in Table 6.4 is not valid for reactive transactions.

Furthermore, a consistent transaction recovery is not possible at all with the Two-Phase Commit protocol described in Chapter 4. As a counter example assume the transaction in Figure 6.7 regarded from the perspective of tr_i. The process executing tr_c encounters a terminal fault in its phase of uncertainty, hence, at some point in time after finishing its own validation phase but before getting a commit or abort command. If the process ceases at t_1, it may be correct to abort or to commit the transaction. Although tr_i cannot be certain of the correct recovery means, it could theoretically find out about them by communicating with all other reactive transactions $tr_j \in TR \setminus \{tr_i\}, i \neq j$. One could implement different recovering strategies in this case. The original decision could be restored or a preference either to abort or to commit the transaction could be predefined.

If the process ceases at t_2, it is correct to commit the transaction. Again, tr_i is not certain about the correct recovery means but could find out about them by communicating with all other reactive transactions $tr_j \in TR \setminus \{tr_i\}, i \neq j$. As tr_1 is already committing tr_i would decide to also commit its transaction to maintain consistency.

However, if the process executing tr_c ceases at t_3, the situation is worse. Transaction tr_i is uncertain and could try to find out the correct decision by communicating with all remaining reactive transactions. At t_3 transaction tr_1 has already committed. Unfortunately, committing a transaction finally terminates it thus removing it from the reactive transaction set TR_2, $TR_2 = \{tr_1, \ldots, tr_n\} \setminus \{tr_1\}$. Transaction tr_i, now communicating with all other remaining participating transactions $tr_j \in TR_2 \setminus \{tr_i\}, i \neq j$, would decide to abort or commit depending on the implemented strategy yielding a possibly inconsistent and potentially blocked transaction.

As a consequence, our current DSTM protocol is not suited to properly recover from all transactional faults. We solve this problem by replacing the Two-Phase approach with a robust Three-Phase DSTM protocol.

6. Implementing Robustness

6.3. Robust DSTM Protocol

We have seen in Section 2.3 that the idea of software transactional memory is an adaptation from transactions in database systems where it has long since been used and researched. Database systems are, in general, used to manage large amounts of data. Database system designers put their main emphasis on transaction throughput thereby possibly limiting system recovery properties. Currently available commercial distributed databases, though efficient, are susceptible to blocking and, thus, cannot properly recover from permanent process (total site) failures [AHS09a]. However, these systems successfully recover from intermittent process failures.

Our focus in respect to DSTM failure is on permanent process failures (see Section 6.1.1). Despite the differences it is well possible to adapt solutions to the recovery problem from database technology.

6.3.1. Database Transactions and STM

We look at established methods in database management to possibly utilize them for our purpose of developing a robust DSTM protocol. As this book is not primarily about database technologies, we refer to the literature for a thorough database discussion. A very comprehensive guide to database technology can be found in [LÖ09]. Bernstein, Hadzilacos, and Goodman thoroughly analyze the recovery aspect of distributed databases [BHG87]. This is the main inspiration for us to adapt the Three-Phase Commit solution to our DSTM protocol.

Distributed database systems require commit protocols such as Two-Phase and Three-Phase Commit [Tok09] to achieve distributed atomicity and ensure transaction consistency. Commercial distributed database systems, however, are exclusively based on variations of the Two-Phase Commit protocol [AHS09b] due to efficiency and ease of implementation.

The Three-Phase Commit protocol is based on the Two-Phase Commit protocol augmented with a third phase inserted between the validate and the commit phase to maintain consistency even under terminal failure of the transaction coordinator. The intermediate phase is often called the precommit phase. It is essentially another protocol message from the coordinating transaction tr_c to all participating reactive transactions tr_i issued after passing the point of no return when validation yields a commit decision.

In each phase the transaction coordinator sends out a cascade of messages,

6.3. Robust DSTM Protocol

one to each participating transaction as shown in Figure 6.8. Each message takes some time to be sent. Thus, for the coordinator itself, each phase takes as long as the combined phases of all participants. The protocol guarantees that *all* messages of a preceding phase are sent *before* the first message of a succeeding phase. Hence, the additional precommit phase guarantees that all participating transactions know about the commit decision before the first one actually executes it. The remaining participating transactions have sufficient information to continue the transaction at every point in time. Thus, the original coordinator is not required, as we will see in the remainder of this section.

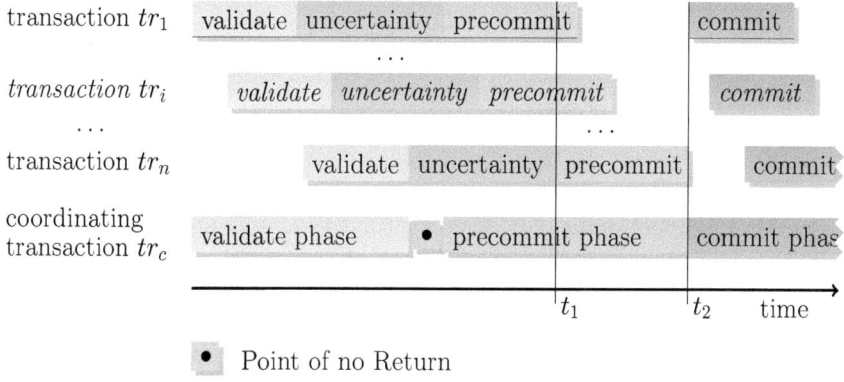

Figure 6.8.: Three-Phase Protocol Time Line

At time t_1 in Figure 6.8, all transactions tr_i have reached their precommit phase and thus ended their phase of uncertainty. At time t_2 the commit phase begins. The Three-Phase protocol ensures that $t_1 < t_2$ always holds. At no time any tr_i is uncertain while any tr_j is committing.

If now a communication fault occurs before t_1, leaving tr_i potentially uncertain about the decision, the protocol guarantees that no reactive transaction has yet terminated. Thus, the set of participating transactions $TR = \{tr_1, \ldots, tr_n\}$ is still complete. Therefore, tr_i can find out the transaction status by communicating with all other reactive transactions $tr_j \in TR \setminus \{tr_i\}, i \neq j$. In case of a fault after t_1 every tr_i even knows the decision itself. Still, the protocol has to be continued by a new coordinator to end the transaction in a consis-

6. Implementing Robustness

tent state. Hence, one of the communicating reactive transactions becomes the new coordinator $tr_{cnew} \in TR$ through the *election protocol* described in Section 6.3.5.

FAULT	ERROR DETECTION	RECOVERY
Transaction	Life-check	Election Protocol

Table 6.5.: Reactive Transaction Recovery

Table 6.5 illustrates that a reactive transaction encountering a coordinator fault always recovers by executing the election protocol independent of the transaction phase the fault occurred in.

6.3.2. Reactive Transaction Status

We have seen that the Three-Phase Commit protocol is well suited to recover from process failure without causing deadlocks. Analyzing the Two-Phase protocol problem again reveals that participating reactive transactions might have already committed when the coordinator fault occurs, as with a fault at t_3 in Figure 6.7. As a consequence, the process executing transaction tr_1 in Figure 6.7 cannot easily reply to requests from other reactive transactions about the decision it had taken in the past.

One might argue that every process should maintain a conceptually infinite database of all reactive transactions ever executed. Then the process could report the decision even when its transaction has already ended. Such a protocol could avoid a third commit phase and the associated protocol messages at the price of an ever growing database. However, in order to keep the protocol scalable, the reactive database entry could be removed as soon as the *active* transaction has ended faultlessly. It could then broadcast a message to all reactive transactions to delete the current transaction status information. Then, of course, we do have a three-phase protocol again.

Hence, when moving to the Three-Phase Commit protocol in our implementation, we maintain a process global database with the state of all reactive transactions that are currently executing in that process. Therefore, we define a `TransID` type (line 1) uniquely identifying a transaction throughout the distributed system as a tuple of its executing process environment and the software transaction identifier. We can then extract the transaction coordinating

6.3. Robust DSTM Protocol

process from a `TransID`.

```
1 type TransID = (EnvAddr , STMID)
```

Note that our nomenclature differs slightly from the terms used in the literature describing the Three-Phase Commit protocol. The second phase is usually called *Precommit* while we call the corresponding protocol step either *Commit* or *Retry* depending on the transaction result. We name the third protocol step the *End* phase (Table 6.6).

PHASE	THREE-PHASE COMMIT	ROBUST DSTM
1	Validation	Validation
2	Precommit	Commit / Retry
3	Commit	End

Table 6.6.: Three-Phase Protocol Nomenclature

We define the `DistTransCont` data type (line 5) as a pair of the `TransID` key and a Concurrent Haskell channel `Chan RemCont`. A channel is an abstract synchronization data type `Chan a` based on `MVars` as proposed in [PJGF96]. Channels can be used to build even higher synchronization abstractions as shown in [SH02]. The function `newChan` creates a new channel. We write to it with `writeChan` and read from it with `readChan`. Writing to a channel never blocks while reading from an empty channel blocks until data is written to it.

```
2 newChan   :: IO (Chan a)
3 writeChan :: Chan a -> a -> IO ()
4 readChan  :: Chan a -> IO a
```

The `RemCont` data type enumerates the possible reactive transaction state *transitions* (line 6). Possible state transitions are commit (`Com`), retry (`Ret`), end (`End`), and error (`Err`).

```
5 type DistTransCont = (TransID, Chan RemCont)
6 data RemCont = Com | Ret | End | Err
```

We use a channel to allow multiple threads to concurrently alter the state of a reactive transaction. The threads store their state transitions in the channel. In regular operation the active transaction, as the transaction coordinator,

6. Implementing Robustness

transitions the state from an initial, implicit, validation via either committed or retried to ended.

In case of a failing transaction coordinator, however, at first the error recovery thread propagates the reactive transaction into an error state and eventually the new elected coordinator resumes the interrupted transaction control. Thus, three threads concurrently control a recovering transaction. Figure 6.9

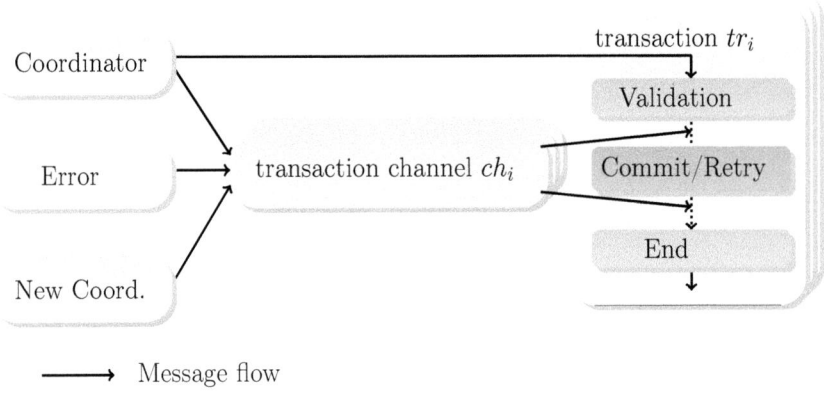

Figure 6.9.: Robust Reactive Transaction Synchronisation

illustrates the messages being sent to advance the three transaction phases, omitting the *error* states for clarity, in a reactive transaction tr_i. We initialize each reactive transaction with a separate transaction channel ch_i sequencing the upcoming state transitions. The concurrent coordinators asynchronously write to the transaction specific channels. Each transaction itself reads and executes the synchronized channel sequence of state transitions independent of their origin.

```
7  gDistTransCont :: MVar [DistTransCont]
8  gDistTransCont = unsafePerformIO (newMVar [])
```

We keep the transaction dictionary in the global **gDistTransCont** variable.

6.3. Robust DSTM Protocol

6.3.3. Controlling Reactive Transactions

Both, the regular coordinator and a possibly elected new coordinator control a reactive transaction by sending Robust DSTM protocol messages which the receiving process executes. Therefore, we extend the `handleMsg` function (lines 9–17) with transaction control entries replacing the non-robust versions described in Section 5.4.3. Each message controls a specific transaction identified by its `TransID`.

The protocol starts a reactive transaction with the `RemStartTrans` message (line 13). Additional parameters are the description of the transactional modifications of all `TVars` hosted in the reactive transaction process and a higher-order function generating the validation reply message. The description is a list of type `ValidRemVal`, representing all processes cooperating in that transaction.

`RemContTrans` commands (line 15), additionally parametrized with a transition command being either `Com`, `Ret`, or `End`, invoke regular state transitions.

```
9   handleMsg :: Handle -> STMMessage -> IO ()
10  handleMsg h msg =
11    case msg of
12      ...
13      RemStartTrans trId idVRs trEnvs ->
14        startRemTr trId idVRs trEnvs (hPutStrLn h . toString)
15      RemContTrans trId cont -> contRemTr trId cont
16      RemElectedNewCoord trId cont trEnvs ->
17        contWNewCoord trId cont trEnvs
```

The `RemElectedNewCoord` message (line 16) indicates that this process has been designated the new coordinator for a specific transaction. Besides the transaction identifier parameters are the state transition, the election took place in, and a list of all remaining transaction participants. This command invokes the new coordinator protocol execution shown in Section 6.3.5.

```
18  startRemTr :: TransID -> [ValidRemVal] ->
19                [EnvAddr] -> (Bool -> IO ()) -> IO ()
20  startRemTr trId idVRs trEnvs reValid = do
21    updateAutoTrans (+1) trId
22    chan <- newChan
23    modifyMVar_ gDistTransCont (return . ((trId, chan) : ))
24    forkIO (ctrlTrans chan trId idVRs trEnvs reValid)
25    return ()
```

6. Implementing Robustness

When a new reactive transaction starts, `startRemTr` initializes the global process channel dictionary (line 23) adding a fresh transaction channel and forks a thread actually controlling the transaction (line 24). Additionally, we update a global state (line 21) used for refining process failure checking as described in Section 6.3.6.

```
26  contRemTr :: TransID -> RemCont -> IO ()
27  contRemTr trId msg = do
28    conts <- readMVar gDistTransCont
29    case lookup trId conts of
30      Just chan -> writeChan chan msg
31      Nothing   -> return ()
```

A reactive transaction state advances by `contRemTr` writing the current transition into its transaction channel (line 30) looked up in the global dictionary (line 29). We ignore commands referring to an unknown transaction (line 31) as they are duplicate messages generated from multiple processes during transaction recovery.

Controller Automaton

We synchronize the three DSTM phases with an independent channel for each robust reactive transaction. In order not to block the message parsing thread, the transaction executes in a separate controller thread.

```
32  ctrlTrans :: Chan RemCont -> TransID ->
33               [ValidRemVal] -> [EnvAddr] ->
34               (Bool -> IO ()) -> IO ()
35  ctrlTrans chan trId idVRs trEnvs reValid = do
36    mapM_ (lockTVarFromId.fst) idVRs
37    isValid <- foldr valValidIds (return True) idVRs
38    catch (reValid isValid)
39          (\(_::SomeException) -> writeChan chan Err)
40    ctrlContTrans chan trId idVRs trEnvs
```

We view the controller as the deterministic finite state automaton shown in Figure 6.10. When started, `ctrlTrans` first locks (line 36) and validates (line 37) all link `TVars` controlled by the reactive transaction. We describe the access of link `TVars` using a `TVar` action dictionary in Section 4.3.1. Validation folds the individual `TVar` validation state to an accumulated result, omitting the straightforward details of `valValidIds`. The validation result is replied back to

6.3. Robust DSTM Protocol

the controlling active transaction (line 38). If this message cannot be properly delivered, the very transaction thread catches the exception and, assuming a terminal process fault of the active transaction, fills its own channel with the Err token. Otherwise, the coordinator would eventually have filled the channel with a Com, Ret or End token.

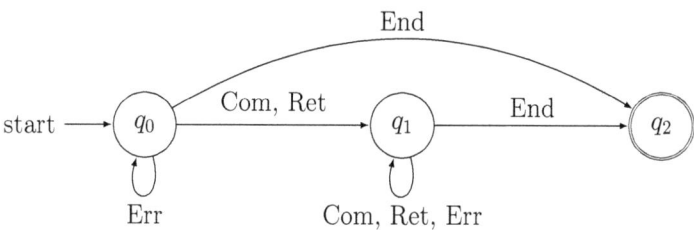

Figure 6.10.: Finite State Automaton of the Reactive Transaction Controller

The controller thread continues with function ctrlContTrans representing the automaton start state q_0. The first token read from the channel determines how the transaction continues (line 45). An Err token (line 55) represents a lost connection to the transaction coordinator, the active transaction. According to our Robust DSTM protocol, we elect a new transaction coordinator and loop back into state q_0 waiting for the End token sent from the new coordinator.

```
41  ctrlContTrans :: Chan RemCont -> TransID ->
42                   [ValidRemVal] -> [EnvAddr]
43                   -> IO ()
44  ctrlContTrans chan trId idVRs trEnvs = do
45    msg <- readChan chan
46    case msg of
47      Com -> do
48        mapM_ contWriteTVar idVRs
49        mapM_ (notifyFromId.fst) idVRs
50        ctrlEndTrans chan trId Com idVRs trEnvs
51      Ret -> do
52        mapM_ contExtWaitQ idVRs
53        ctrlEndTrans chan trId Ret idVRs trEnvs
54      End -> finishTrans trId idVRs
55      Err -> do
56        electNewCoord trId trEnvs End
57        ctrlContTrans chan trId idVRs trEnvs
```

151

6. Implementing Robustness

An End token read in state q_0 (line 54) corresponds to an aborted transaction which we terminate properly in `finishTrans` (lines 58 – 63) by unlocking the TVars again and cleaning up the global states, thus, reaching the accept state q_2.

```
58  finishTrans :: TransID -> [ValidRemVal] -> IO ()
59  finishTrans trId idVRs = do
60    mapM_ (unLockTVarFromId.fst) idVRs
61    updateAutoTrans (+ (-1)) trId
62    modifyMVar_ gDistTransCont
63      (return . filter ((/= trId) . fst))
```

A `Com` (line 47) or `Ret` (line 51) token read from the channel both advance to the next state q_1 calling `ctrlEndTrans` while executing the necessary TVar write and notify respectively wait queue extending actions. Again, we omit the evident technical details of executing link TVar actions.

State q_1 corresponds to the Three-Phase Commit *precommit* phase. We proceed depending on the next read token (line 68). Reading an End token (line 70) symbolizes a successfully terminated transaction, having either committed or retried. We perform the same administrative `finishTrans` cleanup as in the abort case and advance to the accepting state q_2.

Again, an Err token (line 71) represents a lost transaction coordinator. Thus, we elect a new transaction coordinator and loop back into state q_1.

```
64  ctrlEndTrans :: Chan RemCont -> TransID -> RemCont
65                  -> [ValidRemVal] -> [EnvAddr]
66                  -> IO ()
67  ctrlEndTrans chan trId remCont idVRs trEnvs = do
68    msg <- readChan chan
69    case msg of
70      End -> finishTrans trId idVRs
71      Err -> do
72        electNewCoord trId trEnvs remCont
73        ctrlEndTrans chan trId remCont idVRs trEnvs
74      tok -> ctrlEndTrans chan trId tok idVRs trEnvs
```

We might also see `Com` and `Ret` tokens (line 74) in this state as our election algorithm allows the new coordinator to be elected concurrently by multiple other participating reactive transactions. We simply ignore such duplicate tokens doing nothing and looping back to state q_1 waiting for the final End token.

6.3.4. Library Exception

In Section 2.1.5 we have shown how dynamically-typed exceptions allow to naturally define and use application, and in our case, library specific Haskell exceptions.

```
75  data SomeDistTVarException =
76    PropagateDistTVarFail String SomeDistTVarException
77    | CommunicationFail String EnvAddr SomeException
78    | NodeConnectionFail String EnvAddr SomeException

79  instance Exception SomeDistTVarException
```

We simply define a SomeDistTVarException distributed exception type (line 75) and make it an instance of the Exception class (line 79). Since we do not build our own exception hierarchy, we do not need to overload the class methods. Instead, we define exception type alternatives for a failure connecting a remote process node (line 78) and a communication failure in an already established connection (line 77).

We use both exceptions to initiate the library failure handling. The main purpose of these exceptions is to carry the failed process EnvAddr identification to where we catch and recover from the failure. Further parameters of SomeDistTVarException are the underlying run-time system error of the generic type SomeException and an error message text.

We use the PropagateDistTVarFail exception (line 76) for recursive failure handling. We recover our library from any SomeDistTVarException and, in addition, propagate the distributed exception up to the application-level to allow the user to recover on application-level.

Within our library, when catching distributed exceptions, we use the helper function distTVarExEnv to extract the faulty process environment from the exception.

```
80  distTVarExEnv :: SomeDistTVarException -> EnvAddr
81  distTVarExEnv eDist = case eDist of
82    (PropagateDistTVarFail _ e)  -> distTVarExEnv e
83    (CommunicationFail _ env _)  -> env
84    (NodeConnectionFail _ env _) -> env
```

We now define the application interface predicate isDistErrTVar that enables the application programmer to discriminate available from unavailable TVars when catching a DSTM library exception.

6. Implementing Robustness

```
85  isDistErrTVar   :: SomeDistTVarException -> TVar a -> Bool
86  isDistErrTVar e t = distTVarExEnv e == tVarEnv t
```

6.3.5. Coordinator Election

A reactive transaction encountering a transaction coordinator fault communicates with the other reactive transactions to elect a new coordinator to continue the transaction control.

```
87  electNewCoord  :: TransID -> [EnvAddr] -> RemCont  -> IO ()
88  electNewCoord trId@(env, _) trEnvs remCont =
89    catch (do
90    let upEnvs = filter (/= env) trEnvs
91        newC = minimum upEnvs
92    if newC == gMyEnv
93      then contWNewCoord trId remCont upEnvs
94      else remPutMsg newC
95           (RemElectedNewCoord trId remCont upEnvs)
96    )
97    (\e -> let eEnv = (/= distTVarExEnv e)
98           upEnvs = filter eEnv . filter (/= env)
99                  $ trEnvs
100   in electNewCoord trId upEnvs remCont
101   )
```

As any of the remaining transaction participants `upEnvs` (line 90) could take over the job, we arbitrarily elect the minimum of the `EnvAddr` typed participants (line 91). In our DSTM protocol the minimum participant progressed the transaction the furthest, in general, which potentially makes the recovery slightly more efficient. The reactive transaction may either elect its very process itself (line 93) or one of the other participating processes (line 94), in which case we send the election message.

The latter case could expose another fault. The newly chosen coordinator might be unaccessible as well hence evoking an exception (line 98), in which case we remove both faulty processes from the participants list and in turn start a new recursive instance of `electNewCoord`.

The elected coordinator continues the coordination of the interrupted transaction in lieu of the terminally unaccessible original active transaction by executing `contWNewCoord`.

6.3. Robust DSTM Protocol

```
102  contWNewCoord :: TransID -> RemCont -> [EnvAddr]   -> IO ()
103  contWNewCoord trId remCont upEnvs = do
104    let remEnvs = filter (/= gMyEnv) upEnvs
105    case remCont of
106      End -> return ()
107      _   ->
108        robustMapM_ (flip remPutMsg
109                          (RemContTrans trId remCont)
110                    ) remEnvs
111    robustMapM_ (flip remPutMsg (RemContTrans trId End)
112                ) remEnvs
113    contRemTrans trId End
```

If called with an End token (line 106), the new coordinator continues the transaction by broadcasting (line 111) this token to the remaining reactive transactions (line 104) and to itself (line 113), thus, aborting the complete transaction.

If called with a Ret or Com token (line 107), contWNewCoord additionally broadcasts the central phase of the Three-Phase Commit protocol to the other reactive transactions. Note that it does not need to execute that phase itself. The new coordinator either has already executed this precommit phase before electing itself or has been elected by another reactive transaction which has finished its own precommit phase. In the latter case, the elected coordinator has also finished this phase because our election scheme selects transactions further advanced in the protocol.

Also, note that we map the communication onto the remaining reactive transactions using a robust version of mapM_. The robustMapM_ function (line 114) ignores io actions generating an exception and continues the communication mapping (line 120).

```
114  robustMapM_ :: (a -> IO ()) -> [a] -> IO ()
115  robustMapM_ _ []     = return ()
116  robustMapM_ io (x:xs) = catch (do
117     io x
118     robustMapM_ io xs
119    )
120    (\(_::SomeDistTVarException) -> robustMapM_ io xs)
```

6. Implementing Robustness

6.3.6. Life-check

The idea to regularly send a message to verify that the queried process is still accessible follows the notion behind the UNIX `ping` command created in need of a network problem solving tool [Muu83]. However, the ping command uses the internet layer protocol-level underneath the TCP-level we use. We call this a *life-check* mechanism. A `RemLifeCheck` message extends the `STMMessage` protocol data type.

The *Erlang* (see Section 7.3.1) distributed functional programming language has a built-in function allowing a process to set a bidirectional *link* to another process. This functionality, provided by the run-time system, allows the application programmer to implement robustness requiring error messages from terminated processes similar to our library requirements for inactive and reactive transactions. The run-time system of one Erlang node transparently starts regular life-check messaging ticks to the run-time system of the linked node [SF07]. The life-check frequency defaults to a tick message every 15 seconds. It is independent of the application program. The run-time system generates an error message after four unsuccessful tick messages [Eri10].

The tail recursive `lifeCheck` function (line 121) periodically polls a system process described with its `EnvAddr` by sending a `RemLifeCheck` (line 123) message which does nothing when it is received (line 133) while the Erlang tick protocol requires the queried process to reply to any tick. However, the Haskell run-time system throws an exception if the life-check message cannot be delivered. We use one unidirectional message and the run-time system exception mechanism for efficiency and design reasons. We catch any exception (line 127), thus, detecting the error, and recover the system as we will see in detail in this chapter.

```
121  lifeCheck :: EnvAddr -> IO ()
122  lifeCheck env = catch (do
123     remPutMsg env RemLifeCheck
124     threadDelay 1000000
125     lifeCheck env
126     )
127     (\(e::SomeException) -> do
128     ... -- system recovery)
```

We use a delay of one second[2] (line 124) as an example. Note that this function actively polls the other process. Although `threadDelay` suspends the

---
[2] The `threadDelay` function requires a delay specified in microseconds.

6.3. Robust DSTM Protocol

thread, thus, avoiding *busy waiting*, the resource intense polling message itself puts a similar *busy checking* burden onto the system. Therefore, the delay has to be carefully chosen to fulfill the system needs. A long delay reduces the resource consumption and a short delay accelerates the reaction on unavailable system processes.

```
129  handleMsg :: Handle -> STMMessage -> IO ()
130  handleMsg h msg =
131    case msg of
132      ...
133      RemLifeCheck -> return ()
```

Each process is potentially executing both reactive and inactive transactions. Thus, we use the global link environment dictionary `gLinks` (line 137) organizing the link surveillance. For each surveyed process, we keep track of the pending transactions it controls (line 134), and maintain a list of all `RetryVars` (line 135) to be resumed if their dependent `TVars` vanished unexpectedly with a terminated linked process.

```
134  data AutoLink = AutoLink {autoTrans :: Int,
135                            autoRetry :: [RetryVar]}
136  type Link     = (EnvAddr, AutoLink)

137  gLinks :: MVar [Link]
138  gLinks = unsafePerformIO (newMVar [])
```

Polling

We control the frequency of life-check message polling. More importantly, we activate life-check polling only when necessary. It is well possible that an application requires regular polling in a phase of high transaction activity followed by a phase of no transaction activity followed by transactions again. Therefore, we switch polling on and off completely as needed. This is fully transparent to the application programmer.

The completed `lifeCheck` function (lines 139–164) chooses its polling action based on the surveillance dictionary `gLinks`. If there is no entry for the linked process, the thread silently exits in line 143. In case of a pending reactive (line 144) or an inactive (line 148) transaction surveillance, we *ping* the linked process, suspend for a predefined context dependent delay, and repeat the task.

157

6. Implementing Robustness

If the dictionary entry indicates no further need for surveillance, we remove the linked process entry completely (line 154) and terminate the `lifeCheck` thread after performing a last poll.

```
139  lifeCheck :: EnvAddr -> IO ()
140  lifeCheck env = catch (do
141    links <- readMVar gLinks
142    case lookup env links of
143      Nothing -> return ()
144      Just link | autoTrans link > 0 -> do
145                    ping
146                    threadDelay 1000000
147                    lifeCheck env
148                | autoRetry link /= [] -> do
149                    ping
150                    threadDelay 3000000
151                    lifeCheck env
152                | otherwise -> do
153                    ping
154                    rmLink
155    )
156    (\(e::SomeException) -> do
157        recoverBrokenReactiveTrans env
158        recoverBrokenInactiveTrans env
159        rmLink
160    )
161    where
162      ping = remPutMsg env RemLifeCheck
163      rmLink = modifyMVar_ gLinks
164               (return . filter ((/= env) . fst))
```

We catch any exception thrown by possibly unsuccessful `RemLifeCheck` message calls to recover from a terminated process by cleaning up possible reactive (line 157) and inactive (line 158) transactions and remove the just broken link from the global link dictionary (line 159).

Recovering

We use the `recoverBrokenReactiveTrans` function to insert an `Err` token into any broken reactive transaction channel (line 169) listed in the global `gDistTransCont` dictionary (line 168). We call a transaction broken, if it originates in an unavailable process. Section 6.3.3 describes the transaction channel synchronization in detail.

6.3. Robust DSTM Protocol

```
165  recoverBrokenReactiveTrans :: EnvAddr -> IO ()
166  recoverBrokenReactiveTrans env = do
167    conts <- readMVar gDistTransCont
168    let brokenTrans = filter ((== env).fst.fst) conts
169    mapM_ ((flip writeChan Err).snd) brokenTrans
```

In case of an unavailable TVar, the recoverBrokenInactiveTrans function resumes every inactive, hence suspended, transaction on its retryVar (line 176). Thus, this recovery function prohibits potential deadlocks, substituting the resume task of the dependent TVars. We look up the retryVar values with the environment key of the unavailable process stored in the gLinks dictionary (line 173).

```
170  recoverBrokenInactiveTrans :: EnvAddr -> IO ()
171  recoverBrokenInactiveTrans env = do
172    links <- readMVar gLinks
173    case lookup env links of
174      Nothing                             -> return ()
175      Just AutoLink{autoRetry=retryVars} ->
176        mapM_ coreResume retryVars
```

If the RetryVar is hosted in the current process itself (line 179), we directly execute the resume action resumeRetryVarAct. Note that we call the non-blocking tryPutMVar function (line 185) to fill the RetryVar, as potentially many TVars will try to resume the inactive transaction.

```
177  coreResume :: RetryVar -> IO ()
178  coreResume (RetryVar retryMVar _) =
179    resumeRetryVarAct retryMVar
180  coreResume (LinkRetryVar (VarLink env retVarId)) =
181    catch (remPutMsg env (RemResume [retVarId]))
182      (\(e::SomeException) -> return ())
```

In case of a link RetryVar, we send a message to the hosting process (line 181) to have executed the resume action. Note that we catch a possible exception to just ignore it (line 182). Such an exception indicates an inaccessible process hosting the RetryVar. Thus, the inactive transaction is inaccessible itself. There is no point in resuming a transaction in a process not being executed anyway.

```
183  resumeRetryVarAct :: MVar () -> IO ()
184  resumeRetryVarAct retryMVar =
185    tryPutMVar retryMVar () >> return ()
```

159

6. Implementing Robustness

Preparing

We use the life-check functionality, the surveillance thread, only when necessary. It is necessary, if there are reactive or inactive transactions in other processes. In such a case we maintain a link to each other process. The default dictionary link entry `gDefaultLink` contains the empty link entry. Initially, there is no linked reactive transaction and no linked retry variable. Any reactive or inactive transaction updates these entries throughout the process life-time. We end the surveillance thread, whenever the link is no longer required, to save inter-process messages.

```
186  gDefaultLink :: AutoLink
187  gDefaultLink = AutoLink {autoTrans = 0,
188                           autoRetry = []}
```

We use `updateAutoTrans`, parameterized with an update function, and the controlling transaction, identified by its `TransID`, to update the number of pending reactive transactions. There is at most one entry for each linked process generated for a new process (lines 193–197) or updated, if there are already linked processes (lines 198–201). We fork a fresh surveillance thread for every newly linked process (line 196).

```
189  updateAutoTrans :: (Int -> Int) -> TransID -> IO ()
190  updateAutoTrans f (env, _) = do
191    links <- takeMVar gLinks
192    case partition ((== env).fst) links of
193      ([], others) -> do
194        putMVar gLinks
195          ((env, gDefaultLink{autoTrans=1}) : others)
196        forkIO (lifeCheck env)
197        return ()
198      ([(env, lnk)], others) ->
199        putMVar gLinks
200          ((env, lnk{autoTrans = f (autoTrans lnk)})
201           : others)
```

A suspended transaction waits to be resumed at some point in time which depends on potentially any one of the `TVars` read in that transaction. Before suspending, the transaction adds its `retryVar` to the `gLink` dictionary referenced with all processes, hosting the potentially resuming `TVars`, as keys. We add the entries with `insertRetryLinks` and remove the entries using `deleteRetryLinks` after the transaction resumes.

6.3. Robust DSTM Protocol

We map `insertRetryLinks` over the cooperating process environments and parameterize it with the transaction information for that environment. If there are no process links yet listed in the `gLink` dictionary (line 206), we set possible `retryVar` dictionary links for the process key based on the empty `gDefaultLink`. In case of existing links (line 211) for that process, we accumulate the additional links. Note that we also fork a fresh `lifeCheck` thread for every newly linked process (line 209).

```
202  insertRetryLinks :: EnvAddr -> [ValidRemVal] -> IO ()
203  insertRetryLinks env idVRs = do
204    links <- takeMVar gLinks
205    case partition ((== env).fst) links of
206      ([], others) -> do
207        putMVar gLinks
208          ((env, retrylink gDefaultLink) : others)
209        forkIO (lifeCheck env)
210        return ()
211      ([(e, link)], others) ->
212        putMVar gLinks ((e, retrylink link) : others)
213    where retrylink l = foldr insertRetryLink l idVRs
```

Within `insertRetryLink` (line 215) and `deleteRetryLink` (line 227) we reveal `retryVar` links by matching the respective `retryVar` values in the `ValidRemVal` dictionary. There is no `retryVar` information for `TVars` only written to in a transaction (lines 218 and 230). The link remains unchanged.

```
214  insertRetryLink :: ValidRemVal -> AutoLink  -> AutoLink
215  insertRetryLink (_, (Just (_, rVar), _))
216                  link@AutoLink{autoRetry=rVars}
217                    = link{autoRetry=rVar:rVars}
218  insertRetryLink _ link = link


219  deleteRetryLinks :: EnvAddr -> [ValidRemVal] -> IO ()
220  deleteRetryLinks env idVRs = do
221    links <- takeMVar gLinks
222    case partition ((== env).fst) links of
223      ([(e, link)], others) ->
224        putMVar gLinks ((e, retrylink link) : others)
225    where retrylink l = foldr deleteRetryLink l idVRs
```

6. Implementing Robustness

```
226  deleteRetryLink :: ValidRemVal -> AutoLink -> AutoLink
227  deleteRetryLink (_, (Just (_, rVar), _))
228                  link@AutoLink{autoRetry=rVars}
229    = link{autoRetry = filter (/= rVar) rVars}
230  deleteRetryLink _ link = link
```

In Section 5.4.1 we have shown how to accumulate retryVars. The typed list ValidRemVal, distributed to all reactive transactions in a distributed system, contains the dependency information. However, using the Three-Phase Commit protocol for our *Robust* DSTM implementation, we must incorporate the complete transaction information in the ValidRemVal data type right from the start of the transaction. In Section 6.3.8 we look at the implications of that change.

6.3.7. Controlling Active Transactions

In Chapter 4 we have described a coarse implementation of the active transaction controller function atomic. We have since changed both our main data structures to enable a more efficient protocol shown in Chapter 5 and the DSTM protocol itself to incorporate precautions for failing processes as highlighted in this chapter. Both changes are reflected in a slightly more sophisticated atomic control function.

The structure of atomic remains unchanged. When called by the application, atomic monadically runs all STM actions starting on a fresh STM state (line 234). The action result may be Success, Exception or Retry, all yielding a new STM state and a possible exception or result value.

For any resulting newState of the atomic actions, the gatherStmState function merges both transaction logs. The validate log of the resulting gState also contains the commit information. Hence, the Three-Phase Commit protocol requires only the consolidated validate log and can safely ignore the commit log. We explain the details in Section 6.3.8.

```
231  atomic :: STM a -> IO a
232  atomic stmAction = do
233    iState <- initialState
234    stmResult <- runSTM stmAction iState
235    case stmResult of
236      Success newState res -> do
237        let gState = gatherStmState newState
238        ...
```

6.3. Robust DSTM Protocol

```
239        Exception newState e -> do
240          let gState = gatherStmState newState
241          ...
242        Retry newState         -> do
243          let gState = gatherStmState newState
244          valid <- startTrans gState
245          if valid
246            then do
247              retryTrans gState
248              endTrans gState
249              let retryVar = stmRetryVar gState
250              insertRetryVarAct retryVar
251              suspend retryVar
252              deleteRetryVarAct retryVar
253              unRetryTrans gState
254            else endTrans gState
255        atomic stmAction
```

Apart from the state modification, both, the **Success** and the **Exception** cases are identical to our basic implementation shown in Section 4.2.3. We reveal their protocol functions in Section 6.3.9. However, in the **Retry** case, in addition, we take precautions to provide for proper garbage collection of **RetryVars** yielding scalability of the library. Also, we prepare possible automated resuming of suspended transactions in case of a failure.

Garbage Collection

Remote-controlling link **TVars** as well as link **RetryVars** requires stub functions in their hosting process. If we created these functions statically with a new variable, the variable itself would never become garbage collected. In Section 4.3.4 we have detailed the measures necessary to allow **TVars** to become garbage when the application no longer references them.

We follow a similar approach with our distributed **RetryVars**. Luckily, the solution is much simpler than the **TVar** measures because we know exactly when **RetryVars** are possibly accessed. A transaction may suspend itself on its **RetryVar**. Eventually, a **TVar** resumes its dependent transactions. Hence, the **RetryVar** itself is only accessed in between suspending and resuming its transaction. Thus, we create the **RetryVar** function stub (line 250) before the **atomic** transaction suspension (line 251) and remove it just afterwards (line 252).

We create a corresponding global dictionary map (line 256) and store the

6. Implementing Robustness

only one necessary `IO ()` function to resume a transaction. Our resuming strategy is highly redundant, in that we enable all possible `TVars` to resume the transaction. As only the first `TVar` actually resumes the transaction we ensure that further attempts do not block the resuming thread by calling the non-blocking `tryPutMVar` (line 262).

```
256  gRetryVarActMap :: MVar (Map VarID (IO () ))
257  gRetryVarActMap = unsafePerformIO (newMVar empty)


258  insertRetryVarAct :: RetryVar -> IO ()
259  insertRetryVarAct (RetryVar retryMVar retryVarId) =
260    modifyMVar_ gRetryVarActMap $
261      return . insertWith (flip const) retryVarId
262               (resumeRetryVarAct retryMVar)


263  deleteRetryVarAct :: RetryVar -> IO ()
264  deleteRetryVarAct (RetryVar _ retryVarId) =
265    modifyMVar_ gRetryVarActMap $
266      return . delete retryVarId
```

The `resumeFromId` function stub actually reveals the `RetryVar` function and executes it (line 271). Note that the `Nothing` case of no dictionary entry (line 272) is required. A first `TVar` resumes its dependent transaction which in turn deletes the `RetryVar` action dictionary entry (line 252). Further, and thus redundant, `TVar` attempts to resume the already resumed inactive transaction must therefore be ignored.

The stub function is called either through the regular notify mechanism (see Section 6.3.9) when writing `TVars` or when recovering inactive transactions from a detected life-check error (see Section 6.3.6).

```
267  resumeFromId :: VarId -> IO ()
268  resumeFromId retryVarId = do
269    gMap <- readMVar gRetryVarActMap
270    case Data.Map.lookup retryVarId gMap of
271      Just act -> act
272      Nothing  -> return ()
```

6.3. Robust DSTM Protocol

Auto Resume

A process executing a transaction resumes the transaction itself to recover from any unavailable `TVar` it depends on. Section 6.3.6 details the logging of necessary recovery information initiated from the `atomic` protocol.

Before suspending itself, `atomic` calls `retryTrans` (line 247) to extend the wait queues of all read `TVars`. We execute the actions directly on hosted `TVars` in the active transaction itself (line 279) and communicate the `Ret` token transition information to link `TVars` in the associated reactive transactions (line 281). Extending the wait queues is necessary to fulfill the regular DSTM protocol without failure handling. Note that we map the processes using `robustMapM_` (line 275), thus, skipping any unavailable process in the protocol.

```
273  retryTrans :: STMState -> IO ()
274  retryTrans state =
275    robustMapM_ (doRetryAction (stmId state))
276               (stmValidLog state)

277  doRetryAction :: TransID -> ValidLog -> IO ()
278  doRetryAction _ (env, Left (_, valLog)) =
279    extWaitQAct valLog
280  doRetryAction trId (env, Right idrs) = do
281    remPutMsg env (RemContTrans trId Ret)
282    insertRetryLinks env idrs
```

We map `insertRetryLinks` (line 282) before suspending a transaction and `deleteRetryLinks` (line 289) afterwards on all dependency link `TVars` to maintain the recovery log.

```
283  unRetryTrans :: STMState -> IO ()
284  unRetryTrans state = mapM_ doUnRetryAction
285                              (stmValidLog state)

286  doUnRetryAction :: ValidLog -> IO ()
287  doUnRetryAction (_, Left _)      = return ()
288  doUnRetryAction (env, Right idrs) =
289    deleteRetryLinks env idrs
```

6.3.8. Consolidated Log

The transaction logs as outlined in Section 5.4.1 reflect the communication optimizations discussed in Chapter 5. Each of the logs is a recursive sorted dic-

6. Implementing Robustness

tionary with the process environment as the key. The dictionary itself contains another dictionary with the **TVar** identifier as its key.

The high-level concurrent STM implementation [HK05] as well as our first distributed attempts use multiple logs. The robust implementation, however, requires that all log information is distributed to all cooperating reactive transactions when needed. In our Three-Phase Commit protocol solution the active transaction, after logging the information, distributes it when starting the DSTM protocol. Therefore, a single consolidated log structure reduces the traversal cost in each cooperating process when executing the reactive transaction.

However, during the collection phase in an active transaction, a single log structure is certainly less than ideal. The possibly recursive **orElse** transaction combinator applications require that we stack just the commit log which can be elegantly achieved as shown in Section 4.2.3. Therefore, a separate commit log, independent of the other logs, reduces the **orElse** interpretation cost.

Our solution to this dilemma is to collect two separate logs, a commit log accumulating information from **TVars** written during a transaction and a validate log collecting information from **TVars** both read and written. We then consolidate both logs into a single one just before executing the DSTM protocol by applying **gatherStmState** to the new transaction state returned from the monadic run in **atomic** (see Section 6.3.7). Note that we consolidate only the link **TVar** log information as only this data needs to be communicated to the cooperating reactive transactions. The host **TVar** logs remain unchanged.

The single log structure requires one addition in regards to link **TVars**. We replace the dictionary type **MaybeRead** with **MaybeRW** allowing to also store the to be written **String** converted value of a **writeTVar** command. This log structure modification entails an obvious technical adaptation to the collection functions described in Chapter 5 which we omit here.

```
290  type ValidRemVal = (ID, MaybeRW)
291  type MaybeRW     = (MaybeRead, Maybe String)
292  type MaybeRead   = Maybe (VersionID, RetryVar)

293  gatherStmState :: STMState -> STMState
294  gatherStmState state = state {stmValidLog =
295    map (gatherValidRemVal (stmCommitLog state))
296       (stmValidLog state) }
```

We replace the validate log in **gatherStmState** by mapping it over all collected environments and applying **gatherValidRemVal** to each of it. As de-

6.3. Robust DSTM Protocol

scribed above, we keep the validate host logs unchanged (line 298). Also, we keep validate link logs unchanged, if there are no write entries for the currently mapped environment (line 302). Just in case of existing write entries for the looked up environment (line 303), we map addComRemVals over all listed TVar identifiers in that environment to complete the consolidated validate log with possible write entries (line 309).

```
297  gatherValidRemVal :: [CommitLog] -> ValidLog -> ValidLog
298  gatherValidRemVal _ (env, Left stActs) =
299    (env, Left stActs)
300  gatherValidRemVal comLogs (env, Right valRemVals) =
301    case lookup env comLogs of
302      Nothing -> (env, Right valRemVals)
303      Just (Right (comVals, _)) ->
304        (env, Right (map (addComRemVals comVals)
305                          valRemVals))

306  addComRemVals :: [CommitRemVal] -> ValidRemVal
307                 -> ValidRemVal
308  addComRemVals comVals (tId, (readVal, _)) =
309    (tId, (readVal, lookup tId comVals))
```

Alternatively, one could collect only a single log and replace the commit information scattered throughout the log before each orElse interpretation. However, our solution performs better, if we assume a frequent usage of orElse statements and a relative small number of aborted transactions.

6.3.9. Robust Protocol for Active Transactions

We conclude the description of the transaction control mechanism with the robust protocol for active transactions called in atomic. For any of the Success, Exception, or Retry transaction results, the protocol starts with validating the transaction calling startTrans with the transaction state where we fold all validate log based validation results to the compound transaction validation result (line 310). Parameters are the transaction identifier (line 312), a list of all cooperating reactive transactions in addition to the active one (line 313), the base folding value, and the validate log list.

Although the idea behind robustFoldValidAct (lines 317–329) is to create a robust version of foldM like robustMapM_ (lines 114–120) represents a robust version of mapM_, we have refrained from generalizing the former one as its

6. Implementing Robustness

recovery mechanism is very specialized. The function not only folds the validate results but also starts all cooperating transactions. Therefore, the recovery measure in case of a failure is the termination of all started transactions.

```
310  startTrans :: STMState -> IO Bool
311  startTrans state =
312    robustFoldValidAct (stmId state)
313                       (fst . unzip $ valLogs)
314                       True
315                       valLogs
316    where valLogs = stmValidLog state
```

We catch communication exceptions in a validation instance (line 323) and terminate the started transaction in this folding instance (line 326). Note that we simply ignore a failing termination itself (line 327) as we exclude unavailable reactive transactions from execution. We finally terminate all started transactions in the reverse order by propagating the exception to the enclosing folding instance (line 329) using the helper function **propagateEx** (line 331).

```
317  robustFoldValidAct :: TransID -> [EnvAddr]
318                     -> Bool -> [ValidLog]
319                     -> IO Bool
320  robustFoldValidAct _ _ isValid [] = return isValid
321  robustFoldValidAct trId envs isValid (v:vs) =
322    catch (do
323      isV <- doValidAction isValid v trId envs
324      robustFoldValidAct trId envs isV vs
325    )(\(e::SomeDistTVarException) -> do
326      catch (doEndAction trId v)
327            (\(_::SomeDistTVarException) -> return ())
328      )
329      propagateEx "robustFoldValidAct" e
330    )

331  propagateEx :: String -> SomeDistTVarException -> IO a
332  propagateEx loc e =
333    throw (PropagateDistTVarFail (loc ++ " -> ") e)
```

The **doValidAction** function really starts either the active or an inactive transaction and cumulates and returns the validation result. In case of the active transaction, we lock all its hosted **TVars** (line 337). We then validate those **TVars** and combine the result lazily with the cumulated result (line 338). We start reactive transactions by sending them the **RemStartTrans** message

6.3. Robust DSTM Protocol

(line 340). The reactive transaction then replies with the validation result (see Section 6.3.3) which we also lazily combine with the cumulated result (line 341). Note that `fromString` converts the communicated `String` into a boolean value.

```
334  doValidAction :: Bool -> ValidLog -> TransID
335                    -> [EnvAddr] -> IO Bool
336  doValidAction isV (_, Left (lActs, rAct)) _ _ = do
337     mapM_ (lockAct.snd) lActs
338     isV +>> validAct rAct
339  doValidAction isV (env, (Right vals)) trId trEnvs =
340     remGetMsg env (RemStartTrans trId vals trEnvs)
341     >>= return . (isV &&) . fromString
```

A valid transaction continues conducting its protocol according to its result. In Section 6.3.7 we have looked at the `Retry` protocol details. A valid transaction returning `Success` commits its results calling `commitTrans` which robustly maps `doCommitAction` over the `CommitLog` dictionary (line 344). Note that it is not sufficient to map over the `ValidLog` dictionary as `gatherStmState` only consolidates link `TVar` data. Thus, the validate log never contains host `TVar` commit information.

```
342  commitTrans :: STMState -> IO ()
343  commitTrans state =
344     robustMapM_ (doCommitAction (stmId state))
345                 (stmCommitLog state)
```

The new `TVar` values of the active transaction are committed (line 348) and the dependent transactions are notified (line 349) executing the logged actions. Reactive transactions are simply sent a message (line 352) advancing their automaton state as described in Section 6.3.3. Note that before delegating the commit actions to the reactive transactions, we execute possibly logged register `TVar` commands (line 351) for `TVars` included in the committed values. Hence, the register commands are executed before exporting the `TVars`.

```
346  doCommitAction :: TransID -> CommitLog -> IO ()
347  doCommitAction _ (env, Left idCommits) = do
348     mapM_ (commitAct.snd) idCommits
349     mapM_ (notifyAct.snd) idCommits
350  doCommitAction trId (env, Right (_, regAct)) = do
351     regAct
352     remPutMsg env (RemContTrans trId Com)
```

169

6. Implementing Robustness

Every transaction includes a terminal protocol call to `endTrans`. It is called once for both, valid and invalid transactions independent of the transaction result. We map, again using the robust version, `doEndAction` over the `ValidLog` dictionary.

```
353  endTrans :: STMState -> IO ()
354  endTrans state =
355     robustMapM_ (doEndAction (stmId state))
356                 (stmValidLog state)
```

We terminate the active transaction unlocking all `TVars` (line 359) and reactive transactions by advancing their automaton state (line 361).

```
357  doEndAction :: TransID -> ValidLog -> IO ()
358  doEndAction _ (env, Left stLog) =
359     mapM_ (unLockAct.snd) (fst stLog)
360  doEndAction trId (env, Right stIds) =
361     remPutMsg env (RemContTrans trId End)
```

6.4. Synchronization Caveats

The major part of this chapter and this book, in general, discusses distributed software transaction synchronization. The goal is to free the application programmer as much as possible from thinking about deadlocks when designing programs. Depending on the particular application program, this can be very challenging for a Robust DSTM library as the solution has to work for every possible schedule.

6.4.1. Protocol Inversion

Even very simple application programs might generate deadlocks with our current Robust DSTM implementation. Each philosopher in the distributed example of the STM-based Dining Philosopher application program, illustrated in Chapter 3, is represented by an tail-recursive function in a separate process. In each function iteration we atomically check the value of two separate `TVars`, symbolizing the sticks. We either rewrite the sticks or suspend the function, depending on the stick value. Different philosopher processes mutually share the stick `TVars`. Our example application is designed such that each process

6.4. Synchronization Caveats

Time	$phil_1$ STM	$phil_1$ Library	$phil_2$ STM	$phil_2$ Library
...	...	...	...	...
t_1	retry	suspend		
t_2			writeTVar $tvar_1$	commit
t_3				notify
t_4			writeTVar $tvar_2$	commit
t_5				notify
t_6		resume		
t_7	readTVar $tvar_1$	read		
t_8	readTVar $tvar_2$	read		read
t_9		commit		
t_{10}		notify		
...	...	...	...	...

⟶ Control flow

Table 6.7.: Protocol Inverting Schedule

works with one TVar hosted in the current process and one TVar hosted in a cooperating process.

Assuming two processes, $phil_1$ hosting $tvar_1$ and $phil_2$ hosting $tvar_2$, the schedule shown in Table 6.7 results in an inconsistent application, thus, leading to a possible deadlock. Table 6.7 symbolizes the execution of a small portion of the program separated into STM application program statements (STM) and Robust DSTM Library actions (Library) each shown for two philosopher processes ($phil_1$, $phil_2$) at consecutive points in time (Time). The library actions printed in regular font symbolize active transaction execution. Actions printed in *italic* font denote reactive transactions controlled in the current process and executed in the other process.

At time t_2 process $phil_2$ writes $tvar_1$ hosted in process $phil_2$. The reactive transaction in process $phil_1$ synchronizes the commit and notify actions using a channel (see Section 6.3.2) and executes them at t_9 and t_{10}[3]. Before that, however, $phil_1$, resumed by the notify action executed by $phil_2$ at t_5, reads

---
[3]Note that both commit and notify use asynchronous unidirectional messaging.

6. Implementing Robustness

$tvar_1$ at t_7 which contains an inconsistent not yet committed value. The order of the circled library protocol actions is inverted. We read a logically committed value before it is actually physically committed thus leading to an inconsistent view of the transaction.

We could prohibit this protocol inversion using bidirectional communication for commit messages thus forcing a synchronization between the process writing a TVar and the process hosting this TVar. This solution would, however, reduce a possible parallel execution and, thus, the performance of the distributed system.

We found a more efficient solution taking advantage of the fact that to be committed TVars are locked until the transaction has ended reaching its final state. We also lock TVars even when they are just read. Thereby, we synchronize each read command with possibly pending reactive transactions only when necessary without additional communication. Thus, we encapsulate reading a host TVar value in coreReadTVar as described in Section 5.5 with a read lock (line 553). Similarly, we lock the read stub in the TVar actions dictionary (see Section 4.3).

```
552  coreReadTVar   :: Dist a => TVar a -> IO (a,VersionID)
553  coreReadTVar (TVar tVarRef _ lock _) =
554    takeMVar lock
555    v <- readMVar tVarRef
556    putMVar lock ()
557    return v
558  coreReadTVar (LinkTVar (VarLink tEnv tId)) = do
559    ...
```

6.4.2. Transaction Trap

The authors of the original Haskell STM abstraction highlight a possible problem with STM implementations [HMPJH05]. We assume a transaction $trans_a$ (line 560) reading two TVars $tvar_1$ and $tvar_2$ while another transaction $trans_b$ (line 567) writes new values to the same TVars. Note that similar problems arise when reading either two different TVars or the same TVar twice.

Further, assuming the schedule illustrated in Figure 6.8 where $trans_a$ first reads $tvar_1$ followed by $trans_b$ modifying both $tvar_1$ and $tvar_2$ followed by $trans_a$ reading $tvar_2$. Then, $trans_a$ reads an inconsistent view on its TVars hence invalidating the atomic transaction.

6.4. Synchronization Caveats

A problem exists, however, if $trans_a$ evaluates both read values *before* the atomic validation. The transaction program might then unintentionally loop forever because of inconsistently read values, prohibiting the transactional validation. The application designer, however, assumes consistent transactions. Such an inconsistent transaction evaluation would then lead to an incorrect application program.

```
560  transA :: TVar Int -> TVar Int -> IO ()
561  transA tVar1 tVar2 = do
562    atomic $ do
563      v1 <- readTVar tVar1
564      -- transB might commit here
565      v2 <- readTVar tVar2
566      if v1 == v2 then retry else loop

567  transB :: TVar Int -> TVar Int -> IO ()
568  transB tVar1 tVar2 = do
569    atomic $ do
570      writeTVar tVar1 1
571      writeTVar tVar2 1

572  main = do
573    tVar1 <- atomic $ newTVar 0
574    tVar2 <- atomic $ newTVar 0
575    forkIO (transA tVar1 tVar2)
576    transB tVar1 tVar2
```

The original low-level concurrent STM implementation solves this problem by validating each transaction after a context switch. This is feasible because the low-level implementation has access to the scheduler itself and because memory comparisons are relatively inexpensive in a concurrent environment.

High-level concurrent and distributed implementations ought to be scheduler independent. The approach in [HK05] suggests a partial solution to maintain consistency with repeatedly read **TVar**s within a transaction. As mentioned in [Rec08], a comprehensive but expensive solution includes an additional transaction validation whenever reading a **TVar**. Naturally, in a distributed environment the resulting additional network messages are hardly acceptable.

An innovative and promising solution for the transaction validation problem, indicated in [Rec08], has been implemented in a concurrent STM library in [Sch09a]. The idea is to invert the validation approach of the regular STM protocol. It is based on the fact that the protocol already uses a mechanism

6. Implementing Robustness

Time	$trans_a$		$trans_b$	
	STM	Library	STM	Library
...	...	...	...	...
t_1	readTVar $tvar_1$	read ←		→ read
t_2			writeTVar $tvar_1$	commit
t_3				notify
t_4			writeTVar $tvar_2$	commit
t_5				notify
t_6	readTVar $tvar_2$	read ←		→ read
...	...	...	...	...

⟶ Control flow

Table 6.8.: Inconsistent Transaction Schedule

to notify suspended transactions which essentially is an invalidation message. The transaction state causing the suspension is no longer consistent. Therefore, restarting the transaction makes sense. The implementation now modifies the notification mechanism to become an invalidation mechanism completely replacing the former validation protocol.

Therefore, reading a TVar immediately extends its wait queue with the transaction information rather than performing all wait queue extension actions just before a suspension. Notified transactions that have not been suspended no longer ignore these notifications but use this information to invalidate themselves. Such an invalidation check can be implemented as an inexpensive token check performed both, whenever reading a TVar and during the commit phase replacing the regular validation protocol. It might even be efficient to perform this check more often as it makes no sense to proceed any further with already invalid transactions.

Our implementation currently shows the aforementioned scheduling problem. We believe that most applications will naturally avoid program constructs evoking such errors, however, it is good practice to fix that problem in an update of our distributed implementation.

Chapter 7

Conclusions and Related Work

The Robust Distributed Software Transactional Memory library presented in this book is in itself a combination of two computing abstractions. It provides a synchronization interface for concurrent computations and combines it with a communication interface for distributed applications.

Although this combination in itself is not unique, the fact that the presented library is entirely written in a pure[1], lazy, strongly typed functional language, to the best of our knowledge, is new. While we have discussed the benefits of Haskell in Chapter 2 in general, its strong type system is especially advantageous to the application programmer when using the STM abstraction to enforce the separation of synchronizing transactional and independent actions. Note that we have used the unsafe function `unsafePerformIO` exclusively to implement global variables. A pure solution would be to replace all global variables by implicit parameters. However, we used the more readable and more efficient approach described in [Mar02].

7.1. Conclusion

With this book, we have presented a distributed implementation of the software transactional paradigm for the functional language Haskell taking full benefit from its strict type system.

We effectively liberate the application programmer from worrying about accidentally creating deadlocks when designing a distributed system. Adding robustness becomes as simple as eliminating erroneous transactional variables

---

[1] Although we use an impure language extension, we adhere to the pure concept of Haskell.

7. Conclusions and Related Work

from the application and replacing them by redundant ones to ensure continued services.

With DSTM we have created an abstraction for fault-tolerance, raising distributed programming to a new level, similar to the STM abstraction for synchronization. As a domain specific communication implementation, our library is able to react to process node and communication failures, abstracting from the concrete application. This failure abstraction in turn relieves the programmer from completely understanding the failure details and from recovering on low communication levels.

In this book, we have developed and shown low-level communication enhancements to raise the library performance onto a level where it can be used even for soft real-time applications. We have shown a non-trivial example application together with a performance comparison.

7.2. Transactional Systems

The STM abstraction we chose as the basis of our work is not unique. In recent years a huge amount of work has been published on transactions and especially on software transactions. We show exemplary adaptions to other languages and proposed improvements to the Haskell STM abstraction.

7.2.1. Data Invariants

The Software Transactional Memory Interface used as the basis for our work meanwhile has been augmented by transactional data invariants described in [HPJ06]. The idea is to enable the application programmer to assert arbitrary conditions on transactional variables used within atomic transactions *before* the transaction commits. The programmer would add transactional invariant statements to one of the application transactions. Then this invariant would be checked before committing this transaction and, in case it fails, exit the uncommitted transaction with a raised exception. After adding such an invariant, all invariants are checked in all subsequent transactions. Transactional invariants are implemented in the ghc STM library and in the lightweight transactional memory implementation used in [Rec08]. In a possible distributed implementation the transactional protocol remotely executes each invariant in the process where it had been created.

7.2. Transactional Systems

7.2.2. STM optimizations

Being an abstraction, the transactional paradigm to synchronize concurrent and distributed systems potentially reduces the overall performance. It obeys schematic protocols. Hand-crafted solutions might lead to more efficient solutions. This sets the goal to improve the protocols used in the STM libraries themselves.

The empirical observations on different transactional approaches shown in [DS06] support the naive notion that the shorter the locking period of the transactional variables is, the better the overall performance will be. Therefore, an individual locking of variables that have been read in a transaction, the read-set, and those that ought to be written in a transaction, the write-set, might be worth investigating.

A different optimization approach, presented in [HPST06], suggests lower level measures like decomposing the concise STM API enabling the application programmer to give optimization hints. Then, the compiler more efficiently performs its code optimizations on the decomposed library calls. Although this approach seems realistic, especially in concurrent rather than distributed systems, we see a disadvantage in decomposing a concise and easy-to-use interface because it diminishes the transactional abstraction for the application programmer.

A technique, recently proposed in [GVS10], is switching from commit-time validation to commit-time *in*validation claiming a speed improvement of up to three times. Instead of validating each transaction at the beginning of its commit phase to determine the commit decision, each commit attempt analyzes existing validation conflicts before the actual commit. Then the transactional system decides to solve these conflicts by either aborting the commit, suspending the commit, or invalidating the other transactions.

In our view, this is a very promising attempt. It resembles the implementation in [Sch09a] where each successful commit invalidates potentially conflicting transactions. Both findings differ in their locking and consequently serializing strategy. Additional research is necessary to adapt either solution to our distributed approach.

7.2.3. STM in Mainstream Languages

Implementations of the software transactional memory paradigm, some of which are referred to in this book, are not unique to Haskell. The functional program-

7. Conclusions and Related Work

ming language is potentially at the verge of evolving to an immortal language, though not quite there [PJ07]. In fact, the implementation in [ST95], coining the notion STM, is imperative, like most STM implementations thereafter. STM has been well adapted to mainstream languages like C/C++ and Java. However, by definition, the aforementioned imperative languages seem to be only second best to implement an STM abstraction. They are not referentially transparent and do not encapsulate side effects with a sophisticated type system like Haskell does.

Thus, the program data cannot easily be segregated into transactional and other mutable data. This problem leads to more complex transactional definitions, like *strong* and *weak atomicity* [BLM06] and the respective implementations like a Java based strong atomicity solution in [SMAT[+]07]. Essentially, the strong atomicity implementation statically analyzes the program code to detect transactional memory accesses and encapsulates them automatically within a transaction. Weak atomicity leaves the responsibility to access transactional memory exclusively within transactional code with the application programmer [MBS[+]08].

Languages featuring even less type safety consequently put an even bigger liability on the application designer. The C/C++ implementation API in [NWAT[+]08] features constructs to let the programmer assert to the compiler that a transaction uses only pure code or not. Furthermore, transactional exceptions inevitably lead to committing the transaction, simply because it is impossible to implement otherwise. This leads to an, in our view, unexpected semantics because the exception, causing the transaction commitment, might not have been raised in the first place in an invalid transaction.

In the end, the interesting question is, how large the benefit of such complex STM semantics compared to the simpler lock-based solutions is. In our view, the benefit to the application designer cannot, by far, be compared with Haskell based solutions.

7.3. Distributed Systems

The advances in computer hardware development originally motivated the rise of distributed systems (see Section 2.2.1). Nowadays, a general language needs to support distribution, in our view. This includes also functional languages. We show exemplary implementations of distributed functional languages.

7.3. Distributed Systems

7.3.1. Erlang

Erlang is a concurrent functional programming language with strict evaluation. The principal design decision of installing lightweight processes, exclusively using message passing synchronization banning shared resources, and a process *link* mechanism[2], enables highly fault tolerant programs. Erlang processes are so lightweight that a system can easily cope with hundreds of thousands of them. Distribution is seamlessly integrated into Erlang, although not implemented in its beginnings.

The Erlang white paper [Eri09] describes the programming language as sharing many features commonly associated with an operating system like concurrent processes, scheduling, distribution, networking, and hot code swapping. The thesis [Arm03] supports that fault-tolerance of distributed large-scale programs is fundamental to Erlang. A very concise rendition is that *Erlang was designed for writing concurrent programs that "run forever"* [Arm07]. Several highly robust industrial applications, containing up to millions of lines of Erlang code, validate this claim.

While Erlang focuses clearly on concurrency and fault tolerance, features found in other functional languages are missing. Besides not being lazy, the programmer cannot enforce purity as there is no static type system. Hence, Erlang programs are not, in general, referentially transparent. Although a missing type system and possible side effects tend to lead to more programming faults, in practice, the built-in fault tolerance mechanisms seem to compensate for that. An approach to combine the Erlang message passing style with pure and strictly typed Haskell has been made in [Huc99].

7.3.2. Curry

Curry is a functional logic programming language [HKMN95]. It has much of its roots in Haskell, adding non-deterministic choice with overlapping rules and free (logic) variables to design logic programs like with Prolog. One of these additions is already sufficient [AH06] to allow logic programming. Curry supports application driven, concurrent constraint solving, synchronized on logic variables.

Like Haskell, Curry is strongly typed and provides lazy evaluation. Other than Haskell, it lacks function overloading with type classes and thus monads

---

[2]One process installs a link to another process. If the linked-to process fails, the linking process gets a failure notification.

7. Conclusions and Related Work

except the explicit monadic IO. However, there is experimental work on adding type classes to Curry [Ber04] as well.

In [Han99] a distributed extension to Curry is shown. It provides process synchronization on logic variables, based on asynchronous communication which is integrated as constraints into ports. It smoothly interacts with the functional logic language.

7.3.3. Oz

Oz [VRH02, VRH04] is a programming language combining the claimed essential features of object-oriented, functional, and logic languages. It supports concurrent and distributed programming using data flow dependent thread blocking and transparent network distribution.

The language Oz adopts and mixes abstractions from object-oriented languages like Java, functional languages like Haskell, Scheme, Erlang and Curry, logical languages like Prolog and Curry, concurrent systems like Curry and Distributed Haskell, and distributed systems like Erlang and Curry. Oz is dynamically typed.

As a multi-paradigm language both syntax and semantics of Oz are quite overwhelming[3]. As an example, Oz knows both procedures and functions which the programmer should use at his discretion. Also, there are multiple paradigms for synchronization like locks and logic variables.

One of the main Oz notions is the *entity*. There are stateful, single assignment, and stateless entities. The former encompass objects enabling three different distribution strategies, threads, ports, cells as mutable object links, and thread-reentrant locks. Single assignment entities consist of logic variables, futures as read-only logical variables, and logic variable streams. The latter category contains procedures and records, both with further derivates.

The application programmer selects from a choice of many configurable strategies to distribute entities. One example is entity replication using an atomic Two-Phase Commit protocol. The run-time system offers automatic distributed garbage collection, dynamic code update similar to Erlang, and failure handling by assigning a fault stream to every entity listing all occurred faults. Distributed entity faults are limited to permanent failure of the distributed node like in our DSTM library.

---

[3] As a lighthearted note with respect to the DSTM library, Oz defines an `orelse` function which other than the transactional function with that name is the Oz version of a lazy Boolean `or` function. Oz uses strict evaluation, in general.

7.3.4. Glasgow Distributed Haskell

Glasgow Distributed Haskell (GdH) extends Concurrent Haskell to support the distribution of threads and their synchronization, both, explicitly by the programmer and implicitly by Gdh itself [PTL01]. GdH establishes implicit communication by allowing IO actions to be executed as distributed closures similar to Java remote message invocations and explicit communication by a distributed version of mutable variables.

Fault tolerance is realized through the extension of the Haskell exception mechanism to distributed systems. Exceptions can be thrown across process boundaries. However, the described implementation currently cannot guarantee program consistency in the advent of faults.

7.3.5. Haskell with Ports

The idea to build a communication and synchronization paradigm with ports, known also from the languages Oz and Curry, is adapted to Haskell with Ports [HN00]. Ports are abstract communication entities that can be communicated themselves. A name server controls the initial exchange. Ports allow a dynamic program design. We use a similar technique with distributed **TVars** in DSTM. However, while ports loose their type information when communicated back and forth, our reimported **TVars** can still be accessed in a properly typed manner. Here, ports are restricted to be written by multiple processes and read from just one process. There is a mechanism to realize basic robustness by a link surveillance of processes and fault tolerant port writing.

7.3.6. Holumbus

In [Sch09b] a distributed storage system based on Holumbus, a Haskell framework for creating powerful indexing and search applications [Sch10], is described. It uses a domain-specific port-based communication implementation. It extends port-based unidirectional messages with precautions for submitting replies similar to our intermediate dedicated line approach. A further efficiency improvement to Holumbus communication might be realizable with our line stack solution.

7. Conclusions and Related Work

7.4. Future Work

Our DSTM implementation has already gone through some, in part significant, refactoring. However, there is some promising work worth doing, in our view.

The protocol flaw described in Section 6.4.2 should be repaired by reverting the validation protocol. In turn, this would enable further protocol efficiency improvements most likely leading to an even more scalable library. We expect the necessary effort to be moderate.

The API should be augmented with assertions enabling the application programmer to write more efficient and concise transactional code. The implementation effort should be moderate, as well.

In this work, we restrict the robustness of our library to the total or permanent failure of a distributed system process. This obviously excludes some practical cases where processes provide fluctuating services as it is typical for mobile network devices. A future DSTM library, properly handling temporal process node failures and fluctuating communication, would clearly realize an additional benefit to the application programmer. Unfortunately, this is a very complex subject. Such a system would have to deal with situations where a fault has been detected and the recovery is progressing while the fault vanishes and hence the system would probably have to recover from the recovery process. We envision a significant effort implementing transactional memory robustness for fluctuating services.

Once, the next generation DSTM protocol has been defined, it makes sense to refactor this protocol to improve the communication efficiency by further bundling independent, asynchronous messages that a transaction exchanges between participating nodes.

Appendix A

Application Programming

The presented Distributed Software Transactional Memory (DSTM) library enables the designer of robust distributed applications to focus on the application logic itself rather than on complex synchronization techniques. This appendix explains the requirements to use our library. The application programmer needs to:

- Initialize the distributed functionality
- Run a name server application on one node
- Register with the name server `TVars` to be shared with other nodes
- Lookup from the name server `TVars` shared from other nodes

The application programmer should encapsulate each of the node main programs in a `startDist` call to properly initialize the distributed system.

A.1. Name Server

The name server thread maintains a dictionary of distributed link `TVars` (line 1). It accepts messages of type `NameServerMsg` to register, unregister, and lookup `TVars` (line 2).

The application programmer starts a name server implicitly on every node within the distributed system. We show the straightforward name server thread (lines 5–26). It creates a socket listening on a TCP port we have randomly chosen from the private port section [IAN10], continuously checks for messages, and maintains the `TVar` dictionary depending on the received messages.

183

A. Application Programming

```
1  type TVarDict = [(String, VarLink)]

2  data NameServerMsg = Reg    String VarLink
3                    | UnReg  String
4                    | Lookup String
```

Note that we create a new connection for every name server message (lines 11, 15) unlike the optimized DSTM communication. Name server communication occurs relatively seldom in a distributed system. Also, note that we unregister a possibly registered **TVar** before registering it, thus, remapping the dictionary entry (line 21).

```
5  nameService :: IO ()
6  nameService = do
7      s <- listenOn (PortNumber 60000)
8      readMsg [] s

9  readMsg :: TVarDict -> Socket -> IO ()
10 readMsg tVarDict s = do
11     (h, _, _) <- accept s
12     str <- hGetLine h
13     newTable <- case reads str of
14         ((msg,_):_) -> handleMsg h msg tVarDict
15     hClose h
16     readMsg newTable s

17 handleMsg :: Handle -> NameServerMsg -> TVarDict
18               -> IO TVarDict
19 handleMsg h msg tVarDict = case msg of
20     Reg name tVar -> return $
21         (name, tVar) : filter ((name/=) . fst) tVarDict
22     UnReg name -> return $
23         filter ((name/=) . fst) tVarDict
24     Lookup name -> do
25         hPutStrLn h (toString (lookup name tVarDict))
26         return tVarDict
```

The DSTM library interface provides functions for a proper communication with the name server. The application should use **registerTVar** to register a **TVar** with its name server. Note that the function also registers the **TVar** actions with the library (line 31) because of a potential **TVar** export out of the host process. The **deregisterTVar** function is added for completeness. It is not required in a DSTM system.

A.1. Name Server

```
27  registerTVar :: Dist a => TVar a -> String -> IO ()
28  registerTVar tVar name = do
29    putServerLn "localhost"
30                (Reg name (tVarToLink tVar))
31    regTVars gMyEnv tVar


32  deregisterTVar :: String -> IO ()
33  deregisterTVar name =
34    putServerLn "localhost" (UnReg name)
```

The `lookupTVar` function provides the interface to reveal a `TVar` from a name server. It also properly handles finalizing the registered `TVar` actions (line 42). Note that we annotate the `TVar` type when converting the generic link `TVar` (line 41) thus enabling the type system to select the type correct `finTVars` instance. In order to use the type variable `a` inside the function body we have to declare it `forall` quantified.

```
35  lookupTVar :: forall a . Dist a =>
36                String -> String -> IO (Maybe (TVar a))
37  lookupTVar server name = do
38    answer <- getServerLn server (Lookup name)
39    case fromString answer of
40      Just link -> do
41        let tVar::TVar a = LinkTVar link
42        finTVars tVar
43        return (Just tVar)
44      _ -> return Nothing
```

The message exchange routines `putServerLn` and `getServerLn` form the counterpart to the simple socket communication described before.

```
45  putServerLn :: String -> a -> IO ()
46  putServerLn nameServer msg = do
47    h <- connectTo nameServer (PortNumber 60000)
48    hPutStrLn h (toString msg)
49    hClose h


50  getServerLn :: String -> a -> IO String
51  getServerLn nameServer msg = do
52    h <- connectTo nameServer (PortNumber 60000)
53    hPutStrLn h (toString msg)
54    hFlush h
```

A. Application Programming

```
55    answer <- hGetLine h
56    hClose h
57    return answer
```

In addition to `lookupTVar`, the name server provides a `lookupWaitTVar` function to reveal a `TVar` even if its name is not yet known to the server. The name server repeatedly tries to resolve the name during a period of time, defined in seconds by a timeout parameter. The function returns immediately after a successful `TVar` lookup or after the timeout period with a `Nothing` result.

```
58  lookupWaitTVar :: forall a . Dist a =>
59                    String -> Int -> String
60                    -> IO (Maybe (TVar a))
61  lookupWaitTVar server timeout name =
62    parIO (repeatGetServerLn server name)
63          (threadDelay (timeout * 1000000)
64           >> return Nothing)


65  repeatGetServerLn :: forall a . Dist a =>
66                       String -> String
67                       -> IO (Maybe (TVar a))
68  repeatGetServerLn server name = do
69    answer <- getServerLn server (Lookup name)
70    case fromString answer of
71      Just link -> do
72        let tVar::TVar a = LinkTVar link
73        finTVars tVar
74        return $ Just tVar
75      _ -> repeatGetServerLn server name
```

The timeout mechanism uses the `parIO` function (line 76) described in [PJ01].

```
76  parIO :: IO a -> IO a -> IO a
77  parIO a1 a2 = do
78    m <- newEmptyMVar
79    c1 <- forkIO (a1 >>= putMVar m)
80    c2 <- forkIO (a2 >>= putMVar m)
81    r <- takeMVar m
82    killThread c1
83    killThread c2
84    return r
```

In the next section we show the complete DSTM library application programmer interface (API) for reference.

A.2. Complete DSTM Library API

```
85   data STM a    -- abstract
86   instance Monad STM

87   -- Running STM computations
88   atomic :: STM a -> IO a
89   retry  :: STM a
90   orElse :: STM a -> STM a -> STM a

91   -- Transactional variables
92   data TVar a    -- abstract

93   newTVar   :: Dist a => a -> STM (TVar a)
94   readTVar  :: Dist a => TVar a -> STM a
95   writeTVar :: Dist a => TVar a -> a -> STM ()

96   -- Exceptions
97   throw :: SomeException -> STM a
98   catch :: STM a -> (SomeException -> STM a) -> STM a

99   -- Additional distributed interface
100  class Serializable a => Dist a where
101    regTVars :: EnvAddr -> a -> IO ()
102    finTVars :: a -> IO ()

103  runDist         :: IO a -> IO a
104  registerTVar    :: Dist a =>
105                     TVar a -> String -> IO ()
106  deregisterTVar  :: String -> IO ()
107  lookupTVar      :: Dist a =>
108                     String -> String
109                     -> IO (Maybe (TVar a))
110  lookupWaitTVar  :: Dist a =>
111                     String -> Int -> String
112                     -> IO (Maybe (TVar a))

113  -- Additional robustness interface
114  data SomeDistTVarException    -- abstract

115  isDistErrTVar :: SomeDistTVarException -> TVar a -> Bool
```

Appendix B

Sample Applications

This appendix shows three example DSTM applications, each focusing on a special aspect of using our library. The first application is a distributed version of the classic *Dining Philosophers* problem used to demonstrate problems of and solutions for concurrent and distributed programming. We use it as an example to introduce the basic idea of designing an application with distributed TVars.

The next application is a simple internet *chat* program. With this example we show how to use a custom data type for TVar values and thus how to define class Dist instance functions that unwrap the custom TVar type constructors. We also introduce the usage of the library robustness functions to make the application itself robust against unexpected faults like suddenly unavailable chat participants.

Our final example is a distributed *bomberman* game implementation. Naturally, the focus is on the application being a useful example of utilizing our library rather than the game being a breathtaking entertainment. We use this example, however, to show that the DSTM library can be used also in a soft real-time environment like a distributed game and scales well with a larger amount of TVars. Also, we make a more elaborate approach to application robustness in case of disappearing game participants.

B.1. Dining Philosophers

The hallmark example of a concurrent application is the *Dining Philosophers* problem formulated by Edsger Wybe Dijkstra in 1971. We show a simple distributed example program running each one of a total of three philosopher processes. Each process is initialized with a unique number as argument.

B. Sample Applications

We import the DSTM library `DistributedSTM` in line 2. We synchronize solely on the sticks between the philosophers modeled as `TVar`s of type `Bool` (line 6). For simplicity we run all philosopher processes on the same process node. Figure B.1 symbolizes the output of three philosopher processes just started, each on a separate terminal shell.

```
1  module Main where
2  import DistributedSTM
3  import Prelude
4  import System
5  import System.IO

6  type Stick = TVar Bool

7  takeStick :: Stick -> STM ()
8  takeStick s = do
9    b <- readTVar s
10   if b
11     then writeTVar s False
12     else retry

13 putStick :: Stick -> STM ()
14 putStick s = writeTVar s True

15 phil :: Int -> Int -> Stick -> Stick -> IO ()
16 phil i n l r = do
17   atomic $ do
18     takeStick l
19     takeStick r
20   putStrLn (show n ++ ". Phil is eating "++show i)
21   atomic $ do
22     putStick l
23     putStick r
24   phil (i+1) n l r

25 main :: IO ()
26 main = startDist $ do
27   (arg:_) <- getArgs
28   let n = read arg
29   l <- atomic $ newTVar True
30   registerTVar l arg
31   (Just r) <- lookupWaitTVar "localhost" 60
32                     $ show ((n 'mod' 3) + 1)
33   phil 1 n l r
```

B.2. Chat

```
> main 1                  > main 2                  > main 3
1. Phil is eating 1       2. Phil is eating 1       3. Phil is eating 1
1. Phil is eating 2       2. Phil is eating 2       3. Phil is eating 2
1. Phil is eating 3       2. Phil is eating 3       3. Phil is eating 3
1. Phil is eating 4       2. Phil is eating 4       3. Phil is eating 4
1. Phil is eating 5       ...                       3. Phil is eating 5
1. Phil is eating 6                                 ...
...
```

Figure B.1.: Dining Philosopher Sample Output

B.2. Chat

The *chat* application is a classic example for a distributed program. An arbitrary number of users, each at a computer network connected to the internet, communicates with each other. There is one dedicated host server. The client users register with the server and subsequently send messages to the server which broadcasts them to all registered clients.

We show both, a simple chat server and a simple chat client communicating with each other using **TVars** to synchronize. Therefore, we design a custom data type **ServerCmd** providing commands to join (line 38) and leave (line 40) a chat and to distribute messages (line 39). The **ServerCmd** alternative *join* contains a mutually recursive defined type **CmdTVar** (line 43). This **TVar** may contain a command generated by a chat client and interpreted by the chat server.

In order for the DSTM library to properly communicate **TVars**, we make the custom **TVar** type an instance of type classes **Serializable** and **Dist** which are defined in respective modules (lines 36,37). Both, **regTVars** (line 45) and **finTVars** (line 47) methods unwrap the application defined constructor from the **TVar**. Alternatives containing no **TVars** simply return the unit value.

```
34  module ChatData where
35  import DistributedSTM
36  import Dist
37  import Serializable

38  data ServerCmd = Join String CmdTVar
39                 | Msg String String
40                 | Leave String
41     deriving (Show,Read)
```

B. Sample Applications

```
42  instance Serializable ServerCmd

43  type CmdTVar = TVar (Maybe ServerCmd)

44  instance Dist ServerCmd where
45    regTVars env (Join _ cmd) = regTVars env cmd
46    regTVars _ _ = return ()

47    finTVars (Join _ cmd) = finTVars cmd
48    finTVars _ = return ()
```

We designate one **CmdTVar** to each participating process discriminating the chat server **TVar**. The chat server application registers its own **TVar** with the name server (line 60).

```
49  -- Chat Server
50  module Main where

51  import ChatData
52  import Control.Exception as CE
53  import DebugTrans
54  import DistributedSTM
55  import Maybe
56  import NameService

57  main :: IO ()
58  main = startDist $ do
59    inVar <- atomic $ newTVar Nothing
60    registerTVar inVar "Chat"
61    chatServer inVar []
```

The **chatServer** function (line 64) loops forever watching its **TVar** for client messages. It dynamically builds and updates a dictionary of all participating client **CmdTVar**s with the client name as key. The server realizes the watch mechanism by reading the **TVar** (line 66) and suspending itself calling **retry** if it contains **Nothing**. Note that it also reads all dictionary client **TVar**s without using their values (line 69) and suspends itself calling **retry**. We use this construct to perform a simple failure recovery. If some client becomes unavailable and no other client is sending a chat message, the transparent DSTM link mechanism still detects the fault and throws a library exception.

If the server **TVar** contains a chat command (line 71), it resets the message, broadcasts a corresponding message to all dictionary clients, and maintains the dictionary accordingly.

B.2. Chat

```
62  chatServer :: CmdTVar -> [(String, CmdTVar)]
63                 -> IO ()
64  chatServer inCmd dict = CE.catch (do
65    newDict <- atomic $ do
66      cmd <- readTVar inCmd
67      case cmd of
68        Nothing -> do
69                   mapM_ (readTVar . snd) dict
70                   retry
71        Just serverCmd -> do
72          writeTVar inCmd Nothing
73          case serverCmd of
74            Join name msgVar -> do
75              mapM_ (flip writeTVar msg . snd) dict
76              return ((name,msgVar): dict)
77              where msg = Just (Msg name " joint")
78            Msg _ _ -> do
79              mapM_ (flip writeTVar cmd . snd) dict
80              return dict
81            Leave name -> do
82              mapM_ (flip writeTVar msg . snd) d
83              return d
84              where msg = Just (Msg name " left")
85                    d = filter ((/=name) . fst) dict
86    chatServer inCmd newDict
87    )
88    (\e -> chatServer inCmd (removeErrDict e dict))
```

We catch any **SomeDistTVarException** arising from unavailable **TVars**. Hence, we detect unexpectedly disappearing chat clients and continue the server loop with a dictionary cleaned from any disappeared client (line 88). The DSTM predicate **isDistErrTVar** facilitates the erroneous **TVar** detection (line 93).

```
89  removeErrDict :: SomeDistTVarException
90                 -> [(String, CmdTVar)]
91                 -> [(String, CmdTVar)]
92  removeErrDict e dict =
93    [d | d <- dict, not (isDistErrTVar e (snd d))]
```

The chat client application first looks up the chat server represented by its **CmdTVar** (line 106). If found, it joins the chat submitting its new empty client **TVar** (line 112). Then the client starts **stdinClient** to manage the user input and **serverClient** to handle chat server messages.

193

B. Sample Applications

```
94  -- Chat Client
95  module Main where

96  import ChatData
97  import Control.Concurrent
98  import DistributedSTM
99  import Maybe
100 import NameService
101 import System.IO

102 main :: IO ()
103 main = startDist $ do
104   putStrLn "Your Name: "
105   name <- getLine
106   serverTVar <- lookupTVar "localhost" "Chat"
107   case serverTVar of
108     Nothing -> putStrLn "Chat server not reachable"
109     Just cmdTVar -> do
110       myTVar <- atomic $ do
111         new <- newTVar Nothing
112         writeTVar cmdTVar (Just (Join name new))
113         return new
114       forkIO (serverClient myTVar)
115       stdinClient name cmdTVar
```

We simply encode any user message into a client `TVar` command (line 125). If the user message is to terminate the chat, we encode the according command (line 122) and terminate the client itself.

```
116 stdinClient :: String -> CmdTVar -> IO ()
117 stdinClient name cmdTVar = do
118   putStrLn (name ++ " >")
119   msg <- getLine
120   if msg == "bye"
121     then atomic $
122       writeTVar cmdTVar (Just (Leave name))
123     else do
124       atomic $
125         writeTVar cmdTVar (Just (Msg name msg))
126       stdinClient name cmdTVar
```

The `serverClient` thread watches its own client `CmdTVar` (line 130), suspends using `retry` when there is no message, and prints and resets any received message.

B.2. Chat

```
127  serverClient :: CmdTVar -> IO ()
128  serverClient myTVar = do
129    s <- atomic $ do
130      cmd <- readTVar myTVar
131      case cmd of
132        Nothing -> retry
133        Just (Msg name msg) -> do
134          writeTVar myTVar Nothing
135          return (name ++ ": " ++ msg)
136        _ -> return ""
137    putStrLn s
138    serverClient myTVar
```

Note that the shown program is very elementary. A more useable chat application would probably synchronize using a transactional channel thus prohibiting the loss of single messages if the server is not able to respond to all requests in time.

```
> main                          > main
Your Name:                      Your Name:
Curry                           Haskell
Curry >                         Haskell >
Haskell: Hello Curry            Curry: joint
Oh, hi Haskell                  Hello Curry
Curry >                         Haskell >
Curry: Oh, hi Haskell           Haskell: Hello Curry
Haskell: Good to see you        Curry: Oh, hi Haskell
You Too. Got to go              Good to see you
Curry >                         Haskell >
Curry: You Too. Got to go       Haskell: Good to see you
bye                             Curry: You Too. Got to go
>                               Curry: left
                                ...
```

Figure B.2.: Chat Sample Output

Figure B.2 shows the output of a sample chat session with two clients. Note that we show each output in a self-contained sequence side by side with the other. There is no common time line among the two terminal transcripts.

B. Sample Applications

B.3. Bomberman

With the *bomberman* game application we provide a somewhat more complex distributed program probing the performance of the DSTM library in a soft real-time environment. The idea of the game is that all participating players move around in a shared game field. The players can walk in four directions. There is empty space allowing to walk around. There are arbitrary walls in the field to block the player from passing.

The goal is to eliminate the opponents by dropping bombs, hence, the name of the game. A dropped bomb explodes delayed to allow the player to leave the area. An exploding bomb destroys the field position it is on itself plus the four surrounding positions. Exploding bombs destroy wall elements and opponents and immediately ignite dropped but not yet exploded bombs. Figure B.3 shows a screen shot of the terminal of one player while gaming with two opponents.

```
W W W W W W W W W
W   @           W
W     W W W
W   W W W W
W     W W W
W  X X W W             o: player
W X X X X    .@        @: opponent
W  X X       .         .: bomb
W            o         X: explosion
W W                W   W: wall element
```

Figure B.3.: Bomberman Game Screen Shot

In this appendix section we describe the major design ideas behind our bomberman adaptation rather than every concrete implementation detail for the sake of clarity.

The bomberman main data structure is the `GameState` record of system states (lines 147–162) represented by various `TVars` properly synchronizing the process state view of each bomberman thread with other threads and with the other player processes. The game field (line 141) consists of rows and columns of possible field elements as shown in Figure B.3.

```
139  data Element = Empty | Wall | Player | Opponent
140               | Bomb | XPlosion
141  type Field   = [[Element]]
```

B.3. Bomberman

We design player positions as points, bombs as a list of points, and explosions surrounding each bomb as a list of lists of points. Each bomberman instance records its user commands as moves. A Dead move symbolizes a killed player.

```
142  data Point = Point Int Int
143  type Bombs = [Point]
144  type Xplos = [Bombs]

145  data Move = MoveLeft | MoveRight | MoveUp | MoveDown
146            | DropBomb | Dead
```

The GameState record consists of TVars like repaint (line 149) designed for *intra*-process synchronization [1] while others are designed for an additional *inter*-process synchronization like the repaints TVar (line 150).

```
147  data GameState = GameState {
148    move        :: TVar (Maybe Move),
149    repaint     :: TVar Bool,
150    repaints    :: TVar [TVar Bool],
151    field       :: TVar Field,
152    player      :: TVar Point,
153    opponents   :: TVar [TVar Point],
154    plBombs     :: TVar Bombs,
155    plXplosion  :: TVar Xplos,
156    plBCount    :: TVar Int,
157    bombs       :: TVar [TVar Bombs],
158    xplosion    :: TVar [TVar Xplos],
159    bCounts     :: TVar [TVar Int],
160    quit        :: TVar Bool,
161    quits       :: TVar [TVar Bool]
162  }
```

Each bomberman instance runs in either autonomous, master, or slave mode. The first mode is a concurrent one process game. The last two are used in a distributed game with exactly one master player and an arbitrary number of slave players. The master player hosts all unique status elements like the playing field. Each player hosts individual status elements like its next move.

After initialization, each player node starts the game calling launchGame. The function starts threads to concurrently display any change of the field elements (line 165), to control the player (line 166), and to read the user input

---
[1] We distinguish here between intra-process (thread to thread) and inter-process (node to node) synchronization for explanatory reasons, only. Its application is fully transparent.

B. Sample Applications

(line 167). The player thread, when dropping bombs, in turn forks a new thread for each bomb. Any bomb thread autonomously manages the behavior of its bomb including the delayed explosion.

```
163  launchGame :: GameState -> IO Int
164  launchGame gameState = do
165    forkIO (view gameState)
166    forkIO (player gameState)
167    input gameState
```

Table B.1 gives an overview of the synchronization task each TVar manages. We explain the idea behind it with the *repaint* example. A similar mechanism operates on the other TVar combinations.

Intra-Process TVars	Inter-TVars	View-	Input- Threads	Player-	Bomb-
	field	✗		✗	✗
move			✗	✗	
player		✗		✗	✗
	opponents	✗		(✗)	(✗)
repaint		✗			
	repaints	(✗)		✗	✗
plBombs plBlasts plBCount					✗ ✗ ✗
	bombs	✗		(✗)	(✗)
	blasts	✗		✗	✗
	bCounts	(✗)	✗	✗	✗
quit			✗		
	quits		✗		

Table B.1.: Regular ✗ and Recovery (✗) TVar Synchronization

Each player creates a repaint TVar predicate initialized to False. The view thread checks repaint and redraws the field if the predicate holds. Otherwise, the view retries thus suspending itself. The other threads set repaint to True whenever they change a field element and hence schedule a redraw. This mechanism is sufficient for a concurrent scenario with a single player.

B.3. Bomberman

In order to manage a distributed game we include a repaints TVar containing a list of repaint TVars. The master player hosts the repaints TVar. Each slave player hosts its own repaint TVar and inserts it into repaints. In this design, scheduling a redraw simply requires to set all repaint predicates in the repaints list. The view thread design is identical to the concurrent scenario.

We also provide system recovery in case of unavailable slave players. The other players, including the master, properly remove all references to the faulty player and continue with the game. The master itself is essential to our implementation of the game. However, one could implement recovery means to replace a faulty master player as well. Providing a backup master player or designing a system that enables clients to take over the master player functionality, however, results in a significantly higher system complexity.

The DSTM library requires all data types of TVar values to be made both a Serializable and a Dist type class instance. Other than the types used in the *chat* sample program (see Section B.2), the *bomberman* types are standard compound Haskell types like Maybe and [] for which we have already defined the necessary instance functions within the library. Therefore, we make the instance functions simply returning (). None of the custom data types include any TVars themselves (lines 171–179).

```
168  instance Serializable Move
169  instance Serializable Point
170  instance Serializable Element

171  instance Dist Move where
172     finTVars _    = return ()
173     regTVars _ _  = return ()

174  instance Dist Point where
175     finTVars _    = return ()
176     regTVars _ _  = return ()

177  instance Dist Element where
178     finTVars _    = return ()
179     regTVars _ _  = return ()
```

Appendix C

Proof of STM Monad Laws

In this appendix we show a semi-formal proof of the monad laws (Table C.1) of the STM monad that we implemented in the DSTM library. We have defined the STM monad similarly to other commonly used state monads that are based on the IO monad. Therefore, intuitively, we are confident that the STM monad obeys the monad laws.

left identity   return x >>= f   <=>   f x
right identity   m >>= return   <=>   m
associativity   (m >>= f) >>= g   <=>   m >>= (\x -> f x >>= g)

Table C.1.: Monad Laws

```
1  newtype STM a = STM (STMState -> IO (STMResult a))


2  data STMResult a =
3          Success STMState a
4        | Retry STMState
5        | Exception STMState
6                    Control.Exception.SomeException


7  instance Monad STM where
8     -- (>>=)  :: STM a -> (a -> STM b) -> STM b
9     (STM trans1) >>= f =
10        STM (\st -> do
```

201

C. Proof of STM Monad Laws

```
11                stmRes <- trans1 st
12                case stmRes of
13                  Success newSt v ->
14                    let (STM trans2) = f v
15                    in trans2 newSt
16                  Retry newSt ->
17                    return (Retry newSt)
18                  Exception newSt e ->
19                    return (Exception newSt e)
20                )
21    --return :: a -> STM a
22    return x = STM (\st -> return (Success st x))
```

We show a semi-formal proof and add some intuition to gain additional confidence that our implementation is not compromised or even invalidated by an incorrectly defined STM monad which is at the core of our implementation.

Note that we use a `newtype` definition of the STM monad. Haskell handles this constructor more efficiently than a data constructor. As a consequence, the constructor evaluates strictly and STM $\bot$ = $\bot$ holds, where $\bot$ denotes non-termination. Therefore, we may use let-floating in our proof.

We start each proof by inserting an arbitrary STM action `m` and an STM action `return` as required by the respective law. For the left and right identity proofs, we insert the STM action on the left hand side of the equation and apply equivalence transformations to reach the right hand side of the rule. For the associativity proof, we start on each side and motivate the equivalence of both sides intuitively.

The STM action `m` is of type `STM (STMState -> IO (STMResult a))`. We assume `m` to be expressed as `m = STM (\state -> io_return_stm)` and we assume `io_return_stm` to either return a value of type `IO (STMResult a)` or to be an arbitrary IO action `io` that returns a value of type `IO (STMResult a)`. Thus, we consider the following six cases for `io_return_stm`:

$$\text{io\_return\_stm}_1 = \text{return}\,(\text{Success state x}) \quad (C.1)$$
$$\text{io\_return\_stm}_2 = \text{return}\,(\text{Retry state}) \quad (C.2)$$
$$\text{io\_return\_stm}_3 = \text{return}\,(\text{Exception state}) \quad (C.3)$$
$$\text{io\_return\_stm}_4 = \text{io} \gg\!= \backslash x \to \text{io\_return\_stm}_1 \quad (C.4)$$
$$\text{io\_return\_stm}_5 = \text{io} \gg\!= \backslash x \to \text{io\_return\_stm}_2 \quad (C.5)$$
$$\text{io\_return\_stm}_6 = \text{io} \gg\!= \backslash x \to \text{io\_return\_stm}_3 \quad (C.6)$$

and a helper function s being the case expression within the STM monad (>>=) operator:

$$s = \backslash r \to \text{ case r of}$$
$$\text{Success newSt v} \to \text{let (STM tr2)} = \text{f v in tr2 newSt}$$
$$;\ldots \tag{C.7}$$

We use some side calculations to keep the proofs more concise. With the application of the IO monad associativity law ($\Leftrightarrow_a$), the application of the IO monad left identity law ($\Leftrightarrow_i$), and the insertion of equation (C.7) ($\Leftrightarrow_s$) the following equivalences hold:

$$\text{io\_return\_stm}_1 \ggg= s$$
$$\Leftrightarrow_a \text{ return (Success state x)} \ggg= s$$
$$\Leftrightarrow_i \text{ s (Success state x)}$$
$$\Leftrightarrow_s \text{ let (STM tr2)} = \text{f x in tr2 state} \tag{C.8}$$

$$\text{io\_return\_stm}_2 \ggg= s$$
$$\Leftrightarrow_a \text{ return (Retry state)} \ggg= s$$
$$\Leftrightarrow_i \text{ s (Retry state)}$$
$$\Leftrightarrow_s \text{ return (Retry state)} \tag{C.9}$$

$$\text{io\_return\_stm}_3 \ggg= s$$
$$\Leftrightarrow_a \text{ return (Exception state)} \ggg= s$$
$$\Leftrightarrow_i \text{ s (Exception state)}$$
$$\Leftrightarrow_s \text{ return (Exception state)} \tag{C.10}$$

C. Proof of STM Monad Laws

$$\begin{aligned}
&\texttt{io\_return\_stm}_4 \gg= \texttt{s} \\
\Leftrightarrow_a\ &\texttt{io} \gg= \backslash\texttt{x} \to (\texttt{return (Success state x)} \gg= \texttt{s}) \\
\Leftrightarrow_i\ &\texttt{io} \gg= \backslash\texttt{x} \to (\texttt{s (Success state x)}) \\
\Leftrightarrow_s\ &\texttt{io} \gg= \backslash\texttt{x} \to \texttt{let (STM tr2)} = \texttt{f x in tr2 state} \quad\text{(C.11)}
\end{aligned}$$

$$\begin{aligned}
&\texttt{io\_return\_stm}_5 \gg= \texttt{s} \\
\Leftrightarrow_a\ &\texttt{io} \gg= \backslash\texttt{x} \to (\texttt{return (Retry state)} \gg= \texttt{s}) \\
\Leftrightarrow_i\ &\texttt{io} \gg= \backslash\texttt{x} \to (\texttt{s (Retry state)}) \\
\Leftrightarrow_s\ &\texttt{io} \gg= \backslash\texttt{x} \to \texttt{return (Retry state)} \quad\text{(C.12)}
\end{aligned}$$

$$\begin{aligned}
&\texttt{io\_return\_stm}_6 \gg= \texttt{s} \\
\Leftrightarrow_a\ &\texttt{io} \gg= \backslash\texttt{x} \to (\texttt{return (Exception state)} \gg= \texttt{s}) \\
\Leftrightarrow_i\ &\texttt{io} \gg= \backslash\texttt{x} \to (\texttt{s (Exception state)}) \\
\Leftrightarrow_s\ &\texttt{io} \gg= \backslash\texttt{x} \to \texttt{return (Exception state)} \quad\text{(C.13)}
\end{aligned}$$

With the definition of m and the STM (>>=) operator the following holds:

$$\texttt{m} \gg= \texttt{f} \Leftrightarrow \texttt{STM }(\backslash\texttt{state} \to \texttt{io\_return\_stm} \gg= \texttt{s}) \quad\text{(C.14)}$$

Inserting (C.1)–(C.6) into (C.14) yields the following six cases using the above equivalences, (C.8)–(C.13), let floating, eta reduction, and the definition of m:

$$\begin{aligned}
&\texttt{STM }(\backslash\texttt{state} \to \texttt{io\_return\_stm}_1 \gg= \texttt{s}) \\
\Leftrightarrow\ &\texttt{f x} \quad\text{(C.15)}
\end{aligned}$$

$$\begin{aligned}
&\texttt{STM }(\backslash\texttt{state} \to \texttt{io\_return\_stm}_2 \gg= \texttt{s}) \\
\Leftrightarrow\ &\texttt{STM }(\backslash\texttt{state} \to \texttt{io\_return\_stm}_2) \\
\Leftrightarrow\ &\texttt{m} \quad\text{(C.16)}
\end{aligned}$$

$$\begin{aligned}
&\text{STM } (\backslash\text{state} \to \text{io\_return\_stm}_3 \ggg= s) \\
\Leftrightarrow\ &\text{STM } (\backslash\text{state} \to \text{io\_return\_stm}_3) \\
\Leftrightarrow\ &\text{m}
\end{aligned} \qquad (C.17)$$

$$\begin{aligned}
&\text{STM } (\backslash\text{state} \to \text{io\_return\_stm}_4 \ggg= s) \\
\Leftrightarrow\ &\text{STM } (\backslash\text{state} \to \text{io} \ggg= \backslash x \to \\
&\qquad \text{let } (\text{STM tr2}) = \text{f } x \\
&\qquad \text{in tr2 state})
\end{aligned} \qquad (C.18)$$

$$\begin{aligned}
&\text{STM } (\backslash\text{state} \to \text{io\_return\_stm}_5 \ggg= s) \\
\Leftrightarrow\ &\text{STM } (\backslash\text{state} \to \text{io\_return\_stm}_5) \\
\Leftrightarrow\ &\text{m}
\end{aligned} \qquad (C.19)$$

$$\begin{aligned}
&\text{STM } (\backslash\text{state} \to \text{io\_return\_stm}_6 \ggg= s) \\
\Leftrightarrow\ &\text{STM } (\backslash\text{state} \to \text{io\_return\_stm}_6) \\
\Leftrightarrow\ &\text{m}
\end{aligned} \qquad (C.20)$$

With equation (C.14), m = return x, the definition of STM return, and equations (C.1) and (C.15) we immediately get:

$$\text{return } x \ggg= f \Leftrightarrow f\ x \qquad (C.21)$$

which is the proof of the left identity law.

With equation (C.14), f = return, equation (C.15), and the definitions of m and STM return we get:

C. Proof of STM Monad Laws

$$\begin{aligned}&\mathtt{m} \ggg= \mathtt{return} \\ \Leftrightarrow\ &\mathtt{return\ x} \\ \Leftrightarrow\ &\mathtt{STM}\ (\backslash\mathtt{state} \to \mathtt{io\_return\_stm_1}) \\ \Leftrightarrow\ &\mathtt{m}\end{aligned} \qquad (C.22)$$

With equation (C.14), $\mathtt{f} = \mathtt{return}$, equation (C.18), the definitions of $\mathtt{m}$ and STM $\mathtt{return}$, pattern matching, and beta reduction we get:

$$\begin{aligned}&\mathtt{m} \ggg= \mathtt{return} \\ \Leftrightarrow\ &\mathtt{STM}\ (\backslash\mathtt{state} \to \mathtt{io} \ggg= \backslash\mathtt{x} \to \\ &\qquad \mathtt{let}\ (\mathtt{STM\ tr2}) = \mathtt{return\ x} \\ &\qquad \mathtt{in\ tr2\ state}) \\ \Leftrightarrow\ &\mathtt{STM}\ (\backslash\mathtt{state} \to \mathtt{io} \ggg= \backslash\mathtt{x} \to \\ &\qquad \mathtt{return}\ (\mathtt{Success\ state\ x})) \\ \Leftrightarrow\ &\mathtt{STM}\ (\backslash\mathtt{state} \to \mathtt{io\_return\_stm_4}) \\ \Leftrightarrow\ &\mathtt{m}\end{aligned} \qquad (C.23)$$

Equations (C.16), (C.17), (C.19), (C.20), (C.22), and (C.23) are the proof of the right identity law:

$$\mathtt{m} \ggg= \mathtt{return} \Leftrightarrow \mathtt{m} \qquad (C.24)$$

In order to proof the STM monad associativity law (C.33) we argue intuitively. We conclude ((C.25)–(C.33)) that if equivalence (C.32) holds then (C.33) holds also. One side of the equivalence ($\backslash\mathtt{x} \to \mathtt{s_f\ x} \ggg= \mathtt{s_g}$) can be seen as unwrapping the STM constructors of $\mathtt{f}$ and $\mathtt{g}$ individually, calculating the (>>=) operation and then bind the two wrapped results. The other side of the equivalence ($\mathtt{s_{fg}}$) first calculates the wrapped (>>=) operation of $\mathtt{f}$ and $\mathtt{g}$ and then unwraps the combined result.

We define three more case expression helper functions $s_f, s_g,$ and s_{fg}:

$$s_f = \backslash r \to \text{case } r \text{ of Success newSt } v \to \text{let (STM tr2)} = f\ v \text{ in tr2 newSt}; \ldots \quad (C.25)$$

$$s_g = \backslash r \to \text{case } r \text{ of Success newSt } v \to \text{let (STM tr2)} = g\ v \text{ in tr2 newSt}; \ldots \quad (C.26)$$

$$s_{fg} = \backslash r \to \text{case } r \text{ of Success newSt } v \to \text{let (STM tr2)} = (\backslash x \to f\ x \gg\!\!= g)\ v \text{ in tr2 newSt}; \ldots \quad (C.27)$$

With the definition of m, the definition of the STM (>>=) operator for f, and beta reduction we yield the equivalence:

$$(m \gg\!\!= f) \gg\!\!= g \Leftrightarrow \text{STM } (\backslash state \to io\_return\_stm \gg\!\!= s_f) \gg\!\!= g \quad (C.28)$$

The application of the definition of the STM (>>=) operator for g and beta reduction yields the equivalence:

$$(m \gg\!\!= f) \gg\!\!= g \Leftrightarrow \text{STM } ((\backslash state \to io\_return\_stm \gg\!\!= s_f) \gg\!\!= s_g) \quad (C.29)$$

With the application of the IO monad associativity law we get the equivalence:

$$(m \gg\!\!= f) \gg\!\!= g \Leftrightarrow \text{STM } ((\backslash state \to io\_return\_stm) \gg\!\!= (\backslash x \to s_f\ x \gg\!\!= s_g)) \quad (C.30)$$

With the definition of m, the definition of the STM (>>=) operator, and beta reduction we yield the equivalence:

$$m \gg\!\!= (\backslash x \to f\ x \gg\!\!= g) \Leftrightarrow \text{STM } (\backslash state \to io\_return\_stm \gg\!\!= s_{fg}) \quad (C.31)$$

C. Proof of STM Monad Laws

Comparing equations (C.30) and (C.31) and assuming an identical STM state in m, we see that if (C.32) holds:

$$(\backslash x \rightarrow s_f\ x \ggg= s_g) \Leftrightarrow s_{fg} \quad (C.32)$$

the associativity law proof holds:

$$(m \ggg= f) \ggg= g \Leftrightarrow m \ggg= (\backslash x \rightarrow f\ x \ggg= g) \quad (C.33)$$

Bibliography

[AH06]   S. Antoy and M. Hanus. Overlapping Rules and Logic Variables in Functional Logic Programs. In *Proceedings of the International Conference on Logic Programming (ICLP 2006)*, pages 87–101. Springer LNCS 4079, 2006.

[AHS09a]   Yousef J. Al-Houmaily and George Samaras. Three-Phase Commit. In Liu and Özsu [LÖ09], pages 3091–3097.

[AHS09b]   Yousef J. Al-Houmaily and George Samaras. Two-Phase Commit. In Liu and Özsu [LÖ09], pages 3204–3209.

[ALR02]   Algirdas Avizienis, Jean-Claude Laprie, and Brian Randell. Fundamental Concepts of Dependability. In *Proceedings of 3rd Information Survivability Workshop ISW 2000 (Boston, USA)*, pages 7–12, Oct 2002.

[ALRL04]   Algirdas Avizienis, Jean-Claude Laprie, Brian Randell, and Carl E. Landwehr. Basic Concepts and Taxonomy of Dependable and Secure Computing. *IEEE Trans. Dependable Sec. Comput.*, 1(1):11–33, 2004.

[Arm03]   Joe Armstrong. *Making Reliable Distributed Systems in the Presence of Software Errors*. PhD thesis, KTH, Sweden, 2003.

[Arm07]   Joe Armstrong. A History of Erlang. In *HOPL III: Proceedings of the third ACM SIGPLAN conference on History of programming languages*, pages 6-1–6-26, New York, NY, USA, 2007. ACM.

Bibliography

[Ber04]   Diego Berrueta. Zinc Project. http://zinc-project.sourceforge.net/, 2004.

[BHG87]   Philip A. Bernstein, Vassos Hadzilacos, and Nathan Goodman. *Concurrency Control and Recovery in Database Systems*. Addison-Wesley, 1987.

[BLM06]   Colin Blundell, E. Lewis, and Milo Martin. Subtleties of Transactional Memory Atomicity Semantics. *IEEE Computer Architecture Letters*, 5, 2006.

[CC07]   Mark Chu-Carroll. The Theory of Monads and the Monad Laws : Good Math, Bad Math. http://scienceblogs.com/goodmath/2007/01/the_theory_of_monads_and_the_m_1.php, Jan 2007.

[Chu85]   Alonzo Church. *The Calculi of Lambda Conversion. (AM-6) (Annals of Mathematics Studies)*. Princeton University Press, Princeton, NJ, USA, 1985.

[Cla99]   Koen Claessen. A poor man's Concurrency Monad. *Journal of Functional Programming*, 9(3):313–323, 1999.

[DdMY05] Evgueni Dodonov, Rodrigo Fernandes de Mello, and Laurence Tianruo Yang. A Network Evaluation for LAN, MAN and WAN Grid Environments. In Laurence Tianruo Yang, Makoto Amamiya, Zhen Liu, Minyi Guo, and Franz J. Rammig, editors, *EUC*, volume 3824 of *Lecture Notes in Computer Science*, pages 1133–1146. Springer, 2005.

[Dij68]   Edsger W. Dijkstra. Letters to the Editor: Go To Statement Considered Harmful. *Commun. ACM*, 11(3):147–148, 1968.

[Dij71]   Edsger W. Dijkstra. Hierarchical Ordering of Sequential Processes. *Acta Informatica*, 1(2):115–138, 1971.

[Dor98]   Chris Dornan. Tcl + Haskell = TclHaskell. In *Glasgow FP Group Workshop, Pitlochry, Scotland*, September 1998. http://www.dcs.gla.ac.uk/ meurig/TclHaskell/.

Bibliography

[DS06] D. Dice and N. Shavit. What Really Makes Transactions Faster? In *Proc. of the 1st TRANSACT 2006 workshop*, 2006.

[Eri09] Ericsson. Open Source Erlang. www.erlang.org, 2009.

[Eri10] Ericsson. kernel. www.erlang.org/documentation/doc-5.7.5/lib/kernel-2.13.5/doc/html/kernel_app.html, 2010.

[Gar04] Vijay K. Garg. *Concurrent and Distributed Computing in Java*. IEEE Press ; Wiley-Interscience, [Piscataway, N.J.]; Hoboken, N.J., 2004.

[GMPS97] Li Gong, Marianne Mueller, Hemma Prafullchandra, and Roland Schemers. Going beyond the Sandbox: an Overview of the new Security Architecture in the JavaTM Development Kit 1.2. In *USITS'97: Proceedings of the USENIX Symposium on Internet Technologies and Systems on USENIX Symposium on Internet Technologies and Systems*, pages 10–10, Berkeley, CA, USA, 1997. USENIX Association.

[Gra81] Jim Gray. The Transaction Concept: Virtues and Limitations (Invited Paper). In *Very Large Data Bases, 7th International Conference, September 9-11, 1981, Cannes, France, Proceedings*, pages 144–154. IEEE Computer Society, 1981.

[GVS10] Justin E. Gottschlich, Manish Vachharajani, and Jeremy G. Siek. An Efficient Software Transactional Memory using Commit-time Invalidation. In *CGO '10: Proceedings of the 8th annual IEEE/ACM international symposium on Code generation and optimization*, pages 101–110, New York, NY, USA, 2010. ACM.

[Han99] M. Hanus. Distributed Programming in a Multi-Paradigm Declarative Language. In *Proc. of the International Conference on Principles and Practice of Declarative Programming (PPDP'99)*, pages 376–395. Springer LNCS 1702, 1999.

[HHPJW07] Paul Hudak, John Hughes, Simon Peyton Jones, and Philip Wadler. A History of Haskell: Being Lazy With Class. In *HOPL III: Proceedings of the third ACM SIGPLAN conference on History of programming languages*, pages 12–1–12–55, New York, NY, USA, 2007. ACM.

Bibliography

[HK05] Frank Huch and Frank Kupke. A High-Level Implementation of Composable Memory Transactions in Concurrent Haskell. In Andrew Butterfield, Clemens Grelck, and Frank Huch, editors, *IFL*, volume 4015 of *Lecture Notes in Computer Science*, pages 124–141. Springer, 2005.

[HKMN95] M. Hanus, H. Kuchen, and J.J. Moreno-Navarro. Curry: A Truly Functional Logic Language. In *Proc. ILPS'95 Workshop on Visions for the Future of Logic Programming*, pages 95–107, 1995.

[HLR10] Tim Harris, James Larus, and Ravi Rajwar. Transactional Memory, 2nd edition. *Synthesis Lectures on Computer Architecture*, 5(1):1–263, 2010.

[HM93] Maurice Herlihy and J. Eliot B. Moss. Transactional Memory: Architectural Support for Lock-free Data Structures. In *Proceedings of the 20th annual international symposium on Computer architecture*, ISCA '93, pages 289–300, New York, NY, USA, 1993. ACM.

[HMPJH05] Tim Harris, Simon Marlow, Simon Peyton Jones, and Maurice Herlihy. Composable Memory Transactions. In *PPoPP '05: Proceedings of the tenth ACM SIGPLAN symposium on Principles and practice of parallel programming*, pages 48–60, New York, NY, USA, 2005. ACM Press.

[HN00] Frank Huch and Ulrich Norbisrath. Distributed Programming in Haskell with Ports. In *Proceedings of the 12th International Workshop on the Implementation of Functional Languages*, volume 2011 of *Lecture Notes in Computer Science*, pages 107–121, 2000.

[Hoa74] C. A. R. Hoare. Monitors: an Operating System Structuring Concept. *Commun. ACM*, 17(10):549–557, 1974.

[HPJ06] Tim Harris and Simon Peyton Jones. Transactional Memory with Data Invariants. In *TRANSACT'06: Proceedings of the 1st ACM SIGPLAN Workshop on Languages, Compilers, and Hardware Support for Transactional Computing*, June 2006.

Bibliography

[HPST06] Tim Harris, Mark Plesko, Avraham Shinnar, and David Tarditi. Optimizing Memory Transactions. In *PLDI '06: Proceedings of the 2006 ACM SIGPLAN conference on Programming language design and implementation*, pages 14–25, New York, NY, USA, 2006. ACM.

[HR83] Theo Haerder and Andreas Reuter. Principles of Transaction-oriented Database Recovery. *ACM Comput. Surv.*, 15(4):287–317, 1983.

[Huc99] Frank Huch. Erlang-style Distributed Haskell. In *In Draft Proceedings of the 11th International Workshop on Implementation of Functional Languages, September 7th 10th*, 1999.

[IAN10] IANA. Port Numbers. http://www.iana.org/assignments/port-numbers, Mai 2010.

[IR08] Damien Imbs and Michel Raynal. A Lock-Based STM Protocol That Satisfies Opacity and Progressiveness. In *OPODIS '08: Proceedings of the 12th International Conference on Principles of Distributed Systems*, pages 226–245, Berlin, Heidelberg, 2008. Springer-Verlag.

[KR07] James F. Kurose and Keith W. Ross. *Computer Networking: A Top-Down Approach (4th Edition)*. Addison-Wesley Longman Publishing Co., Inc., Boston, MA, USA, 2007.

[Lam74] Leslie Lamport. A New Solution of Dijkstra's Concurrent Programming Problem. In *Communications of the ACM*, volume 17, pages 453–455, 1974.

[Lea08] Quantum Leaps. Dining Philosophers Problem Example. http://www.state-machine.com/resources/AN_DPP.pdf, Aug 2008.

[LÖ09] Ling Liu and M. Tamer Özsu, editors. *Encyclopedia of Database Systems*. Springer US, 2009.

[Mar02] Simon Marlow. Developing a high-performance web server in Concurrent Haskell. *J. Funct. Program.*, 12(5):359–374, 2002.

Bibliography

[Mar06]   Simon Marlow. An Extensible Dynamically-Typed Hierarchy of Exceptions. In *Haskell '06: Proceedings of the 2006 ACM SIGPLAN workshop on Haskell*, pages 96–106, New York, NY, USA, 2006. ACM.

[Mar10]   Simon Marlow. The Glasgow Haskell Compiler. http://www.haskell.org/ghc/, Apr 2010.

[MBS+08] Vijay Menon, Steven Balensiefer, Tatiana Shpeisman, Ali-Reza Adl-Tabatabai, Richard L. Hudson, Bratin Saha, and Adam Welc. Practical Weak-Atomicity Semantics for Java STM. In *SPAA '08: Proceedings of the twentieth annual symposium on Parallelism in algorithms and architectures*, pages 314–325, New York, NY, USA, 2008. ACM.

[MPJMR01] Simon Marlow, Simon Peyton Jones, Andrew Moran, and John Reppy. Asynchronous Exceptions in Haskell. In *PLDI '01: Proceedings of the ACM SIGPLAN 2001 conference on Programming language design and implementation*, pages 274–285. ACM Press, 2001.

[Muu83]   Mike Muus. The Story of the PING Program. http://ftp.arl.army.mil/~mike/ping.html, 1983.

[NWAT+08] Yang Ni, Adam Welc, Ali-Reza Adl-Tabatabai, Moshe Bach, Sion Berkowits, James Cownie, Robert Geva, Sergey Kozhukow, Ravi Narayanaswamy, Jeffrey Olivier, Serguei Preis, Bratin Saha, Ady Tal, and Xinmin Tian. Design and Implementation of Transactional Constructs for C/C++. In *OOPSLA '08: Proceedings of the 23rd ACM SIGPLAN conference on Object-oriented programming systems languages and applications*, pages 195–212, New York, NY, USA, 2008. ACM.

[OY06]   OGI and Yale. hugsonline. http://www.haskell.org/hugs/, Sep 2006.

[Pep03]   Peter Pepper. *Funktionale Programmierung in OPAL, ML, HASKELL und GOFER*. Springer-Lehrbuch. Springer-Verlag, 2 edition, 2003.

Bibliography

[Pet81] Gary L. Peterson. Myths About the Mutual Exclusion Problems. *Inf. Process. Lett.*, 12(3):115–116, 1981.

[PF06] Thomas Peschel-Findeisen. *Nebenläufige und verteilte Systeme.* mitp-Verlag, 1 edition, 2006.

[PH06] Peter Pepper and Petra Hofstedt. *Funktionale Programmierung - Weiterführende Konzepte und Techniken.* Springer-Lehrbuch, 2006. ISBN 3-540-20959-X.

[Pie05] Benjamin C. Pierce, editor. *Advanced Topics in Types and Programming Languages.* MIT Press, 2005.

[PJ01] Simon Peyton Jones. Tackling the Awkward Squad: monadic input/output, concurrency, exceptions, and foreign-language calls in Haskell. In *Engineering theories of software construction, Marktoberdorf Summer School 2000, NATO ASI Series.* IOS Press, 2001.

[PJ+02] Simon Peyton Jones et al. Haskell 98 Language and Libraries. www.haskell.org/onlinereport/, Dec 2002.

[PJ07] Simon Peyton Jones. Taste of Haskell. http://research. microsoft.com/en-us/um/people/simonpj/papers/haskell-tutorial/TasteOfHaskell.pdf, Jun 2007.

[PJGF96] Simon Peyton Jones, Andrew Gordon, and Sigbjorn Finne. Concurrent Haskell. In *POPL '96: Proceedings of the 23rd ACM SIGPLAN-SIGACT symposium on Principles of programming languages*, pages 295–308, New York, NY, USA, 1996. ACM.

[PTL01] Robert F. Pointon, Philip W. Trinder, and Hans-Wolfgang Loidl. The Design and Implementation of Glasgow Distributed Haskell. In *IFL '00: Selected Papers from the 12th International Workshop on Implementation of Functional Languages*, pages 53–70, London, UK, 2001. Springer-Verlag.

[PVE93] Rinus Plasmeijer and Marko Van Eekelen. *Functional Programming and Parallel Graph Rewriting.* Addison-Wesley Longman Publishing Co., Inc., Boston, MA, USA, 1993.

Bibliography

[Qui08]　　Michael Quinion. English Affixes: the Building Blocks of English. http://www.affixes.org/t/trans-.html, 2008.

[RBP09]　　Charles Reis, Adam Barth, and Carlos Pizano. Browser Security: Lessons from Google Chrome. *Commun. ACM*, 52(8), 2009.

[Rec08]　　Fabian Reck. Erweiterung des Concurrent Haskell Debuggers für transaktionsbasierte Kommunikation. Master's thesis, Christian-Albrechts-Universität, Kiel, 2008.

[Sch09a]　　Jan Schaumlöffel. Optimierung transaktionsbasierter Kommunikation in Haskell für Multicore-Architekturen. Master's thesis, Christian-Albrechts-Universität, Kiel, 2009.

[Sch09b]　　Stefan Schmidt. Distributed Computing with MapReduce in Haskell. Master's thesis, FH Wedel, 2009.

[Sch10]　　Uwe Schmidt. Hoλumbus. http://holumbus.fh-wedel.de, 2010.

[SF07]　　Hans Svensson and Lars-Åke Fredlund. Programming Distributed Erlang Applications: Pitfalls and Recipes. In *ERLANG '07: Proceedings of the 2007 SIGPLAN workshop on ERLANG Workshop*, pages 37–42, New York, NY, USA, 2007. ACM.

[SH02]　　Volker Stolz and Frank Huch. Concurrency Abstractions for Concurrent Haskell. Draft. Proc. of IFL, 2002.

[SMAT+07]　　Tatiana Shpeisman, Vijay Menon, Ali-Reza Adl-Tabatabai, Steven Balensiefer, Dan Grossman, Richard L. Hudson, Katherine F. Moore, and Bratin Saha. Enforcing Isolation and Ordering in STM. In *PLDI '07: Proceedings of the 2007 ACM SIGPLAN conference on Programming language design and implementation*, pages 78–88, New York, NY, USA, 2007. ACM.

[ST95]　　Nir Shavit and Dan Touitou. Software Transactional Memory. In *Proceedings of the fourteenth annual ACM symposium on Principles of distributed computing*, PODC '95, pages 204–213, New York, NY, USA, 1995. ACM.

[Tib09]　　Johan Tibell. The Network Package. http://hackage.haskell.org/package/network-2.2.1.7, Dec 2009.

Bibliography

[Tok09] Wee Hyong Tok. Distributed Transaction Management. In Liu and Özsu [LÖ09], pages 925–929.

[Tur37] Alan Turing. On Computable Numbers, with an Application to the Entscheidungsproblem. In *Proceedings of the London Mathematical Society*, volume 42 of *2*, 1937.

[TVS01] Andrew S. Tanenbaum and Maarten Van Steen. *Distributed Systems: Principles and Paradigms*. Prentice Hall PTR, Upper Saddle River, NJ, USA, 2001.

[vN45] John von Neumann. First Draft of a Report on the EDVAC. Technical report, University of Pennsylvania, 1945.

[vN56] John von Neumann. Probabilistic Logics and the Synthesis of Reliable Organisms from Unreliable Components. In C. E. Shannon and J. McCarthy, editors, *Automata studies*, pages 43–98. Princeton University Press, 1956.

[VRH02] Peter Van Roy and Seif Haridi. Teaching Programming Broadly and Deeply: The Kernel Language Approach. In Lillian N. Cassel and Ricardo Augusto da Luz Reis, editors, *Informatics Curricula and Teaching Methods*, volume 245 of *IFIP Conference Proceedings*, pages 53–62. Kluwer, 2002.

[VRH04] Peter Van Roy and Seif Haridi. *Concepts, Techniques, and Models of Computer Programming*. MIT Press, 2004.

[Y$^+$09] Ashley Yakeley et al. Haskell Wiki. http://www.haskell.org/haskellwiki, 2009.

Index

[], 7
(==), 8, 9
(>> +), 114
AutoLink, 157
CommitActs, 109
CommitLogBundle, 108
CommitLog, 65, 108
DistTransCont, 147
Dist
    finTVars, 45, 91
    regTVars, 45, 91
EnvAddr, 61
Eq, 9
Exception
    fromException, 19
    toException, 19
HostCLogBundle, 109
HostVLogBundle, 109
IO, 13
LinkCLogBundle, 110
LinkVLogBundle, 110
Link, 157
LockActs, 109
MVar
    modifyMVar_, 18
    modifyMVar, 18

newMVar, 16
putMVar, 17
takeMVar, 16
MaybeRW, 166
MaybeRead, 110, 166
Monad
    (>>), 11
    (>>=), 11
    fail, 11
    return, 11
MsgID, 99
Read, 85
RemCont, 147
ReplyMsg, 99
RetryLogBundle, 118
RetryLog, 118
RetryVarData, 60
RetryVarID, 60
RetryVar, 61
STMMessageSC, 99
STMMessage, 81
STMMsg, 99
STMResult, 57
STMState, 65
STM, 57, 58
    Dist, 53

219

Index

SomeDistTVarException, 51, 54
TVar, 36, 42, 53
  atomic, 36, 42, 53
  catch, 37, 42, 53
  deregisterTVar, 43, 53
  finTVars, 53
  isDistErrTVar, 52, 54
  lookupTVar, 43, 53
  lookupWaitTVar, 43, 53
  newTVar, 37, 42, 53
  orElse, 36, 42, 53
  readTVar, 37, 42, 53
  regTVars, 53
  registerTVar, 43, 53
  retry, 36, 42, 53
  runDist, 43, 53
  throw, 37, 42, 53
  writeTVar, 37, 42, 53
Serializable
  fromString, 81
  toString, 81
Show, 85
SomeDistTVarException, 153
SomeException, 20
State, 14
TVarActions, 83
TVarID, 60
TVar, 60, 61
ThreadId, 16
TransID, 147
ValidActs, 109
ValidLogBundle, 108
ValidLog, 65, 108
ValidRemVal, 110, 166
VarLink, 61
VersionID, 60
accept, 33

addComRemVals, 167
addEnvToTVarActions, 90
atomic, 66, 67, 68, 162
catch, 18, 19, 69
commitTrans, 169
connectExclTo, 102
connectTo, 33
consumer, 17
contRemTr, 150
contWNewCoord, 155
coreReadTVar, 62, 121, 172
coreResume, 159
ctrlContTrans, 151
ctrlEndTrans, 152
ctrlTrans, 150
delEnvFromTVarActions, 90
deleteRetryLinks, 161
deleteRetryLink, 162
deleteRetryVarAct, 164
distTVarExEnv, 153
doCommitAction, 169
doEndAction, 170
doRetryAction, 165
doUnRetryAction, 165
doValidAction, 169
eatAWhile, 23
electNewCoord, 154
elem, 8, 9
endTrans, 170
enter, 26
finTVars, 90
finalizeLinkTVar, 90
finishTrans, 152
fmap, 11
forkIO, 16
gActions, 83, 89
gDefaultLink, 160

Index

gDistTransCont, 148
gLinks, 157
gPendReplies, 99
gRetryVarActMap, 164
gTCPStacks, 103
gUniqueId, 60
gatherStmState, 166
gatherValidRemVal, 167
getLine, 13
handleMsgSC, 100
handleMsg, 82, 117, 149, 157
head, 6
initialState, 65
insertCommitLog, 111
insertRetryLinks, 161
insertRetryLink, 161
insertRetryLog, 118
insertRetryVarAct, 164
insertTVarAct, 83, 89, 92
insertValidLog, 111
insertWith, 111
intTail, 7
isDistErrTVar, 154
killThread, 16
leave, 26
lifeCheck, 156, 158
listenOn, 33
lockId, 117
lockValid, 117
lookupReply, 100
loop, 17
main, 13
map, 4
mergeRVal, 115
newChan, 147
newReply, 99
newRetryVar, 65

newTVar, 70
nodeReceiver, 80
orElse, 69
popTcpHandle, 103
producer, 17
propagateEx, 168
pushTcpHandle, 103
putReply, 100
putStrLn, 13
putStr, 13
readAction, 82
readChan, 147
readHost, 122
readIntraTransTVar, 120
readMsg, 81
readTVarFromId, 83
readTVar, 71, 120
recoverBrokenInactiveTrans, 159
recoverBrokenReactiveTrans, 159
recvTCP, 102
regTVars, 90
remGetMsgSC, 99
remGetMsg, 84, 102
remPutMsg, 84
resumeFromId, 164
resumeRetryVarAct, 87, 159
retryTrans, 165
retryVarEnv, 118
retry, 67
robustFoldValidAct, 168
robustMapM_, 155
runDist, 80
runSTM, 58
runState, 15
singletonCLog, 115
singletonRLog, 119
singletonVLog, 112, 113

221

Index

startAction, 116
startLinkTVars, 117
startRemTr, 149
startTrans, 116, 168
tVarEnv, 111
tVarToLink, 121
tail, 7
takeReply, 100
test, 15
throwTo, 18, 19
throw, 18, 19, 68
unRetryTrans, 165
uniqueId, 60
updateAutoTrans, 160
updateCLog, 115
updateRLog, 119
updateVLog, 114
update, 15
validateId, 117
writeAction, 82
writeChan, 147
writeRead, 93
writeTVarFromId, 84
writeTVar, 71

Bomberman
    Bombs, 197
    Dist, 199
    Element, 196
    Field, 196
    GameState, 197
    Move, 197
    Point, 197
    Xplos, 197
    launchGame, 198

Chat
    CmdTVar, 192
    Dist, 192
    ServerCmd, 191
    chatServer, 193
    removeErrDict, 193
    serverClient, 195
    stdinClient, 194

Dining Philosopher
    Stick, 38, 48, 190
    phil, 23, 48, 190
    putStick, 38, 48, 190
    startPhils, 39
    startPhil, 48
    takeStick, 38, 48, 190

Name Server
    NameServerMsg, 184
    TVarDict, 184
    deregisterTVar, 185
    getServerLn, 185
    handleMsg, 184
    lookupTVar, 185
    lookupWaitTVar, 186
    nameService, 184
    parIO, 186
    putServerLn, 185
    readMsg, 184
    registerTVar, 185
    repeatGetServerLn, 186

Die VDM Verlagsservicegesellschaft sucht für wissenschaftliche Verlage abgeschlossene und herausragende

Dissertationen, Habilitationen, Diplomarbeiten, Master Theses, Magisterarbeiten usw.

für die kostenlose Publikation als Fachbuch.

Sie verfügen über eine Arbeit, die hohen inhaltlichen und formalen Ansprüchen genügt, und haben Interesse an einer honorarvergüteten Publikation?

Dann senden Sie bitte erste Informationen über sich und Ihre Arbeit per Email an *info@vdm-vsg.de*.

Sie erhalten kurzfristig unser Feedback!

VDM Verlagsservicegesellschaft mbH
Dudweiler Landstr. 99   Telefon +49 681 3720 174
D - 66123 Saarbrücken   Fax   +49 681 3720 1749
www.vdm-vsg.de

Die VDM Verlagsservicegesellschaft mbH vertritt

Printed by Books on Demand GmbH, Norderstedt / Germany